THE
RUDDER TREASURY

Geoff and Mary
Merry Christmas
and
Happy New Year
and
Perfect Sailing

Jim and Kay
Christmas 2006

THE
RUDDER TREASURY

A Companion for Lovers of Small Craft

Edited by Tom Davin

With an Introduction by Boris Lauer-Leonardi
Editor, THE RUDDER

Charles G. Davis

SHERIDAN HOUSE   NEW YORK

This edition first published 2003
By Sheridan House Inc.
145 Palisade Street
Dobbs Ferry, NY 10522
www.sheridanhouse.com

Library of Congress Cataloging-in-Publication Data

   The Rudder treasury: a companion for lovers of small
craft / edited by Tom Davin ; with a foreword by
Peter H. Spectre.
     p. cm.
Includes index.
ISBN 1-57409-160-3 (alk. paper)
1. Boats and boating. 2. Yachts. I. Davin, Tom.
II. Rudder (Greenwich, Conn.)
GV813.R77 2003

796.1—dc21   2002155096

Printed in the United States of America

ISBN   1-57409-160-3

FOREWORD

BACK IN THE 1970s I would hear every once in awhile from William Garden, a yacht designer in the Pacific Northwest who I hadn't met but knew through the mail. I was then deeply involved in a raggedy annual publication called the Mariner's Catalog and at the same time I was the editor of an obscure publishing company that specialized in nautical books. Generally, our theme was that the modern world was going to hell in a hand basket, that we had lost touch with our past, that the last of the Real Sailors was born in the nineteenth century, that we had tapped into the consciousness of our forefathers because we had read what they left behind, and that if all the lost losers of our generation would just listen up, we could make the nautical world whole again (we were young then). Garden seemed to have an appreciation for this—minus the arrogance—and would offer various suggestions for improvement.

One of William Garden's suggestions involved *The Rudder*, which had been founded in 1891, had had a long, glorious run, and was at the time undergoing a pathetic decline. Anyone who knew the magazine in its heyday—roughly from its founding to the middle of the twentieth century—knew also that it had once been the greatest American yachting and boating magazine ever published and that all other magazines in competition with it were basically near beer and hard cheese. Garden suggested that we gain reprint rights to the back issues and republish them serially by subscription, month by month, year by year, beginning with the first issue of 1890 in 1990. If you subscribed to The Centennial Rudder, for example, you would receive the July 1903 issue in July 2003.

What made *The Rudder* so special? The principal reason in my opinion was that it was founded and edited for years by a man, Thomas Fleming Day, who knew what he was talking about. Day was an enthusiast with a deep knowledge of the subject and a well-founded point of view. He treated his readers as intelligent human beings. He didn't pander to advertisers. He recognized yacht design as an evolution, with a connected past, present, and future. Above all, he was a literate, literary man of strong opinion, the author of articles, editorials, poetry, and books.

FOREWORD

The Rudder was Thomas Fleming Day, and Thomas Fleming Day was The Rudder. His influence was so powerful that even after his time the best editors that followed—William Crosby and Boris Lauer-Leonardi—carried the magazine forward with similar dedication and enthusiasm, as if he were still in charge.

Day and his successors were of the school that the doing was more important than the having. As a result, there was little in *The Rudder* about buying stuff off the shelf and more about making it. Cruising wasn't about driving from one marina to another and plugging the air conditioner into the grid; it was about handing, reefing, and steering, and cooking up a meal of boiled potatoes and canned beans when you got there. Racing was about the joys of competition without any chest-pounding braggadocio at the finish line.

William Garden's suggestion to reprint *The Rudder* serially was a brilliant, utopian idea. For a long time I harbored the fantasy that we could pull it off, but too many difficulties—raising the money, gaining the rights, reaching the (dwindling) audience—stood in the way. Besides, after time the obscure book publishing company and I went our separate ways; the Mariner's Catalog itself folded. The scheme never came to pass.

Complete runs of *The Rudder* can be found in a few libraries here and there, and isolated issues show up from time to time in the used book trade, but for regular readers the magazine might as well have never existed. That's why the republication of this book, *The Rudder Treasury*—a sample of the magazine's broad spectrum—is such a treat.

Yes, a few items republished here are somewhat dated, but the vast majority are not. The writing is as fresh as it ever was; so, too, is the writers' enthusiasm for yachts, boats, and the traditions of the sea. As the first edition's jacket flap copy wonderfully promised, *The Rudder Treasury* is "a well rounded bilgeful of dogmatic advice, arbitrary opinion, clever devices and methods—the sort of thing that you are always meaning to paste in your hat. "

Peter H. Spectre
Spruce Head, Maine

CONTENTS

5

INTRODUCTION

ONE OF THE many attractions of being editor of THE RUDDER Magazine is the occasional excursion into a fascinating and colorful past necessitated by requests for information by our readers.

Since the requests rarely pinpoint the time, I find myself leafing through back volumes, looking for a design, a date, a regatta, a picture . . . and before I know it I am captured by the romantic world of days gone by and I find myself pleasantly adrift among a miscellany composed of items such as a cruise to Florida forty years ago (yes, it's changed) a design of a schooner yacht that would stop us all today, sleek power yachts, famous personalities, races in which sail is crowded on so as to make modern sailors gasp, and many other lively and quaint subjects which often have caused me to lose track of my original object of search.

Upon emerging from such an adventure in the past I have been left with the regret that so much material by which our yachting tradition is molded is no longer available to the reader of today. Not only is it instructive, but it gives a yachtsman a perspective and a respect for the oldtimers who, after all, not only knew a lot but tried almost everything.

It was with enthusiasm, therefore, that I greeted Tom Davin's proposal that he compile representative material from back issues of THE RUDDER into a book. Tom combines editorial skill with love of boats and an intimate knowledge of the magazine, which makes him ideally suited for the job. I think he has acquitted himself well and I believe that the glimpse of the past he gives us will make many of us feel closer to the world's greatest sport and a fine way of life.

BORIS LAUER-LEONARDI

EDITOR'S APOLOGY

IT STARTED very simply. One day, while chatting with Boris Lauer-Leonardi, THE RUDDER's editor, I remarked that there must be a lot of good reading buried in the 744 back issues of that magazine. "There probably is," he replied in the manner of a man who has had that remark made to him many times in the past, "but who is going to take the time to dig it out?"

A few months later, I emerged from this literary excavation with a slight eye strain, a half-dozen notebooks filled with article titles, page and volume numbers and a confused picture of 62 years of popular American yachting. There *was* a lot of good reading there; so much, in fact, that it was difficult to select a small sampling that would make up a reasonably sized book.

Of course, every anthology is but a reflection of the editor's own imperfect taste; he cannot explain that away. To those readers who complain that their favorite bits of reading matter are not included, he can only plead lack of space. Or he can advise his critics, irritably, to make their own collection and be damned.

The longer narratives, such as the detailed reporting of the America's Cup races (with one reporter on each of the contenders, noting each puff of breeze and its consequences on board,) are of dubious historical interest. Most of the serial cruising articles have already appeared in book form: such material already published has been left out. All selections have been made from the point of view of their interest or usefulness today.

One personality stands out. Tom Day, THE RUDDER's founder and editor during its early years, was the greatest American yachting writer. Despite handicaps, he launched the sport of popular yachting, as we see it today, practically single handed. Like Captain Cook who explored and discovered large sections of the world to find markets for English cotton goods and other notions, Tom Day inspired the building of thousands of small boats across the country and encouraged the formation of hundreds of small yacht clubs to make readers for THE RUDDER. This oldest and most beloved yachting

11

magazine was conceived and launched in an oddly indirect way, according to Tom Day:

"In the year 1890 I was selling boats at 49 Dey Street, New York. The proprietor of the shop was Mr. John J. Bockée, who was agent for A. Bain & Co., afterwards the St. Lawrence River Skiff, Canoe and Steam Launch Company, with works at Clayton, N. Y. In three years we sold more boats than had ever been sold before in the same time by all the concerns in the city. Frequently we got rid of five to ten in a day; in fact we sold them faster than the Clayton people could build them. Besides selling boats we gave away thousands of catalogs, and it was this free distribution of catalogs that was the embryonic cell whence sprang THE RUDDER.

"Mr. Bockée, who was a perfect genius for devising plans whereby other people had the felicity of paying for things from which he reaped certain benefits free of cost, suggested that it would be a good idea to get out a little paper instead of the expensive catalog and support the publication by obtaining advertising, we getting our publicity gratis for the trouble of running the thing. This I welcomed joyfully as for some time it had been my dream to launch and sail a yachting paper. I had done some writing, descriptive catalogs, introductions, stories and small articles, and having learned to write by years of constant practice knew that part I was fit to tackle, but the business of publishing I knew as much about as a duck does about the motions of the moon.

"Anyhow, I prepared the copy and we went to a printer, Thomson & Co., next door and had one page and a cover set up."

There were trials and tribulations before the publication was finally under way. Today, 62 years later, Thomson & Co. are still getting it out. To the present day Thomsons go my thanks for their genial cooperation in assembling this book. To Boris Lauer-Leonardi, THE RUDDER's greatest editor since Tom Day, my gratitude for his sound but unobtrusive advice and generous encouragement.

TOM DAVIN

NOTICE TO MARINERS

This editorial, by Tom Day, which appeared in the January, 1916, issue of THE RUDDER, *is timelessly apropos; agitational subheads and all. The editor would like to think that it sums up the philosophy of this volume.*

NO BOATS, NO SPORT: ALL HANDS BUILD HULLS.

EVERYTHING bad has been laid at the door of Emperor Nero, so let him have the credit of once giving expression to a humane sentiment. When asked to sign a death warrant, he exclaimed: "Oh, that I had never learned to write!" But, if as how be, the famous fiddler never hated the pen half as much as I do. Give me the spade, sledge, scythe, sword or spike, or any other tool to wield, but the pen. That instrument, I cheerfully curse the inventor of, whenever my hand grasps it. But many of you, from the letters, some of 'em as long as the main royal backstay of a tea clipper, don't seem to share my abhorrence of ink dabbling. One man wrote three pages which, boiled down, was an inquiry to know if he could disagree with my statements, criticise my knowledge, and refute my arguments, and if he did, would I print his letter. Most certainly. We'll print anything a man signs his name to, barring abuse. That is just what I want you to do, and what you people don't do. You are like toadfish, you will swallow anything that is offered, if it is in print. Never believe or accept any statement made by any man, until you have rolled it over and over in your mind, and made certain that it fits snug with your own findings. I am neither the Pope's brother, or first cousin to the Sherif Islam, and my statements are not to be accepted unquestioned, than are those of any other man. Know this, that three-quarters of what you read in trade papers and technical magazines is written by people who don't know any more about the subject they write about than you or I do. They are staff writers, who, without hesitancy or dread, tackle any subject from inseminating beans, to detecting the eccentricity of the moon's orbit. Believe nothing until weighed and found good weight.

NO BOATS, NO SPORT: ALL HANDS BUILD HULLS.

Again and again, I have told you people that the only knowledge that is of value is knowledge based on experience. All closet speculations and opinions are so much trash. I was brought up in a hotbed of science, at a time when science was in the making; white-hot under the blows of controversy. I have sat for hours listening to Huxley, Lord Cole, Ethridge, Newbery, and a dozen other leaders, discussing across the table the length of a man's days on earth, the number of cervical vertebrae in the neck of the ichthyosaurus, or the probable cause and duration of the ice age. In my time, the age of the world has expanded from a few millions to untold billions of years, and man, instead of being a mere infant of a few thousand seasons, is now credited with being a fire-making, house-building creature, with a hundred thousand decades to his credit. One valuable lesson these discussions taught me is this, that there are two distinct breeds of scientific men. First, the one who formed his opinions in the study and then went out into the open to prove them true; and the second, the man who went opened-minded to seek Nature, and after gleaning from her fields a rich harvest of facts, returned to the study to arrange and digest them. To the first type we owe dogmatism, stagnation and retrogression; to the second, opinion, enlightenment and progress. Opinion is knowledge in the making—the soft iron before it is compacted under the blows of the smith. Dogmatism is like hardened steel—no future blows can alter its shape or consistency. In our sport, we have the same types—the man who sits in his study or office and forms his opinions by speculation; and the man who goes out on the water and gathers from experience, facts upon which to base his ultimate findings. The many erroneous ideas regarding the design and handling of boats can be traced to the writings and talkings of the former type. And what is most strange, but seems to be true of all phases of human knowledge, such erroneous and sometimes fatuous opinions find a wide and ready acceptance, whereas the real deductions of the experienced man are declined and derided.

NO BOATS, NO SPORT: ALL HANDS BUILD HULLS.

WINTER READING

A Miscellany of Cruising Yarns, History and Some Opinions

PORTUGUESE-PATACHE

Warren Sheppard

CURIOUS RECORDS OF THE SEA

by RICHARD MAURY

JANUARY, 1941

Now that winter is here and the boat is cradled, covered, and set away to await another spring, the die-hard boatsman will be turning to nautical literature with more ardor than ever. The close-hauled sailings off lee shores, the desperate actions known in squall and gale will all be held at a comfortable distance from his cozy fireplace, while the ship's clock on the mantel ticks calmly away, and the shiny barometer on the wall indicates snow before morning.

He will want, of course, his monthly boating magazine with its timely score of seagoing lore, much of which he will convert from the written word into the spoken word before spring. Likely he will read one or two modern cruise books. Perhaps he will go back into antiquity by joining up with Cook's voyages, or sailing with Dampier to the Savage Isles. Possibly he will turn to a good novel of the sea, Melville's *Moby Dick* or Joseph Conrad's immortal *Nigger of the Narcissus*.

Now there remains another field of paper-bound adventure not so often broached; an interesting field, to my mind, an informative one—at the very least an amazing one. I refer to the plain records of the sea, many of which have been relegated to obscurity, many forgotten, tossed to the winds by time while others are left to lie in the sanctuary of the second-hand book store.

Some of the records are amusing, some tragic, while many border on the fantastic: Ships with eighty miles of rigging, steamers with thirty-two smokestacks, for instance. . . . But here are facts, awaiting to be devoured by an age that insists on facts and yet more facts.

Let us skim over, very much at random, some of the evidence, and let us commence under the general and vague heading of Names.

We have, for example, been told that aboard ship there are only three "ropes" (bell rope, hand rope, bucket rope), that all other

17

pulling stuff is to be named "line." We are also told that it has been considered bad luck to change the name of a ship.

But go over the records. Here is a scrap of information, here we come upon another—and in the end we find a list of no less than fifteen "ropes" used on shipboard—a list that may even be incomplete. Taken alphabetically they are: back rope, bell rope, bolt rope, buoy rope, bucket rope, clew rope, foot rope, gap rope (used for hauling snug the foot of a jib being stowed), grab rope (to aid small boats coming alongside), guest rope, man rope, top rope, tow rope, wheel rope and yard rope.

With two of the above the wording is optional. A grab rope may be called a grab line, a tow rope a tow line. But the rest stand.

Now as to the changing of a ship's name. In that supposedly superstitious Victorian Era of the square-rigger let us see what they were doing. There was a fine British four-masted barque named the Lord Wolseley. Her name was changed to Columbia. Columbia failed to stick. Lord Wolseley again. One would think that enough, but no, she was re-named again, this time the Everett G. Griggs, and when the ship was finally broken up, she bore yet another name, that of E. R. Sterling.

Well, perhaps the English and Americans were not so superstitious after all; let us turn to the Latins a moment. We find first a Spanish vessel with six names, an Italian that has borne seven, and in the east the Turkish barque Sulimanie, ex Elviva, ex Ina, ex Carlo, ex La Virginia, ex Venti Settembre, ex Benedetto.

And most of the great sailing fleet purchased by the Scandinavians when the rest of the world turned to steam had their names changed. As a matter of fact it was generally the fate of the windjammer to lose, sometime in her life, the name by which she was christened. The records testify to this, and thereby explode the theory that the changing of a name was looked upon with great apprehension. Nor was there always any accounting for taste when the change took place. The neat, lofty Spirit of the Morning became plain Ellen; and wasn't it the powerful high-flying clipper, Sovereign of the Seas, that the Germans flatteringly re-named Hans.

Speaking of names, did you know there was once a deep-sea vessel named the Essence of Peppermint?

Still sailing is the Indian Ocean barque Venyagasowpakialetchmye.

But the Venyagasowpakialetchmye by no means bears the longest ship's name. I recall seeing in a Lloyd's Register of a few years ago a craft bearing the unabbreviated name of Port of London Authority Dredger Number 3. Even the word "Number" was spelled out in full. Finally there once sailed out of the port of Jaffna the wooden barque, Thiro Nada Rasa Sivakama Sunthara Letchemy.

Still speaking of names, contrary to popular opinion there is no set method for naming the masts of five-masted ships. In one five-master it might be: fore, main, middle, mizzen and jigger; and in another: bowmast, foremast, mainmast, aftermast, jiggermast. In one five-master the masts were numbered. In six-masted schooners the following system has been used: fore, main, mizzen, jigger, spanker, driver; while the seven masts of the Thomas E. Lawson were supposedly named after the days of the week.

Incidentally the Lawson was the slow coach of all the big sailers, and it is not correct that she was the largest sailing vessel of all time. That distinction goes to a comparatively little-known vessel, the five-masted French barque France II, of the following dimensions: Length, 418'; breadth, 55'; depth, 24'; tonnage, 5,633. It was this mammoth craft which set aloft an estimated 80 miles of rigging, of which 42 was wire, 38 manila rope.

Now to leave the matter of names and take for another general subject that of size.

Although the France II was the largest of sailing ships, she did not set the greatest amount of sail. In 1853, we have the Great Republic, a clipper ship, with a sail area containing 15,653 yards of cotton, and, in more recent times the five-masted barque, Preussen, of the Flying "P" Line, sailing from Hamburg, a mammoth windjammer setting 48 working sails cut out of 59,000 square feet of cloth.

What was the largest mast to be stepped into a ship? We must again go back to the American Clipper, Great Republic, where up through four decks and soaring into the air rose 276 feet of mainmast (not allowing for top doubling). From deck to truck, then, reared 230 feet of wooden mast held aloft entirely by hemp rope and swinging from it six yards, one of which measured 120 feet between yard arms, or more than twice the vessel's beam. This mainmast measured 132 inches in circumference—and that it, together with its massive yards, were held aloft at all, remains a miracle in

Russian hemp and old-fashioned wrought iron. Incidentally, this fabulous ship had no less than 62 feet of bowsprit and jibboom lunging outboard of her figure head.

A paragraph recording big small boats: the craft setting the greatest amount of sail in the World in proportion to her size is a 14 ft. open dinghy: The old Bermudian racing dinghy. With a bowsprit as long as her length, together with a boom considerably longer, and a 30 ft. spar, she sets a spinnaker almost as large as her mainsail—all this clouding up above an open boat that has neither rail nor deck. Curiously enough the 750 square feet of mainsail set by the champion of the Bermudians, the Victory, is stopped to the mast with sail twine, and, come calm or squall it cannot be lowered. Perhaps there is no craft afloat, including the over-masted I sloop, that demands such precise and expert handling. . . . The biggest rowing-gig in the world: Long ago the Samoan Islanders copied the early ships gigs and whale boats which visited their shores, and, in a great inter-village rivalry, continued to add new section after section amidships until, with little alteration to the original beam, they ended up with a gig no less than 130 feet in length, of 60 oars.

In the Merchant Marine humorous reference is often made to a mythical steamer (sometimes known as the Tuscaloosa City) having sixteen smokestacks, an equal number of decks and a straw bottom. Actual history reveals a forgotten steamship no less fantastic. In the 1850's one Darius Davison of New York designed and built, of iron, I believe, the steamship Leviathian, a mammoth cigar-shaped craft with an inverted bow. 700 feet in length, she was designed to carry 3,000 passengers across the Atlantic at a speed of 30 knots. This vessel had not sixteen smokestacks but thirty-two all told, and sixteen engines. She never made 30 knots, for on her trial trip with every engine wide open and her funnels belching out a furious smoke screen, she barely touched 4. She sailed no more, and, was soon forgotten.

Have you ever looked along the graceful waterline of an ocean liner, and wondered what she could do if, freed of superstructure and engines she was allowed to set above her fine hull a network of giant sails? This too has been attempted, the best example being when in 1888 the well-known and crack trans-Atlantic mail steamer "Pereire," a French Liner, was stripped of funnels and engines and rigged as a four-masted sailing ship. Awkward in appearance, over-long and slim, she nevertheless made her name under sail first as the British, then as the Norwegian, Lancing. To this day Norwegian sailormen speak with pride and affection of the old mail steamer which became for them their fastest windjammer. Many critics consider her the most able sailer of her day. Under sail, for example, she once averaged 18 knots for three consecutive days.

Let us move from the vague and general category of size to that of speed.

Under sail alone, what ship has moved fastest over water? The small, swift, South Seas outrigger? Perhaps. But as far as I am aware, records on their performances are completely lacking, although opinions on the subject most certainly are not. We must bear in mind, where eye witness accounts are concerned, that craft the size of canoes appear to be flying at anything over and above 8 knots. For example, a motor launch splitting water at 20 m.p.h. often appears to be outrunning a larger vessel moving sedately and comfortably by at a greater speed. The sailing outrigger often presents a similar illusion, and yet it is certain that, given the "laboratory weather" demanded by a Cup boat, the outrigger can pick up her heels on a beam wind very much like an iceboat. As I say, opinions vary. Having sailed a few of them, and having observed a great many more, my own and not too-final opinion of them is that, their top speed lies somewhere between 13 to 18 knots. But even if they can exceed these and touch 20 no record is thereby broken.

It is claimed that the American Clipper Champion of the Seas topped 22 knots, although the 21 knots of her sister, the James Baines, is more often referred to. This same ship is said to have run down 475 miles in a day, although the more generally accepted record is that of another of her sisters, the Lightning's 436 miles. These are the highest all-out speeds recorded under sail.

While on the subject of the clippers, how many are there who realize that, almost without exception, every American Clipper Ship was either completely or partially dismasted? They were frantically bullied and, with all due respect to their masters, were beaten to death—as an old-timer might say—so much so that, after half a dozen voyages, they were usually in need of rebuilding. They were strained and buckled out of shape to reach the pots of gold in California and Australia. They were severely worked and their backs were broken until they had to be held in shape with chains secured about their sides; they were old ships in five years, and, in most cases, slow coaches within ten. It is a pity that the very mania for speed which brought their beauty into existence, turned upon them and destroyed them so quickly and completely.

Thoughts on the windjammer era always bring forth a sense of salt-water nostalgia, a reflective moment, a sigh for those brave, violent days of iron men and wooden ships. "Iron men and wooden ships!" Yes, they were hard days, but I think any old shellback who has sailed in both wooden and steel windjammers will agree when I say that the later day steel or iron ship was the harder, more dangerous craft to serve in. The high-riding wooden ship was seldom if ever pooped, and she had the buoyancy to lift at least half way up an oncoming storm wave. No, wooden-ship sailors knew little or nothing of the surf bathing variety of seamanship imposed by iron and steel ships—often called half-tide rocks. They knew nothing of helmsmen being swept from the wheel to the forecastle head and even into the fore rigging by violent boarding seas. (Both instances occur several times in the records.) Their decks were comparatively dry, whereas there were times when an iron ship was inhabitable only on the poop and after deckhouse—so often so that in the end, lifting bridges, of the type now seen on oil tankers, were employed. They say sailors never needed to learn the art of swimming until the advent of the iron ship.

Furthermore the wood ship had the warmer forecastle—a very important item. Not in vain were the steel living quarters of a windbag hammering against the Horn known as the ice house.

An iron ship, incidentally, will outlast one of steel by many years. A well-constructed wooden ship will outlast both.

Odds and ends of windjammer facts: even in the remote 1880's there were square-riggers with wheel houses. Then there were others that were commanded and steered from bridges amidships. There have been oil-tank sailing ships and refrigerator sailers. Windjammers struggled on in the passenger service right into this century. Merchant square-riggers are still being built. Where? Imagine—of all places—in unworldly, mystic India. Some will want to know what type of men are employed to crew them? Surely, impractical, gentle-eyed Indians couldn't be expected to handle such a complicated and demanding organism as a three-masted barque. But such is the case; from captain to ship's boy they work their craft with all the finesse of a crew of Western Ocean shellbacks, with one very notable exception—they disdain the use of ratlines in the shrouds, and, night or day, calm or gale, swarm aloft by clamping their toes about the towering coir rope backstays.

Did you know that the first iron sailing ship, the Vulcan, was built in Scotland only six years after the War of 1812? That the first iron craft was in use a year after the American Revolution? That as long ago as 1875 Great Britain, for example, the leading sea power, built 200,000 odd tons of iron sailing ships as against only 45,000 of wood? That blue was the one color sailing ships would not wear? Colors for windjammers have ranged from ships painted unblushingly barn red to the famous pea soup hulls of Shutes' nitrate fleet, but except for waterways, blue was used solely as a sign of mourning—a tradition observed as late as 1935, when, upon the death of George V the vessels of the British Government appeared with mourning streaks of that color.

Do you know that there is still in active service a sailing man-of-war? She is the small frigate Zalee of the French Navy stationed at Papeete, Tahiti. Originally a trading schooner, she carries at least one small gun forward, and holds to her credit the sailing record for the once popular passage, San Francisco to Papeete. That is not her sole claim to fame, for in naval action she has engaged no less a formidable enemy than the notorious German cruiser Emden, that was menacing the Pacific during the first World War; and it must be noted that it was the wooden-built two-masted schooner that opened fire with her single small calibre gun against an armored cruiser bristling with long range pieces.

It seems, from what can be gathered of the tale on the Papeete waterfront, that the Zalee was at anchor off the retaining wall of that Tahitian harbor when the Emden hove in sight, a long, gray shape on the horizon. The German altered course only long enough to observe there was nothing of importance in the harbor, then proceeded peacefully west on a course taking her across the Pacific. So the great Emden was going about her business, when suddenly, the Zalee, still at anchor, opened fire with her single gun. The challenging shot fell short. Lazily the big turrets of the German swung around until a row of wide gun muzzles drew a bead on both schooner and town. The Zalee fired again, and again short. Then the Emden let go a broadside—perhaps two. The Zalee was suddenly missing. She was nowhere to be seen. She had been immediately sunk at her moorings. A few more shots fell into the town. But on the whole this was taken philosophically ashore; the Emden was destroyed by the Australian cruiser Sydney, and the Zalee, of inadequate but heroic action, was raised to continue her existence very much as though nothing at all had happened.

And now to pause for a moment upon such matters as ship's furniture, detail, and the origin of some of the modern improvements afloat to-day. At times, we cannot get away from a feeling of definite superiority over what we imagine to be the easy-going, unenlightened and un-scientific ways of our nautical forefathers. For instance, while many of us realize that, say, the marconi rig and the genoa jib go back into history at least a hundred years, we are apt to think that there the matter ends, and that the bulk of all the other innovations may be labeled, 20th Century.

But those rough and ready clipper-ship days and the days which went before them were not quite so unenlightened as the cheap sea novel or the average moving picture on the subject would have us believe. Steel masts and wire rigging come out of those days—out of the 1860's. Hand winches are equally as old. Turnbuckles were in use in the '70's, known then as bottle screws and rigging screws. The modern sounding machine is a product of that era, the patent log goes back to very near 1800, while the ultra-modern taffrail log was in use in the bygone '70's.

Nor is that all. Thank that same out-dated era for patent blocks, worm-drive steering gear, the modern binnacle, a reliable compass, the patent windlass, and patent davits and falls; for the aneroid barometer, the perfection of chronometer and sextant, great circle sailing, azimuth tables, and Sumner's Line of Position.

One is apt to gather from the brackish, second-rate sea novel, as well as from the average sea motion picture that sailing-ship days demanded only two things of seamen: profound illiteracy coupled with profound incaution. No greater injustice could be placed on a school of men that, as a majority, served this golden rule and served it well: "One hand for the ship and one for yourself." Out of those supposedly hit-or-miss days came the following results, results which, it must be noted, were usually attained not by an isolated group of scientists, but through a close collaboration of scientists and seamen, of which the merchant marine seaman played a part equally as important as that of the naval officer. First, there came about a correct recording of tides, carefully tabulated; then a precise study of winds and currents, resulting in the indispensable winds and currents charts. The ocean was methodically charted, and sounded, meteorological bureaus were established, weather reports issued, sailing directions and ship lanes set down, high latitude ice drifts observed. Those are but a few items of a long and significant list of an era which introduced, among other safety measures, navigational lights, Very lights, britches buoys, . . . and international signal flags.

What part did religion play in sailing ship history? On the whole it proved quite an important factor, but as time and space forbids entering upon it, the following single account must suffice.

In the year 1868 the Scottish firm of Barclay Curle decided to build a full-rigged ship to the exact dimensions of Noah's Ark as interpreted from a reckoning of the Biblical cubit. The vessel was built and launched in 1869 under the name of "Golden Fleece." She sailed the seas for fifteen years, and far from being an atrocity, was looked upon as an unusually handsome ship. The marine historian, Lubbock, refers to her as, "One of the most beautiful iron clippers ever built." Not only handsome, she was also able, an easy ship to work, and one endowed with a good turn of speed. Her dimensions: 223 feet by 37 feet by 22 feet 3 inches.

What is the longest ships' passage on record? In 1890 the schooner Marlborough of Glasgow, sailed homeward bound from New Zealand. She failed to arrive. Months passed. She was posted as missing. One, two, three years went by: four—and she was forgotten. But one morning, twenty-four years later, she was sighted off Cape Horn still afloat, still striving against the weather. The vessel was boarded and on the decks and inside the musty cabins were found the crew: silent, bleached, skeletons. Nothing spoke. The mystery stands to this day.

This ship was probably the victim of Antarctic ice which has a way of working northwards along the course that a sailing vessel running east from New Zealand would normally take. Perhaps at this point, one of the breath-taking gales of those latitudes dismasted her, or perhaps she became so surrounded by floating ice that she could not work clear, allowing the pack to hem her in, until, at another season, it froze about her, holding her in this position until the occurrence of a great thaw many years later, when, at last, the prevailing northerly currents brought her out into the light of day.

All this is but the taste and the odor of what may be found before a crackling fireplace this winter: the records of the sea; the great record of the sea which awaits to inspire or delight all those who sail or steam, race or cruise or row the modern sea; to startle the innocent, to inflame the imaginations of many, and to broaden one's understanding of a vast intricate sea-scape painted by many hands through many ages.

In concluding I would like to tell of a gallant stand put up by the crew of a ship's boat, whose true account I have not read in several years—to be more exact, not since I was fourteen—and that, I trust, will explain why I cannot at this moment put my hands upon the names of any of the men mentioned below.

Sometime during the last century the survivors of a foundered British sailing ship appeared off one of those bleak and dreadfully isolated islands which border upon the empty Antarctic. Short of food, they forced a landing in the surf. The shore was rocky, steep-to, and the boat was completely wrecked.

The crew discovered the island to be nothing more than a cliff that, hung over a wild sea, was blown bare by the almost constant gales of those regions. There was some lichen, and, in the lees, shrubs and a few berries; but nothing else—except birds.

The boat was beyond repair. The nearest habitable land lay hundreds of miles away, while perhaps not once in four years was a ship likely to chance by. The men knew they could not survive there indefinitely—and, to top it off, the Antarctic winter was already setting in.

The British merchant marine mate did not give up. Casting about to make something out of an impossible situation, he at last struck upon an idea. A fantastic idea. Surely he must have known that the odds against it working were at least a thousand to one. Nevertheless he drove the half-frozen men high up the cliffs collecting deposits of bird lime, then to the shore below for quantities of sand. At last, somewhere between cliff tops and shore, began the long laborious processes over a make-shift kiln. The fire was stoked by twigs and fragments of another wreck, parts of which were fashioned into huge crude molds. The wrecked lifeboat was gotten together as much in one piece as possible. Throughout the night the handful of men would scale the windy cliffs scraping the frigid lime, or work to feed the little fire, counting every stick, then to keep a careful watch over it. The result:

at last the old life-boat covered over, turned into a concrete boat, very high about the sides to allow for the extra weight, but sufficiently seaworthy for the mate and the men (whom I believe made the passage entirely on berries and salted bird flesh) to sail successfully across the stormiest ocean in this world.

But here the bare sea record is inadequate. It states that this boat was fashioned entirely out of wood and concrete. It says no more. It leaves it to your own understanding the discovery of at least three other elements buried in the composition of that boat: tenacity, courage, and, as they say, the long faith—good shipmates, able hands in all weathers.

THE LOG OF THE
ABIEL ABBOT LOW

by CAPT. W. C. NEWMAN

MAY, 1903

ONE of the most important events in the history of motor boats is the voyage made in summer 1902 by the launch Abiel Abbot Low across the Atlantic from New York to Falmouth, England. The Abiel Abbot Low is the smallest boat that has ever crossed the ocean on her own bottom under power, and her successful passage has demonstrated the seaworthiness of the modern type of launch as well as the reliability of the motor with which she was fitted.

The credit for the undertaking is due to the New York Kerosene Engine Company, who built and equipped the boat and sent her across in charge of Captain Newman, under whose supervision the boat was constructed in the Company's shops at College Point, New York City. The boat is a double-ender with good freeboard, and has a low trunk cabin with a small cockpit. On the two short masts enough sail is carried to steady the boat in a seaway, and in case of a breakdown of machinery would enable her to make a port, or at least keep in the track of steamers. Her dimensions are: 38 feet over all; 33 feet 6 inches water line; 9 feet beam, 3 feet 8 inches draught; 2 feet

"The day is fair, wind from the southeast and my son is sick.
Engine is doing well . . ."

3 inches least freeboard; and 4 feet 8 inches depth of hold. She is equipped with a 10-horse-power kerosene oil motor installed in the cabin, and started on her voyage with eight hundred gallons of kerosene oil in her supply tanks. Besides her fuel supply she carried two hundred and fifty gallons of fresh water and a supply of food for a sixty-day passage.

The boat was launched on June 30th, 1902, and before starting to cross the ocean made a trip around Long Island, covering the distance of about 250 miles in forty-two and one-half hours. After this preliminary trial the boat was fitted out for the trip across and sailed from New York, on July 9th, in charge of Capt. William C. Newman and his sixteen-year-old son, C. E. Newman. After a stormy passage the launch arrived in Falmouth, on August 14th, at 6 P.M. On the voyage the motor used four hundred and forty gallons of kerosene at the rate of four-fifths of a gallon per hour.

The log, kept each day by Capt. Newman, gives a better idea of the voyage and its hardships than can be given by any written-up account, and is most interesting.—THOMAS FLEMING DAY

July 9. Sailed from College Point at 11:25 A.M. carrying the flag of Messrs. A. A. Low and Brothers at mast head and at rearmast, flag of white ground with a blue cross and star in center, also the code signal "Good Bye." At 3 P.M. bid good-bye to wife and children at Coney Island Point. As Fire Island Light dips out of sight the feelings of my heart cannot be told.

July 10. The day is fair, wind from southwest and my son is sick. Engine is doing well.

July 11. Cooked our first meal since we left home. Engine is doing well. I am off Georges Banks. I can see the fishermen and I have made a mistake; I should have E. S. E. for my true course and my magnetic course by a westerly variation but I have changed my course S. E. ½ S. bound for the southern passage across. I now realize I am on the ocean and must do all I can to get across. Weather cloudy and foggy. We are now about 380 miles from New York.

July 12. The fourth day out, weather fine. Engine doing splendid. I have great difficulty in getting my bearings, the only means I have is the North Star; when it is behind clouds I cannot get it; my only instruments are my compass and barometer.

July 13. The fifth day out and a beautiful Sunday. We feel now reconciled, held our little church service and thanked God for his keeping us. The engine is working away like a good fellow, with no trouble whatever. We sighted a French barque, got our first bearings Lat. 39:10, Long. 62:20.

July 14. The sixth day out, calm. Engine doing well. At one o'clock we stopped the engine on account of some bearings running hot.

July 15. Seventh day out, saw a steamer in the distance going in the same course as we are. Got my bearing of the North Star, variation 20:30, west of true north. I have a good mind to change my course and go further north as I will be more in connection with steamers. Engine working away like a good fellow. At 4 P.M. the sea began to get very high and at 8 P.M. came to on our drag but boat would only lie to by stern; the night is dark and we are in our first storm.

July 16. Eighth day out, stormy, with high sea running from south, wind increasing with violent gushes. I am worried about my boat not lying to the wind. I have resorted to all means, but they are of no avail. Daylight has come and the ocean is something frightful to behold. Seas are like mountains. During the night I used two gallons of fish oil, but during the day the seas were longer and my mind more at ease, as I find the little launch rides the waves in safety. Night is coming with no sign of any let up.

July 17. Ninth day out begins with no hope of good weather and the night has been a trying one. 8 A.M. the wind is going down and the barometer is rising. Made some coffee to warm my body as I am almost exhausted.

July 18. Tenth day out. Started engine at 4 A.M., but am afraid will have to shut down soon. 7 A.M. passed the steamer St. Louis and exchanged salutes. At 8 A.M. the wind backed around to southwest and at 9 A.M. came to our drag again; wind blowing strong with an awful storm from the northwest. 8 P.M. The night is dark, raining and blowing so hard we had to use some more oil, and we tossed about so hard that our kerosene tanks are beginning to leak.

July 19. Eleventh day beginning with little hope of improvement and I have five inches of kerosene in my bilge. 12 o'clock, the wind is going down; at 4 P.M. used my torch for steamer; hard work nights is using me up and my eyes are getting dim; I cannot see so well at night; I think I see a light when it is only a big wave that appears so high in the Gulf Stream; at 9 P.M. started the engine.

July 20. Twelfth day out and our second Sunday at sea; the weather is fair, the wind and sea going down and we are making good time; the engine is doing its best without any trouble; held our little meeting and remembered the Sabbath Day; we passed the Deutschland at 3 P.M. going west.

July 21. Thirteenth day out, begins fair and ocean is coming smooth again, so we have a breathing spell; I mended up my sea anchor and gave the boat a good overhauling; found five of my eighty-five one-gallon cans of kerosene empty; the engine is doing fine and we passed a steamer in the offing to south of us at 1 P.M.

July 22. Fourteenth day out with the sea heaving in from the north and it looks bad in the south with now and then lightning; my boy is not well; I gave him something to take and he showed his first day of homesickness. The day is turning out fine, making good time and engine doing good work.

July 23. Fifteenth day out; at 4 A.M. stopped the engine, as kerosene was leaking from tanks; got a good breakfast and at 11 A.M. got underway with engines, but the sea is so rough and high we cannot make headway, so came to again at 12 P.M.

July 24. Sixteenth day out; the sea is high; I am not feeling well; the voyage is telling on me; the rolling, constant sitting and steering is fast pulling me down, and the sea tosses the boat about so; my after-tank leaks about 15 gallons a day; I figure myself in mid-ocean and the engine is doing well.

July 25. Seventeenth day out; the wind is light; not much sea; stopped the engine at 8 P.M. to pack the pumps and got a good break-

"I have great difficulty in getting my bearings, the only means I have is the North Star, when it is behind clouds I cannot get it; my only instruments are my compass and barometer."

fast; started the engine at 11 A.M., but as wind and sea are against us our progress is slow.

July 26. Eighteenth day out and fine weather; the English Hixham from South Shiels hailed us and asked if we were all right; the Captain gave me my bearings, latitude 43:34 north, longitude 40:26 west; I thanked him, we dipped our flags and sailed on; our engine doing well.

July 27. Nineteenth day out; our third Sunday at sea; wind northeast with high rolling sea; the barometer fell 2-10ths; at 4 A.M. came to on our drag, but started again at 6 A.M. This is the highest sea I ever saw and if we get a storm with it our chances will be small; my boy is in good health but I suffer from weary work and care; the voyage is telling on me and I have much pain; we held our Sabbath Day services at 4 P.M.; the steamer Patrician, from Liverpool, hailed us and we reported all well; engine doing fine.

July 28. Twentieth day out; fair with light winds; engine is doing fine and I am feeling better; emptied my after-tank of oil into the forward-tank; this makes very hard work for me, as the little boat rocks and rolls about so it is hard to move about; it is impossible to get our food regularly as the boy has to steer while I keep things in shape and my hours are from dark to daylight, steering, then to look after things; the oil tanks leaking cause me a lot of trouble but the engine works all right and gives me no bother.

July 29. Twenty-first day out and on account of the fly-wheel of the engine running in kerosene had to stop and repair my tanks; I do not know what I can do as my strength is giving out fast; we stopped at 8 A.M. and slept until 12 o'clock; then tore down bow partition and found leak in tank; at 8 P.M. got ready, and after taking some more rest got underway at 10 P.M., but the night was so dark and a high sea running, came to a stop at 1 P.M. and in my condition thought it better to rest.

July 30. Twenty-second day out and it is not very promising; the wind is ahead; started engine at 10 A.M., but we are not making much headway; our general condition looks blue just now but hope for the best; there is an awful sea and high swell at 7 P.M.; came to a stop to wait for more favorable weather.

July 31. Twenty-third day out and it is fine, the best we have had for a long time; I am somewhat straightened out again; the old tanks leak about 10 gallons a day which causes hard work to put back in tanks; the engine is doing splendid and we are pushing on to England as hard as the engine will drive us; the weather is sunny and warm and our condition a little better.

August 1. Twenty-fourth day out but it does not look very promising and we come to our drag at 12 A.M., then went below to get something to eat; in less than half an hour the steamer Kroonland of the American line came right for us and asked if we were all right. I told them yes and wished to be reported; the passengers cheered us and as she went by we dipped flags; at 4 P.M. it looks very bad and wind is increasing; at 8 P.M. the night is dark, raining and wind blowing, and the sea is getting awful high; it is a bad night; I do not know what will become of us.

August 2. Twenty-fifth day out and we are in an awful condition, the sea high, blowing with rain, but I think we have had the worst of the storm; at 4 P.M. wind changed to northwest and it makes a very rough sea; inside we are swimming in kerosene, the tanks leak so; the man that made them ought to be with me; at 12 P.M. the storm is not over yet, heavy squalls and blowing with all its might but the Abiel Abbot Low rides the waves, thank God.

August 3. Twenty-sixth day out and our fourth Sunday; we had our little service and thanked God for our keeping; we are still laboring in high seas, our clothing is all saturated with kerosene, and we have not tasted food in 30 hours; the wind is going down some and at 2 P.M. the steamer Maesland, from Glasgow, bore down on us and asked if we needed any assistance. I told him no but would like to be reported. I also asked him for his longitude but did not get it as the sea was too high to get near her. We did not dip flags, as a big sea broke over the steamer. At 6 P.M. came to our drag again, night dark, raining and blowing; I am very ill, bleeding and very tired; my son is keeping up bravely.

August 4. Twenty-seventh day out and we have another breathing spell for ourselves; there is not much wind but it looks bad all around; we started our engine at 4 A.M., but do not know how long, as the barometer is very low yet, but we are here and have to make the best of it; I have my kerosene under control, I think I have lost about 25 gallons to the best of my judgment; my sea anchor was nearly gone when I hauled it up, the bridles and eyelets being badly chafed; at 7 P.M. came to on the drag again, the wind is strong from the northeast, I cannot take chances in my condition, will wait till daylight.

August 5. Twenty-eighth day out and we have another storm on us; it is frightful; we are tossed about in an awful manner, the hardships of this voyage are more than I thought for, we cannot hold out much longer; the barometer is rising some; we are making slow progress; the seas are high, the night dark and stormy but we are riding very good, the only fear is my sea anchor giving out on me before I can get it again for repairs.

August 6. Twenty-ninth day out and we are still lying to on our drag anchor with no sign of letting up, the wind and sea are creeping up, the barometer is 29.90; at 10 A.M. we started engine and are mak-

"Twenty-eighth day out . . . we are tossed about in an awful manner, the hardships of this voyage are more than I thought . . ."

ing good time; the weather is bad but we are pushing so hard to get across the Atlantic; my sea anchor was badly damaged when I hauled it up, but, thank God, I can mend it all right; at 8 P.M. came to our drag again, as the night was squally and I am worn out and sick.

August 7. Thirty days out and it is fair with a good breeze; started engine at 5 A.M. and we are doing good work; passed a steamer to the north of us going west; at 5 P.M. stopped to clean valves and started again at 9 P.M.; my health is very poor, I am losing ground fast.

August 8. Thirty-first day out; the wind is east and blowing very fast and we came to a stop at 8 A.M. for rest; my health is poor and I suffer much pain; I cooked a good meal and then straightened things; we have found another source of trouble—the barnacles are on our bottom about one inch long. I tried to get them off, but they have come to stay. I hope we will get to land soon.

August 9. Thirty-second day out; started engine at 3 A.M., but wind breezed up again at sunrise and came to a stop at 9 A.M. This is hard, but I have to take what comes. Started again at 2 P.M., and we are struggling against wind and sea. Came to again at 9 P.M., as my strength gave out.

August 10. Thirty-third day out and wind remains the same; I fell asleep and my boy calls me at 1 P.M.; I feel better now, my son stood watch over me four hours this night; started engine at 3 A.M.; the wind is changing; we are pushing on once more; we held our little Sabbath Day service; the sun is coming out, the first for a long time; the engine is doing fine; two steamers passed us going west; we had our last can of soup to-day; our stores are getting low but we have plenty of bread.

August 11. Thirty-four days out and we are making good time with engine and we are nearing the end of our voyage; if the weather holds good we will see land in a day or so; at 4 P.M. we got on our soundings, saw other birds and our friend the Haglar has left us; at 9 P.M. a steamer passed us going west; if my position is right and the weather stays fine, we are all right; my boy feels happy.

August 12. Thirty-fifth day out; it is raining and wind is fresh from northwest but we are pushing our engine; stopped at 7 o'clock to repack pumps and started again at 8 o'clock; we had a good breakfast. It has been a hard day, same cold and wet from the rain; came to our drag at 6 P.M.; the barometer is falling; have no bearings; my condition is poor; I must keep sea room as I think we are only 50 miles from the Scilly Islands and cannot take chances.

August 13. Thirty-sixth day out; we started engine at 5 A.M; at 8 A.M. made a fishing steamer, got my bearings from him; we are 90 miles from the Scilly Islands now; if the wind and weather remain as they are, we will be in Falmouth to-morrow at 11 A.M.; the wind is going down some and we are speeding for all she can go.

August 14. Thirty-seventh day out; we have not sighted land yet. I am looking for it but my eyes are so poor I cannot see far; it was a trying night; my dear boy sat steering for me whilst I was looking for the Bishop light; at 5 A.M. we made the light; we are not more than two miles from it and, thank God, the wind has gone down, the sun is coming out. Passed the Scilly Islands at 7 A.M.; passed Seven Stones Lightship at 9 A.M., Lands End and Wolf Rock at 11 A.M., and the Lizard Head Light at 3:15 P.M. Here the tide ran with violence against me and the water is very rough; at 6 P.M. cast anchor in Falmouth, and my ocean voyage is ended.

The launch laid at Falmouth from August 14 to September 3, when at 8 A.M. it left for Plymouth; the weather is fine and made the trip in six hours.

Sept. — Left Plymouth at 7 A.M. for Dartmouth; made the trip in seven hours; the tide running swift against us and the coast being from 200 to 500 feet high, makes it dangerous to navigate. We are well received by the people here.

Sept. 10. We are leaving Dartmouth at 6 A.M. for Weymouth; it is a fine day and we have a hard trip before us as the Portland Bill is very dangerous for small boats. We passed the bill at 3 P.M., the water running very swift and the sea is one unbroken sheet. We are well received by the people.

Sept. 13. We are leaving Weymouth for the Isle of Wight at 6 A.M. It is fair, with wind from northwest; arrived at Cowes at 4 P.M. We are well received by the people here. I have come along this dangerous coast to here alone, as I could not get a pilot; they all said that my boat was too small for them to go in.

Sept. 15. We are leaving Cowes Harbor, have got a pilot to take me to London for four pounds sterling; left Cowes at 2 P.M. for New Haven, but had to go in at Bembridge, Isle of Wight, as it turned stormy at 5 P.M.

Sept. 17. We are leaving Bembridge at 5 A.M. for New Haven; we have a good breeze from the northwest and are making good time; the sea is rough from the tide and my pilot is afraid of the boat, but we told him that she was all right and not to get afraid. We entered New Haven at 3 P.M.

Sept. 18. We are leaving New Haven for Ramsgate; we started at 5 A.M.; have a fine day of it; tide in our favor; got in at Ramsgate at 4 P.M. This is a watering place and we are swarmed with people to look at the launch.

Sept. 19. We are leaving Ramsgate at 11 A.M.; it was foggy all the morning but it is clear now and we are off for London; got at Hall Haven at 7 P.M. This is in the Thames River, 35 miles from London. We came to anchor for the night as so many steamers go up and down the river.

Sept. 20. We got under way at 9 A.M. with the turning of the tide; at 11 A.M., at the West India Dock; 3 P.M., the Abiel Abbot Low is safely moored at her pier. Here ends our voyage across the Atlantic with no serious breakdown to the engine. Whatever I have said in this log is the truth. Witness by my son and myself with my right hand, so help me God.

THE GREATEST RACE OF THEM ALL

by GEORGE S. HAWLEY

JANUARY, 1931

IN 1865, the greatest ocean race ever sailed was arranged. The tea-clippers, Ada, Black Prince, Fiery Cross, Chinaman, Serica, Flying Spur, Taitsing, Taeping and Ariel, lay at the Pagoda anchorage, fifteen miles downriver from Foochow, China, hurrying their lading so that all might sail on approximately the same date. Coolie gangs were doubled; papers were put in order as rapidly as possible, and the hundred and one details necessary to fit a ship for sea were attended to.

The Fiery Cross got her final chest of tea aboard and was towed to sea early on the morning of May 29, 1865. The Ariel, Serica, and Taitsing all left at about 10:50 the following day; the Ariel possibly a few minutes in the lead. The Taitsing followed at midnight on the

31st. The other vessels of the fleet, unfortunately, could not get away in time to participate in the race.

The Fiery Cross picked up a light northeast breeze and passed through the Formosa Channel with royal studding sails set. The other four ships following closely behind. This breeze carried them for four hundred miles when the Fiery Cross was becalmed, allowing the other ships to run up on her in short order. She was, however, the first to catch the southwest monsoon and rapidly drew away from her rivals.

On June 8 the Fiery Cross and the Ariel met on opposite tacks, both ships being favored by a strong southwest breeze, and the Fiery Cross passed three miles to windward. She kept this lead through the Sunda Straits, passing Anjer Point on June 19. She was followed by Ariel the next morning and the Taeping on the same afternoon. The Serica and the Taitsing passing the point on the 22nd and 25th respectively.

From Anjer Point to the meridian of Mauritius they all found fresh trade winds and it was on this "leg" that they all made their best twenty-four hours' run—Ariel 317, Serica 291, Taeping 319, Fiery Cross 328 and Taitsing 318 miles.

The Fiery Cross rounded the Cape of Good Hope on July 14, forty-six days out, closely followed by the Ariel. The other ships following in close order in the next few days.

The Fiery Cross reached the Equator August 3, twenty days from the Cape of Good Hope, with the Ariel still dogging her heels. On this stretch the other vessels of the fleet gained considerably and on August 9, in latitude twelve minutes, twenty-nine seconds north, the Fiery Cross exchanged signals with the Taitsing, the two ships keeping in company for about a week.

The Ariel, about thirty miles to the westward, found fresh winds and took the lead from the Fiery Cross. Meanwhile, the Taitsing brought up with a fresh breeze and closed in on the Ariel. The Ariel, not to be outdone, broke out still more sail, left the Taitsing in the rear and was the first to pass the Azores, followed by Taitsing, Fiery Cross, Serica and Taeping in the order named.

After passing the islands the Taeping seems to have shaken her sluggard ways. At any rate she passed the Taitsing and Fiery Cross and, in company with the Serica, closed in on the leader.

At daybreak on September 5, the Ariel and Taeping passed the

Lizard; their lee scuppers smothered in foam and making all of fifteen knots.

After passing the Lizard the winds moderated and each ship had the company of the other in the run up the channel

At three o'clock on the morning of September 6, both vessels were boarded by pilots and, under strange hands, Ariel gained a slight lead on Taeping, passing the Deal, or finish line, at eight o'clock, followed by the Taeping a scant eight minutes later.

The Serica passed the Deal four hours later and all three ships went up the Thames on the same tide. The Fiery Cross followed on the 7th and the Taitsing on the 9th.

It would seem that since the Ariel crossed the line in the lead she would be awarded the victor's crown. Such was not the case, for the Taeping had left the Pagoda anchorage twenty minutes after her rival and therefore was entitled to the premium due the winner.

After a race of 16,000 miles she had won by *twelve minutes!*

RUNNING THE RAPIDS
OF THE COLORADO

by DEVERGNE BARBER

APRIL–MAY, 1931

IN THE FALL of 1928 there gathered on the banks of the Colorado River, at Green River, Utah, a party of thirteen men and one mongrel dog. Pulled up on the edge of this mighty stream lay six white boats. A band struck up a lively air, Governor George H. Dern shook the hands of the thirteen men as they gaily piled into the little craft and one by one drifted from sight below the railroad bridge. Three thousand people cheered. The Pathé Colorado River Expedition was under way.

Before many weeks passed this little band of men were to furnish front page copy for western newspapers and be the object of a prolonged search by the Army Air Service. But now they were a light-hearted bunch of adventurers bound on a trip undertaken by few and finished by fewer still, the navigation of the canyons of the Colorado.

The object of the expedition was varied, as were the men that composed it. The United States Army Signal Service was desirous of testing a new radio set designed by them and for that purpose had assigned Master Signal Sergeant Vernon T. Herrick to the expedition, furnishing him with one of the sets to operate in the depths of the canyons where the iron ore studded walls, thousands of feet deep, would put it to a real test.

In addition to the set with us, the Army had erected a high-powered station on the rim of the Grand Canyon at Shinemu Alter, on the Painted Desert, to work with Herrick and relay my stories to the outside world. This station was to relay to Salt Lake City, Utah. The Pathé film company, always on the lookout for a novelty, had sent several cameramen with the expedition to film completely, for the first time, the wonders of these gorges.

For myself, I was a rather scared and subdued newspaper reporter from the cliff dwellings of Manhattan. I had read of the perils and hardships of a trip like this; and, although when my city editor had handed me a ticket to Los Angeles and solemnly shaken my hand, I had been wild to get started, now I wasn't so sure.

The boats were sixteen feet long. They were completely decked over with the exception of a small cockpit amidships where the boat-man rode; the passenger riding on the open deck. In the center of the decked over space, fore and aft, was a watertight hatch, fastened down with wing-bolts. Under these were stored provisions and equipment. In each boat was an equal share of food, to be used in the event of a separation.

In command of the party was Major E. C. LaRue, a retired United States engineer, who has spent the greater part of his life in and around the Colorado River and is said to be one of the greatest living authorities on the river and its problems. With him was Frank Dodge, chief boatman. In 1921 Dodge and LaRue had led a government expedition down the river on a survey and were well acquainted with the trip before us. They had it on us in that respect. We had no idea what we were up against.

The first few days were a constant repetition of wide open country and slow current, for up in northern Utah, the Colorado is called the Green and is as calm and quiet as an old woman.

For days we drifted with the current, the boatmen only using their oars to keep the boats in some semblance of a line. Occasionally one would ground on a sand bank and the crew of two would drop off into the cold snow water and heave her off. This process was accompanied by a round of applause and "razzberries" from passing boats in the line.

On the bank the trees and shrubs grew close to the water's edge. A deer, drinking, glanced up, stared and returned to its drinking, entirely unafraid. The silence was broken only by the murmur of the water and the gentle splash of an oar. Overhead snowy clouds scudded before a swift wind. In the purple distance a range of mountains reared their peaks far above the horizon. In the evening a halo of orange and purple dropped quickly about them as the sun sank from sight. Then the utter blackness of a desert night.

It was the custom of LaRue to begin his hunt for a camping place as soon as we had finished our dinner. Camping spots were few and far between, being composed of a sand bank long and wide enough to pitch our tents on and in the proper place on the stream to be covered with driftwood, our fuel.

I will always remember the third night out of Green River. It was a high spot in my already checkered career as a news hound. A misty rain was falling and we were all of us wet to the skin. The sun had failed to shine and the cold added to our discomfort. All hands were waiting LaRue's signal to pull for the shore and make a camp. A fire was what we wanted.

Suddenly around a bend in the river the lead boat swung towards the shore. The rest of the line followed. My boat, the Havesue, being the lightest of the lot, was first ashore. With a sigh of relief I saw the nose ground and the stern swing around. I leaped.

The bank was composed of a delightful species of mud that on the surface resembled solid earth. Under half an inch of this was a composition of sand, rotten wood and black mud. When my two hundred pounds landed on this soft crust I went in to my arm pits. Two hours later I was hauled out, cursing the whim that had made me want to be first ashore.

I learned later from Major LaRue that this was one of the most common things along the river and one to guard against. Quicksand. The river always raising and lowering, is in spots merely a current of drifting sand mud along the banks. Over this is a crust of sun-baked mud, very deceptive and uncomfortable to a tenderfoot.

The fourth night out of Green River Sergeant Herrick set up his radio station and attempted to get in touch with either Salt Lake City or the army station on the Painted Desert; but with no luck, although he reported that he could hear the calls of the desert station trying to raise us. When they failed to hear our signals the operator was heard to call Salt Lake and ask for information. Needless to say, Salt Lake also had no news.

As we drifted down the river, it seemed to me, lying on my back on the stern of the boat, that the surrounding country slowly and relentlessly closed in upon us. Inch by inch, foot by foot, the banks grew higher and steeper. The current was a little swifter each day, although we had not yet reached the region of the gorges and rapids. They were still many days away.

The weather grew colder. Owing to the increasing height of the banks on either side, we saw less of the sun each day. By now it only shone directly on us for four hours and the boatmen strived to dodge the patches of shade as long as possible, for the thin air does not hold the heat and out of the sun it is bitter cold.

Each morning, day after day, we rose long before daylight and John the cook, working under handicaps that would have driven an ordinary cook completely crazy, prepared a feast fit for kings. While breakfast was on the fire, the rest of the crew rolled up tents, packed bedding, dismantled the radio, loaded the boats leaving out only the equipment being used by the cook and enough food for a light lunch. Breakfast over, it was the work of but a few minutes to load this and with light hearts we were off again.

As the days passed we drifted through more or less open country again; passed farms long since abandoned by the hardy forefathers of the Mormons. Ancient water-wheels, used a hundred years ago to lift the muddy water up and into irrigation ditches, tiny log cabins that housed the hardy pioneers and the old camp sites of prospectors, searching for gold along the river, dotted the landscape.

Suddenly all this was blotted out by the towering cliffs around us. We were in the canyon country. True, they didn't rate very much as canyons, but to us, tired of the monotony of days, they seemed to be of unplumbed depth.

The river had narrowed and grown swifter. Rocks studded it here and there. Its tune had changed from a merry tinkle to a warning snarl as it whipped around the boulders, as if telling us to turn back before it was too late. And believe me, if I had had an inkling of what we were to go through I will be perfectly frank and say that I would have taken a chance of finding my way out and beat it right then.

It was the second day before Thanksgiving that we entered our first canyon, called Glenn Canyon. This gorge is not dangerous but gave us our first taste of waves and rapids.

Within an hour after entering, LaRue located a sand bank and ordered the boats ashore. After the last boat had been pulled up on the mud he looked us all over as if mentally sizing us up.

"All right, fellows," he said. "You guys have been hollering for some excitement, now you're going to get it. Within the next mile we will strike a formation on the bottom that causes what is known as sand waves. They are not dangerous, but you will find them as wet as any to come.

"Boatmen will reverse their boats at the signal from Dodge. Go down stern first. Passengers will lay on the stern, or bow as it will be then. Everyone put on your kapok life jackets. If you go overboard one of the boats will pick you up at the foot."

To say I was thrilled would be putting it mildly. I have hung to the spray hood of a speeding Coast Guard boat while bullets sung all around and I have hung on to the rear step of roaring fire trucks in my time as a reporter, but never have I felt the shiver that went over my body when I heard LaRue's words. Somehow it seemed different out in that country. Anyone can be a hero when there is a crowd around to admire, but try running a Colorado River rapid and you will change your ideas of what constitutes intestinal fortitude.

All hands rushed to their respective boats, broke out the jackets and donned them. Boatmen looked to their spare oars and rowlocks. All was in readiness for the great adventure.

The mile was covered in a little less than no time. The first warning we had of the nearness of the rapid was a low roaring echoing across the surrounding cliffs. Rapidly this rose to a high pitched scream as the first boat, manned by LaRue and Dodge flashed into it.

Once or twice I sighted the boat as it rose on a wave, but in a few seconds I was too busy hanging on to notice anything. With a death hold on the life lines running around the gunwales, I felt the crash of the boat as it struck the opening wave. From then on it is rather hazy.

I had an impression of thousands of tons of water falling on me and looked up once to see a wall of mud over my head. The next instant I was cowering on the deck with the whole load around my neck. It was a lifetime before the boat ceased its pitching and rolling and grounded gently on a sand bank. It was all over.

All of the boats had come through without turning over, although LaRue said the Dirty Devil had had a close call as she struck the opening wave sideways.

The entire crew was wet to the skin and a great driftwood fire was built to thaw out. The cockpits had to be bailed out and the cargo inspected. Everything was dry under hatches and in an hour we were under way again.

During the afternoon we encountered three of these minor rapids, none of them rocky but all miserably wet, and after running each we were obliged to stop and dry out, owing to the cold. We camped that night on a sand bar and all hands were glad to crawl into their blankets for a short sleep.

Early the next morning I was awakened by a harsh voice singing something about "I want to wake up in the morning where the morning glories grow."

It was LaRue calling his crew. How I learned to hate that song. Every morning without fail it was the first thing I heard and crawling, numb with cold, from a pile of wet blankets I would curse the major and his music until I had warmed myself with my own rage.

It was now the day before Thanksgiving and LaRue told us we had one bad rapid to run before we entered Dark Canyon, the first one of any importance. It was rock studded and dangerous, he said and he doubted we would get through without a wreck.

Three hours after the morning start we heard it and if the sound meant anything, it was some stretch of water. The roar was so loud that conversation between the boats was impossible. The towering cliff on each side confined the noise, multiplying it until it sounded like ten thousand souls in mortal torment.

LaRue signaled the boats to a sand bank and gave his orders. The boatmen would work their way down the bank and take a look from the foot of the rapid. Here they could locate the larger rocks, it being impossible to see them from the head owing to the water flowing over them. The passengers would also make their way down the bank, leaving the boatmen to navigate it alone. I was all for this idea and expressed myself loudly.

It wasn't much trouble to walk the quarter mile to the foot, and arriving there we built a great fire of the ever-present driftwood and prepared to watch the fun.

Dodge came first. His boat, the Little Colorado, entered the rapid slowly, stern first, Dodge pulling at the oars in an attempt to hold a course mapped out from the foot. It was impossible. The boat picked up speed with appalling rapidity and in a few seconds it was traveling like an express train. Dodge ran that quarter mile in a few seconds over a half a minute.

Four other boats followed in quick succession. They came through safely. The sixth, manned by Val Woodbury, California sportsman, managed to get half way through and then with a resounding crash struck a boulder and turned over, catapulting Woodbury out into the cold water.

A cry of "He's over" rose from every throat. A dozen lines snaked out from shore, life jackets on the end. Dodge sprang into his boat and struck for the center of the stream, knowing that Woodbury would come out on the tail of the rapid. He did and it was a wet, spluttering, embarrassed and slightly bruised young man that was bodily dragged into the boat and hoisted close to the fire.

Of course, nobody "razzed" him, *much*, but he felt that his honor had suffered by being the first casualty. Ten days later it was a good man who brought his boat through a rapid and remained attached to it.

An inspection of the boat showed that it had been damaged slightly and would need repairing, so LaRue ordered camp made. We would make Dark Canyon the next day and spend Thanksgiving there, he said.

Once again Herrick set up his radio station but was unable to reach the desert station. By this time their call had become frantic. We were twenty days out of Green River and had not yet been heard from. The desert operator told us to light flares so that Indians scouting along the top of the canyon could see us. This we did, also setting fire to a pile of driftwood that stood nearly 150 feet high and covered a half an acre of ground.

The driftwood fire wasn't such a bright idea. Hotter and hotter grew the air until we were almost forced off the bank by the heat. Paint on the boats blistered and so did we under the withering tongue of LaRue, who had no respect whatever for a young reporter from New York.

Early the next morning we were again broken out by the morning glory song, now cordially hated by one and all. At five o'clock the boats had been loaded and we were off. At seven we heard Dark Canyon Rapid.

Eight o'clock found camp made for the day and good old John toiling over his fire. He was baking a ham for dinner and from the smells that drifted away from the Dutch oven no turkey could ever be better.

A stream of clear cold water came out of a small side canyon and it was a welcome change from river water. We had been forced to settle all our water before drinking it and a milk bottle, set out full, would show three inches of mud on the bottom in an hour.

I spent a few minutes watching the boatmen preparing to line the boats down the rapids, the water being too swift and rocky to run. Stripping to only pants and shoes, the boys were preparing to wade shoulder deep in the bitter cold water and let the boats down with ropes. I thought this process was going to be interesting and was congratulating myself on being a scribe instead of a boatman when Dodge, chief boatman, walked over to my seat and said, "All right, big boy, shed that fancy coat and try the water, it's fine." Ten minutes later I was hip deep in the river, holding a rope for dear life. On the other end was a boat that seemed determined to gallop down stream without benefit of operator. Dodge came to my rescue, mentioning something about reporters in general and one in particular.

After six hours of unceasing struggle the boats were all safely moored at the foot of the rapid. My hands were raw and bleeding from the rough application of saw-toothed manila. It was several days before I could resume my labors on a typewriter. The rest of the boys seemed to enjoy my discomfort and offered many suggestions regarding relief; such as rubbing them with salt, and others too numerous to mention.   ·

Thanksgiving dinner was a huge success. Baked ham, baked potatoes, home-made bread, apples, canned fruit, a pie that John had managed to make, coffee and to top it all off LaRue produced a gallon jug of liquid lightning which he had saved for the event and had kept hidden in his boat.

After dinner, with a few hours of daylight still left, Herrick and I decided to follow the little stream back into the side canyon. The rest of the party being unable to navigate, had spread themselves out around the fire.

For about three miles we followed the stream back into the cliffs. For a short distance it was fairly wide and then the sides slowly closed in until we were almost in a tunnel. The brook tinkled and sang in the dark as we made our way along the side, bent almost double to avoid striking our heads. Far ahead I could see a spot of light.

It took us some time to get through the cave but it was well worth the effort, for as we stepped forth in the light there burst upon us a sight so beautiful that it was several minutes before either spoke.

Before us lay an open valley of green and brown. It extended for at least five miles back before it again raised to a cliff. It was perhaps three miles wide. Deer grazed in the knee deep grass and they seemed either not to see us, or they ignored us entirely.

On our left as we stepped out of the cave entrance was a dwelling made of rocks and mud that had stood for thousands of years. It was the home of a cliff dweller. Inside were the remains of a fire. Broken pottery was scattered around the ashes just as they had been left centuries ago. Directly in front of the cave opening was a watch tower or fort of some kind, evidently intended to defend the valley against invaders.

Several more cliff dwellings were grouped around the first one, which had evidently been a headquarters of some kind. Through each of these we searched, hoping to find a skeleton or some other relic which we could take out. Not finding anything of the sort we had to be satisfied with some bits of pottery.

On the face of the cliff, some hand, long since returned to ashes, had chiseled a story in pictures. Not having a camera with me, for which I berated myself, I copied the pictures as closely as possible, hoping to have them identified after the trip was over.

For two hours Herrick and I wandered through this village of the ancients so engrossed that we did not notice the sun was fast sinking. Back into the tunnel we plunged and it was long after dark when we returned to camp. The rest of the party had long since turned in so Herrick and I were forced to crawl into our blankets without being able to tell of our discovery, although we were burning with the importance of it.

The next morning I told LaRue what we had found and he became an amazing fountain of information. He told us the history of the cliff dwellers who had made their homes in the canyons of the Colorado. Of the villages to be found in the thousands of side canyons. Of the watch towers and forts they had built long before America was thought of. For an hour we listened as he unfolded the lore and tribal stories of the Indians who have handed down for generations the story of the Colorado.

Dark Canyon is well named. The walls tower a thousand feet in the air before they set back a half a mile and reared another two thousand. It was dusk all day with the exception of an hour at noon and the cold was intense. It rained nearly all the time. That is, it was rain where we were. At the top it was snow and the white blanket that covered the peaks and cliffs was beautiful to see, but as it changed to rain as it fell to the bottom, it was extremely uncomfortable.

After leaving Dark Canyon life became a living Hell. Rapids every mile or so to run. Boats turning over and spilling the men into the icy water became a common occurrence, and to make matters worse we were running short of food. Rations had been cut to rock bottom and the noonday lunch now was composed of bread and water. "Cake and Wine," we called it.

Out of Dark Canyon and into Marble Gorge we traveled. The rapids became worse and worse, getting so bad that some days we made only a mile or two. The radio still refused to work, although Herrick could hear the frantic calls of the desert station and Salt Lake begging for some word. Nearly a month had passed and we were still unheard from.

Marble Gorge is so called because of its formation of sandstone. Its sides, cut through by centuries of water action, are as smooth and highly polished as the front of a bank. They rise straight in the air for 3,000 feet and at that time were capped with snow.

Through Marble Gorge we struggled, hungry, cold and tired. The rapids had taken their toll and the boats were patched until they resembled a crazy quilt. Oars had been smashed and lost. Bedding remained water-soaked and we were inured to wet blankets. We had ceased to sleep nights. We merely crawled into our blankets and passed out, to awaken in the morning for a day of horror. All of us were practically deaf by this time from the unceasing roar of the rapids. No unnecessary words were spoken. Every man went about his tasks automatically. An uncomplaining lot of men they were.

After Marble Gorge we struck Sheer Wall Rapids. These must have been conceived by the devil. Straight from the water rose the walls. No chance here to walk around and avoid the drenching we knew would result from a ride through. One by one the boats approached the side and both men of the crew grasped a crack or outcropping to hold the boat from rushing through. LaRue shouted his orders. They were short and simple. Go through one at a time about five minutes apart. After a final glance LaRue let go the wall and like a rifle shot his boat plunged into the maelstrom.

Woodbury went next and disappeared around the bend. We were next in line. With a push I forced the boat away from the wall and dropped flat on the deck, grabbing everything in sight.

Lunging and rolling we hit the opening wave, all of fifteen feet high and hiding a boulder as big as a house. Swiftly we picked up speed and just as I was congratulating myself, I heard a sickening crash and felt myself lifted from the boat.

Landing on my back in the torrent I struck the overturned boat and came up under it. The buoyancy of my life jacket pinned me against the deck and strangling for want of air I attempted to tear the jacket off. A rock struck me between the shoulders, knocking out what little air remained in my lungs, but the momentary stop allowed the boat to slide over my head, tearing two long gashes in my forehead.

More dead than alive I was fished out at the foot of the rapid and allowed LaRue to sew my cuts with cotton thread and a needle I had seen him darning a sock with the night before. I wasn't the only wreck. Five of the six boats had turned over. Only LaRue and Dodge had come through unscathed.

A great fire soon revived us and it was with warming hearts we heard LaRue say that less than two miles below us lay the town of Hite, Utah. He wasn't very explicit regarding the city, but assured us that the town really existed. Light as a feather the boats were as we pushed them from the mud bank and headed for Hite. We arrived in two hours.

Fifty years ago Hite was a flourishing mining village of a thousand souls. But that was fifty years ago. Today it stands uninhabited and forlorn in its loneliness. The log buildings still stand as sturdy as the day they were built.

With great gusto each boat crew moved into a building. The

radio station was set up in the post office building and the kitchen operated in the general store. It was easy to warm the log huts and soon we were in dry clothes and high spirits.

For an hour after supper Herrick tried vainly to reach the outside world. He could hear the desert station still calling as it had every night for a month. Now it was telling us to be on the lookout for an army airplane that would soon be flying over with food.

Pat Gannon, Pathé news cameraman, had set up a Radiola broadcast receiver we had with us, and to our great surprise it burst forth in song. We sat around the hut for many hours listening to the music and changing the tuning, we heard a broadcast from Los Angeles announcing that an airplane was about to set out in search of the lost Colorado River Expedition.

LaRue dryly announced that no man was lost if he knew where he was and surely LaRue had a good idea as to his general whereabouts. If he didn't no one else did.

We were now about thirty miles north of Lee's Ferry, Arizona, which was to be our first contact with civilization. But what a thirty miles. It took us nine days to make it and most of the time we lifted the boats bodily from the water and carried them around the rapids, now too dangerous even to line. It was tough work, but we made it.

On the eighth day, one day out of Lee's Ferry, we made camp at Warm Springs, twenty miles below the junction of the Green and the Grand Rivers.

Used as we were to camping on wet sand banks it was a relief to find a grassy spot a mile long and nearly as wide, high above the waterline. A spiral of smoke rose from the bank as we made our way towards it and all hands thought it to be an advance party of searchers. It turned out to be the camp of a dozen Indian hunters who, taking us for agents, immediately hid their deer meat.

It took some tall talking to convince them we were not Indian agents and they brought forth a hind quarter of venison. To thirteen men who had lived for several days on beans and bread, dreaming of pot roasts and steaming stacks of hot cakes with golden butter, it isn't hard to imagine what happened to the hind quarter. We got it in trade for six sacks of tobacco and some cigarettes.

In the evening Herrick, after again trying to reach the desert, had set up the broadcast receiver, using the long antennae of his set for the smaller one. In a few minutes music poured forth.

The braves carefully inspected the box from which the sound came and, being unable to fathom it, asked if it were a "phoeygraf." Carefully Herrick explained that it was a radio. This being some years ago when radios were not in general use in this great open country, the braves had never heard of them. Suddenly spying the wire leading off to a pole a hundred feet away, the head brave followed it to the end, returning with a triumphant gleam in his eye.

"Ah, telephone," he said.

"No," answered Herrick. "It is a radio."

Still the chief wasn't convinced and, after listening for a few minutes, turned to his friends, with a disgusted toss of his head towards the box, announced, "Huh, hokum."

At three o'clock the following afternoon LaRue's boat disappeared around a bend in the river and ten minutes later I heard three pistol shots. We had arrived at Lee's Ferry.

A great crowd, at least twenty persons, lined the bank as we pulled ashore and jumped out of the boats. The first man I spied was Clyde Eddy, a fellow reporter and an old pal. He had come from New York to join us for the remainder of the trip.

Ten minutes after we landed an airplane flew over our heads, bound up the canyon. It was the army searching plane. Vainly we tried to signal it but it sped on its way, to return that night with the news that we were nowhere to be found.

For two days we were the guests of Preacher Smith, Indian missionary for thirty years, and Deputy Sheriff Buck Lowery. These two, and three families named Johnson, all brothers, comprise the enterprising town of Lee's Ferry. The Johnsons operate the ferry, which was the only connecting link between the north and south banks at that time. Lowery maintains law and order and Smith handles the church business.

After feeding up for two days we pushed on, now numbering fourteen, as Eddy was with us. Ninety miles of roaring river faced us and then the end.

Out of Lee's Ferry for twenty miles the going was smooth. No rapids to contend with; only the bitter cold, but we didn't mind for now the boats were creaking under the load of food and new dry blankets which had arrived at the ferry from Flagstaff, a present from Babbit Brothers.

For a week we ran rapids without complaint. But with the end of the trip in sight we encountered a difficulty that could easily have ended in death for the entire party. The river had dropped so low that it was a constant struggle to keep the boats afloat. The rapids became rock studded pools of slowly running water. It was hard work pushing and pulling to get them over into the next stretch of water.

To understand fully the position we were in it is necessary to know something about the Grand Canyon, which we were now in. The cliffs towering thousands of feet on either side make escape that way impossible. There is only one way to go and that is straight ahead. You can not go back and you can not go up except in two spots. One of these is Bright Angel Trail, which was to be the end of the trip, and the other is Hance Trail, twenty miles above Bright Angel.

By the time we had arrived at Hance the going had become so bad that LaRue decided to abandon the boats and take us out by the trail, intending to hike to the settlement at the head of Bright Angel. But the Hance Trail has not been used for thirty years and has fallen into ruins.

The morning after we had made Hance, LaRue announced his intention of taking us out but said that he would go up first, locate the trail and come back for us. He wanted a companion and, looking the crowd over, decided that I was the most useless of the party, therefore could be spared.

With two chocolate bars each we started the ascent. It was raining in the bottom but it was snow on top. For three hours we climbed, following faint marks that were invisible to my eyes, but told a complete story to LaRue. Soon we hit the snow line and were wading knee deep in it, but LaRue forged ahead, following the unseen trail.

Over the first cliff we made our way and crossed the open space between it and the one set back a half mile. Up the face of this one we climbed. Clambering along on a trail that existed almost entirely in the mind we came to a space where ten feet of the trail had caved off. All our work had gone for nothing. It was only a few feet, but it may as well have been a mile, we could not cross.

With an ache of disappointment in our hearts we retraced our steps and returned to camp nine hours after we had left, having traversed only seven miles in that time.

Knowing that escape was cut off from that direction failed to lower LaRue's spirit and in a calm voice he ordered us to the boats for an attempt to make it by river. It was a sober crowd that pushed the boats away from the bank and began a struggle for their lives.

Unless one has been there it is hard to realize just what we were up against. We were only a few miles from safety but had only a sixty-forty chance of making it. We no longer sang and poked fun at each other, every breath was needed for the work ahead.

For days we fought the numbing cold. Shoulder deep in water we tooled the boats through rapids and over falls. Our clothes froze to our bodies. It was now late in December and winter had set in. The snow streams far north of us, that fed the Colorado, had frozen over and water was no longer forthcoming. As a consequence the river dropped. If LaRue regretted leaving Lee's Ferry and certain safety to finish the job he had started, he never mentioned it.

At last it seemed we could go no farther. LaRue's whiplash voice drove us on. Never did he ask us to do what he wouldn't do himself. Always the first into the water and the last one out, he set an example easy to follow. After what seemed an age of nightmares he told us that with good luck we could make Bright Angel that night.

With renewed effort we fought on. The river had risen and would now float the boats. Herrick had contacted the desert for the first time and told them to expect us within forty-eight hours. New life came into our worn out bodies.

At six o'clock in the evening, we had run Sockdologer Rapid, the longest and worst in the river. It was now dark and to try and make camp was impossible. LaRue shouted we would continue and trust to luck to get through the only remaining rapid after dark, a feat never before attempted. It was plain and undiluted Hell.

Hanging to the boat, I became a part of it as my clothing froze. I had no feeling in my body. The boatman, Dean Farren, pulling at his oars could keep his blood in some semblance of circulation. The rest of us passengers clinging to the decks could only hold tight and hope for the best.

Lurching and plunging we entered the Grapevine Rapid. Tons of water smothered us as we rushed through it with express train speed. How Farren ever managed to keep us upright I never will know. Crashing against boulders and diving into twenty foot waves we emerged at the bottom, and looking up I saw LaRue's flashlight scanning each boat as it came out. Like an old hen who finds herself with a flock of ducks, our leader checked us as we flashed out over the tail of the rapid.

At ten o'clock that night we saw the lights of Phantom Ranch at the foot of Bright Angel Trail. Was it a Bright Angel? No angel in Heaven could ever look better than those first gleams of light we saw.

Shouting at the top of our voices we landed. Buildings spewed forth guides and tourists. Through an open door I could see a great fire in a fireplace.

After a great amount of back slapping and question answering we were hurried inside where kindly cowboy guides furnished dry overalls and hot coffee spiked with something that never came in a coffee can. A bath and shave, the first in seventy days, put new life into us.

Making for a telephone that connects with the rim of the canyon, I placed a call for New York, beating Eddy to the only 'phone by a split second, he was forced to stand helplessly by while I gave my story to the boss, after expressing my opinion of an editor who would send a man on a trip like the one I had just finished.

The next morning a line of pack mules carried us and our equipment to the top. The boats were left on the river to rot or be used again, we cared not what fate befell them.

During the trip, which had taken us through country seldom seen by white men, we had run two hundred major rapids, had carried the boats around over fifty and had lined twenty-seven.

We had passed through Glenn, Marble, Dark, Lava and the Grand Canyon, and had come through without losing a single man, thanks to the leadership of LaRue, who I will always remember as one of the great men of the old West.

I have never stopped to figure how many miles we covered, but it seemed to have been at least a million, although it was probably less than 400. Some day, when this great river is dammed and the resulting lake runs for hundreds of miles back into the mountains, everyone will have an opportunity to see the wonders of the canyons without the hardships endured by us.

A SHIPWRECK ACCORDING
TO ST. LUKE

by EDWIN SMITH

MARCH, 1947

DURING the First World War I spent a winter in the Mediterranean in command of a flotilla of H. M. ships of war based on Taranto, Italy, and Malta, and while there I made a careful survey of St. Paul's Bay where a notable shipwreck took place in A.D. 58 or 59.

In the twenty-seventh chapter of *The Acts of the Apostles* St. Luke gives us a graphic picture of the last voyage and shipwreck of a grain ship of Alexandria in which he and the great apostle to the Gentiles sailed as passengers, bound for Rome.

As I was caught out in a similar storm in December, 1918, while on a voyage from Taranto, Italy, to Malta I became interested in St. Luke's account of their experiences, and later that winter I read again his story of their voyage and shipwreck, in the original Greek, paying particular attention to the sea terms used by him.

Those who happen to know something of the sea, ships and storms, having learned the hard way, are often greatly amused when reading stories written by men who were making their first voyage at sea; and I confess that I expected to find in St. Luke's account something similar, since he was but a passenger on this particular voyage.

I did not read very far, however, before I realized that Luke the physician was at the same time a first class sailorman, and my respect for him was thereby greatly increased. In this account he shows conclusively that he had a thorough knowledge of ships and of seamanship that could be gained only in one way, viz., by experience. No amount of reading or observation of ships from the shore would fit him for the writing of the narrative of St. Paul's shipwreck and his own. Such knowledge and insight as is here displayed comes only

55

by experience. I do not mean to say that he must have followed the sea as a sailor before the mast; in fact the same evidence shows that he did not, but that he went to sea nevertheless, and for more than one or two short voyages. He spent years at sea at some time or other. When we first hear of him he was living at Antioch in Syria where he was known as a clever physician (surgeon). Since Antioch carried on an extensive trade with the west, and since many of the ancient ships were large and carried hundreds of passengers, there is great probability that such ships carried surgeons too, and Luke may have been one of them.

One of the most enthusiastic seamen I ever met was the doctor on board the battle cruiser Endymion when I was navigator in her. His name was Alan Moore, now Sir Alan Moore, and we became close friends on a long and tedious voyage from Gibraltar to Chatham, England, when we towed a monitor all the way, and encountered a violent storm in the Bay of Biscay where we saw a large Dutch freighter sink before our eyes, less than a quarter of a mile from our ship. He was a doctor and a good one, but he was also a first class sailor, greatly interested in the sea and in all kinds of ships. And such a man I believe St. Luke to have been.

Next, what about Paul? Was he a sailor too? He certainly was. Paul, the preacher and missionary, was by far the best sailor in the ship, and it would have been better for all concerned if they had followed his advice. Paul, as we know, was a lawyer before he became a missionary of the Gospel, and this narrative shows plainly that he was not only a good sailor but something of a meteorologist as well. He seems to have had more sea sense than any other man on board. Paul, you may have noticed, is not quite so reticent about himself and his past as is St. Luke. I would like to point out in this connection that there are three years of Paul's life unaccounted for in the New Testament. In Galatians i, 17, 18, we read "I went into Arabia, and returned again unto Damascus. Then, after three years I went up to Jerusalem." Where was he, and what was he doing during those three years? No one knows that now, but I would not be surprised if someone should make the discovery that he spent the whole three of them at sea. Next turn to II Corinthians xi, 25, "Thrice I suffered shipwreck." Now a man does not usually get shipwrecked every voyage, and the mere mention of three shipwrecks would seem to indicate that he had not only a long but bitter experience with the sea.

It only requires a little knowledge of the history of the countries bordering on the Mediterranean to know that by the time of this shipwreck, say A.D. 59, going to sea was a very ancient profession, and that many of the men who commanded these larger vessels were experts at their job. Certain it is that the account of their seamanship given by St. Luke on this occasion leaves little to be desired. In fact his description of what they did is almost word for word what the most modern works on seamanship tell us we should do if we were placed in similar circumstances.

It is when we come to make inquiry about the ships of the ancients that we experience the greatest difficulty. I know of no book on the subject that bears directly upon either their size, shape or rigging, so that we are dependent upon a few indirect references of ancient writers, representations on coins, etc., which in all probability are correct only in general outline and not in detail, except perhaps in detached parts such as the head and stern ornaments, rudders, anchors, etc.

There are two circumstances, however, to which we are indebted for much valuable information respecting the very class of ships with which we are at present concerned.

The Emperor Commodus (A.D. 161-192) during a season of scarcity imported grains from Africa. In commemoration of this a series of coins were struck bearing upon the reverse side figures of ships under sail. One of these Alexandrian wheat ships was driven by stress of weather into the Piraeus. The extraordinary size of the vessel excited much curiosity on the part of the Athenians; and Lucian, who visited her, lays the scene of his dialogue *The Ship, or Wishes* on board of her, in the course of which we learn many interesting things regarding the ship, her voyage and management.

Who would ever have thought of going to Pompeii to find out about the ships of the ancients, or the ships of St. Paul's comparatively modern day? And yet it is there that we get the most real help, for the marbles and frescoes of Pompeii afford valuable details and have the added advantage of synchronizing perfectly with the voyage of St. Paul, the catastrophe to which they owe their preservation having happened less than twenty years after his shipwreck.

I will now endeavor to reconstruct one of these ancient ships of the first century of the Christian era.

In general outline they did not differ greatly from sailing ships of seventy-five years ago in America, especially in their underwater parts, with the exception that the bow and stern were much alike. The bulwarks were open rails, and cabooses or galleries were built at both ends. Perhaps the greatest difference between these and all classes of modern ships is in the steering arrangements. The ancient vessels were not steered as those in modern times by a single rudder hinged to the stern post, but by two great oars or paddles, one on each side of the stern; hence the mention of them in the plural number by St. Luke. Indeed it was not until around the close of the thirteenth century that the modern hinged rudder came into general use.

The point of greatest interest in connection with these ancient craft is their size. Many of the wheat ships plying between Egypt and Italy in St. Paul's day must have been upwards of one thousand tons burden. They must have been of considerable size to make them pay. Small ships are profitable only for short voyages. But we are not left to our reasoning, unaided by any statements of facts, as for example the ship in which Luke and Paul sailed on this occasion had a cargo of wheat and 276 souls in all. To accommodate that many people on board for weeks at a time the ship must be considerably larger than an ordinary coasting vessel in our own day. The ship in which Josephus sailed, and which was wrecked on his voyage to Italy, contained 600 people—a good passenger list for a five or six thousand ton steamer of the present day.

The best account we have of the size of some of these ships is that given by the carpenter of the Isis, the Alexandrian vessel which was driven by contrary winds to Athens. According to the data supplied, and after making full allowance for difference in construction, this ship must have been between 1,100 and 1,200 tons burden. I find that some writers would make her upwards of 1,300 tons.

The rigging of these ancient vessels was simple. For the most part it consisted of one principal mast which carried a long yard, spreading a great squaresail which was furled on the yard aloft. These large grain ships in addition carried topsails. They generally had a smaller mast close to the bow on which they spread a small squaresail called the *artemon*. In addition they carried triangular sails for the purpose of making the ship steer easier under different circumstances, and for the purpose of tacking or wearing ship. These also were made use of in a storm when the larger sails had to be taken in.

We must not forget when we read this story that the ship in which St. Paul sailed was fitted for emergencies. Failure to understand the construction and rigging of these ships is why so many commentators made such unhappy blunders when dealing with the incidents recorded in the twenty-seventh chapter of the *Acts of The Apostles*.

For the sake of brevity we will pass over the details of the voyage until the vessel arrives at Fair Havens on the south coast of Crete. It is from this port that she sailed on what proved to be her last voyage, the narrative of which I now propose to examine.

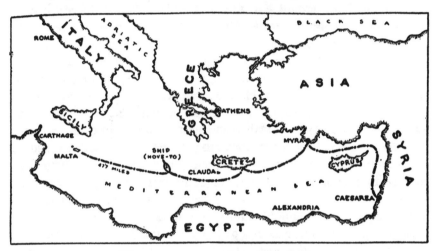

The voyage according to St. Luke.

Though St. Luke fails to make any reference to the condition of the ship, an omission which a real sailor would not have made, I am persuaded that her condition was none too good, for reasons that will appear as we go along. At Fair Havens the skipper first decided to remain there for the winter months; but when later he announced that he was going to shift up the coast to Phenice because the harbor there afforded better shelter for the ship, we find Paul objecting and urging him to remain where he was. He assured them that such a move was fraught with danger "not only of the lading and the ship but also of our lives."

We are told that it was the season when "the south wind blew softly" so that the danger did not manifest itself in the threatening condition of the weather, but we may feel sure that, since the move suggested by the skipper was one which promised greater safety and comfort to all hands, St. Paul would not have opposed it without good reasons. No reasons are given however, another characteristic of St. Luke's narrative, and a second proof that he was not after all a real sailor who had served his time at sea, for a real sailor never fails to give his reasons; indeed he is liable to become tedious in that respect. Nevertheless no sailor can read this narrative and fail to discover what those reasons were. Briefly, I believe, they were these: this ship was none too safe even in the best of weather, and he, for one, would not run the risk of being caught out in a gale in her at this season of the year if it could be avoided. Paul had been in the ship some weeks already; they had had a hard beat to windward in working down to Crete, and in those weeks Paul had made some observations and indulged in some reflections which he had kept to himself. He noticed, for example, that the ship was leaking considerably, and when the squalls blew hardest she strained and worked in a manner far from reassuring; and I can hear him saying to himself, "This ship is hardly seaworthy; she works and leaks even in these sheltered waters and if she is ever caught outside in a Levanter, such as is common in the winter season, she will go to pieces under our very feet." Kindly note at this stage that Paul said the harm and injury would come (1) of the lading, that is, the cargo of wheat which the sea water would injure; (2) to the ship, i.e., she would strain and perhaps break up in a gale; (3) to our lives in consequence, for our safety depends very largely upon the safety of the ship. Paul's contention then was simply this: "Though I concede that Phenice is a better harbor than Fair Havens to winter in, yet I maintain that the risk we run in putting to sea at this time of the year in this ship is too great to make it worth while; and besides all this I don't like to see the balmy south wind at this season, for it generally backs round to the east-northeast and blows a gale, and if it catches us while crossing the Bay of Messara it will blow us off the land altogether, and then look out!"

The skipper discussed the matter with the centurion and decided to sail immediately since the weather was fine and the wind two points abaft the beam. They had thus every prospect of reaching their destination in a few hours. They had not gone far, however, when a sudden change in the weather took place, and the thing that

St. Paul had feared came to pass. The ship was caught in a cyclonic gale which blew with such force that they could not face it and were compelled to run before it. We know that it blew them out of their course toward the island of Clauda, about twenty-three miles west-southwest from Crete. If therefore we know about where the ship was when the gale overtook her, we can form a tolerable estimate of the direction of the wind which drove them thither. From the narrative itself it is easy to see that the wind was east-northeast and that, you will observe, is the direction mentioned by St. Luke in verse fourteen where he calls the wind *Euro-Aquilo* (see the revised version of the New Testament) which is the point midway between *Eurus* and *Aquilo*. Now, according to the twelve winds of the ancients, *Eurus* is east, and *Aquilo* is northeast, and therefore the point midway between the two is *Euro-Aquilo*. The Greek word in the manuscript from which the authorized version was made was *Eurokludon* rendered by the word *Euroclydon*, which evidently is not the word St. Luke used. (*Euroclydon* in Greek does not mean anything sensible so far as I can make out. It evidently is a jumbled word.) All the older manuscripts including *Codex Sinaiticus*, which had not been discovered when the authorized version was made, have the word *Eurakulon*, i.e., *Euro-Aquilo* or east-northeast.

The first thing to be done is to make the ship snug for riding out the gale. The large squaresail must be furled aloft and storm trysails hoisted, and next they must at once resort to frapping the ship. What, undergirding already! Alas, then the worst fears of St. Paul are now confirmed. St. Luke tells us that they frapped her after she had gone only twenty-five miles, a sure indication that she was straining and leaking badly. I may say that frapping is sometimes still resorted to, but in every instance it is where the ship is old and weak, or in consequence of having sustained some damage. I wish to point out here what nearly all the commentators have failed to recognize, but which is of the utmost importance—that the real danger before the ship in which Luke and Paul sailed was the danger of foundering at sea owing to her leaky condition, and that if they had not providentially made the land, and been thereby enabled to save their lives by running the ship ashore, she would have foundered at sea and all on board would have perished.

We are told that, being apprehensive of being driven towards the Syrtis, "they lowered the gear" (see revised version verse seventeen).

It is not easy to imagine a more erroneous translation than that given in our authorized version, "Fearing lest they should fall into the quicksands, strake sail and so were driven." That would have been indeed fatal. Had that been done they would have fallen into them in about one day, for the Syrtis lay to the west-southwest—the direction to which the wind was blowing, and about 200 miles distant.

Since we know that they did not fall into the quicksands we are sure that they did not strike sail and run before the gale, but adopted some other plan. Imagine how that ancient mariner would resent the statement in the authorized version of the Scriptures, which in effect tells us that he was no seaman; that he was a man not only without knowledge of the first principles of seamanship but also lacking in plain common sense. But I know, and every other sailor knows, that he was anything but that. He was a real sailor, a master of his art. I take off my hat to him today.

Follow the steps taken by him from here on to save his ship, cargo and crew.

(1) He hove the ship to, that she might the better ride out the gale, and he hove her to on the proper tack. When a ship is being hove-to in proximity to any danger, the proper thing to do is to heave her to on the tack which, considering her forward motion, will always carry her away from the danger rather than towards it. In this instance they would lay the ship to on the starboard tack, that is, with her right hand side facing the wind. She would thus be pointing about north, or away from the African coast and the Syrtis; and any headway she might make while hove-to would be carrying her on her course towards Italy, while her broadside motion (drift) would be, speaking generally, to the westward.

On the following day when the gale continued unabated they lightened the ship. Every step hitherto taken indicates skillful seamanship, and so here, for all works on seamanship recommend this as one of the things which should be done. They threw overboard everything not necessary now to the working of the ship. The relief which a ship experiences by this would be the same as when a warship throws her guns overboard. She would ride higher and make less water.

A dreary interval of eleven days succeeds, the gale continuing with unabated fury. Neither sun nor stars can be observed, and at length we are told that "all hope of being saved was taken away."

But why? An ancient ship without compass and without celestial observations had no means of keeping a reckoning. This was no doubt a situation of danger, but not necessarily one of despair, for she might have been drifting into safety. The true explanation, as I have already indicated, is this: their exertions to subdue the leak had been unavailing; they could not tell which way to make for the nearest land in order to run their ship ashore, the last recourse for a sinking ship; but unless they did make the land they must founder at sea. Their apprehensions therefore were caused not so much by the fury of the tempest as by the state of the ship.

At length, on the fourteenth night of being driven through the sea of Adria, towards midnight the seamen suspected that land was near. If we take St. Paul's Bay as the actual scene of the shipwreck we can have no difficulty in stating what the indications must have been. No ship can enter it from the eastward without passing within a quarter of a mile of the point of Koura; but before reaching that point the land is too low and too far back from the track of ships being driven from the eastward to be seen on a dark night. When she comes within this distance it is impossible to avoid observing the breakers on the shore, for with northeasterly gales the sea breaks upon it with such violence that one is reminded of Campbell's line, "The white wave foaming to the distant sky."

On the writer's first visit to this spot he remained all night. A *Euro-Aquilo* was in progress and the white spray rose forty or fifty feet in the air. On the shore the noise was deafening. No ship could have entered St. Paul's Bay that dark night without these breakers on the shore being seen.

During a second visit the writer took a boat and sailed out into the bay to make further observations from the sea, and ran a line of soundings with the result that there is now no doubt in his own mind that the point of Koura is the land which drew near them on that eventful night. St. Luke says that they were wrecked on Malta (Melita) and I have shown that their drift would carry them in that direction.

The next point is interesting. How far would the ship have driven from Clauda about midnight when the fourteenth day had come? The answer to that question depends upon the rate of drift and the time elapsed. While in Malta I questioned a good many captains who had sailed the Mediterranean for many years, and who during the war had been running regularly to Crete, as to how far such a ship as I have supposed Paul's to be would drift an hour while hove-to. The general consensus of opinion was from one to two miles an hour, or thirty-six miles in twenty-four hours, and this agreed with my own calculation.

I come now to the time elapsed. The time consumed in driving through the sea of Adria is thirteen days complete and a fraction of a day. Taking then the calculated rate of thirty-six miles a day and the time elapsed as thirteen and one-quarter days, all we have to do is multiply thirty-six by thirteen and a quarter to get the calculated drift, which is 477 miles. The course is west by north and when I measured the actual distance from a point under the lee of Clauda to the entrance of St. Paul's Bay, Malta, I got 476.4 miles. I admit that a coincidence so close as this may be to a certain extent accidental, but it is an accident that could not have happened had there been any inaccuracy on the part of the author of the narrative with regard to the numerous incidents upon which the calculations are founded, or had the ship been wrecked anywhere but at Malta, for there is no other place agreeing either in name or description within the limits to which we are tied down by calculations founded on the narrative.

The ship now approaches the termination of her disastrous voyage. Land has not yet been sighted, but to the watchful senses of the "shipmen" the sound or appearance of breakers tells them that it is near, or in the nautical language of St. Luke, that it is approaching. The hope that was taken away is now restored. They can now adopt the last resource of a sinking ship and run her aground; but to do so before daybreak would be to rush upon certain destruction. They must bring the ship to anchor if it be possible, and hold on until daybreak, when they may find some creek into which they may be able to thrust the ship.

During the interval which remained before day St. Paul exhorted the sailors to take some food, since they had not had a square meal for a fortnight, and this they did. Then with renewed energy they made a last effort to lighten the ship, not only by pumping but by throwing the wheat into the sea—a sure indication that she was settling fast by reason of the water coming in through her weakened hull and empty seams. That man Paul, preacher though he was, had a head on him and was a born leader of men. I would rather go to sea tomorrow in a square rigged ship with Paul in command than with the captain of this grain ship, though I have already said that he was one of the best.

When the day broke, seeing what they thought was a creek (though it was really the opening between Salmonette Island and the Mediterranean) they let down their rudders, slipped their anchors, hoisted the *artemon* (foresail, not mainsail as in the authorized version) and prepared to beach the ship. Selecting a place where two seas meet, they ran the ship aground, bow on, which explains the "anchoring by the stern" since this held the ship in the proper position for beaching. I know this procedure has been severely criticised by persons who have not fully understood the circumstances, as for example the Scotch sailor who was heard to remark that "there was just ae thing in the scriptures that he could na quite gae along wi—St. Paul's anchoring by the stern. Na doot the apostle was an inspired man, but he should hae keepit her head til't." Now all these objections vanish when we come to know that the object was to slip the cables and beach the ship at daylight. I need hardly mention that St. Paul had nothing to do with anchoring her, though doubtless he would approve of the method under the circumstances. I do not mean to say that these vessels were usually anchored by the stern any more than I would say that English ships are usually anchored by the stern because Nelson anchored his fleet that way at the battle of the Nile.

Though there is now no creek in St. Paul's Bay that could possibly be sighted by anyone on a ship, yet at that distance in the early dawn the flat rocky space opposite Salmonette Island on which the sea would then be breaking was probably mistaken for a beach. From the opposite side of the bay it looked like a beach to me too, but when I rowed over I found it to be a flat bed of solid rock formation. For quite a distance from the shore the water was only about two feet deep and then abruptly dropped into perhaps twenty or more feet. No wonder, I thought, that "the fore part stuck fast, but the hinder part of the vessel was broken off by the waves."

It is not stated that they ran the vessel into the supposed creek, but "onto the shore where two seas met," showing either that the supposed creek was nonexistent, or that for some reason they decided upon the other spot after the ship was under way.

We have seen in our examination that every statement as to the movements of this ship, from the time when she left Fair Havens until she was beached at Malta, as set forth by St. Luke has been verified by external and independent evidence of the most exact and satisfying nature; and that his statements as to the time the ship remained at sea correspond with the distance covered; and finally that his description of the place arrived at is in conformity with the place as it is. All of which goes to show that Luke actually made the voyage as described, and has moreover shown himself to be a man whose observations and statements may be taken as reliable and trustworthy in the highest degree.

The twenty-seventh chapter of the *Acts of The Apostles* is a simple statement of facts, and I, a sailor of the old school and a teacher of modern methods in navigation, am thoroughly convinced that this whole book is of the same high order, and of imperishable value.

10,000 MILES—
"AND NEVER A HARSH WORD"

by MARION LOWNDES

SEPTEMBER, 1940

These observations were made during a 15,000 mile scientific expedition in 1937. They also apply to shorter cruises, too, where more than one person is involved.

"BEING in a ship is being in a jail with the added chance of being drowned."

Dr. Johnson must have been gratified, sir, the day he got that one off. Being bound for the East Indies in a schooner we were, according to him, seven people going to jail together for a year. A rolling, pitching, heaving kind of jail. Seven of us in a place the size of a trolley car. Almost never out of one another's sight. And never, alas, out of each other's hearing.

Our jail's name was Chiva and George Adams has already navigated her through the pages of the yachting publications from Gloucester to New Guinea. What follows is simply a discussion of daily life aboard, with notes on a few tricks that added appreciably to the comfort and pleasure of a long, hot, memorable voyage.

Chiva, 60 foot schooner, Frederick Crockett, owner, was one of those roomy, dependable jobs John Alden turns out for ocean cruising. She answered her helm like a bridle-wise horse and with a good stiff breeze on the quarter she could log nine knots with no more trouble than it takes to tell. Below decks she was as comfortable as possible, but it wasn't what you'd call soft.

A year's supply of clothes and ink and toothpowder had to be stored somehow in the per capita allowance of a hammock, a bureau drawer and part of a locker. At sea, all the fresh water used for a week's bathing and cooking and drinking could have been contained easily in one white porcelain bathtub, and the usual delicacies of a ship's table kept body and soul as far apart as possible. When the sun was out in earnest you could evaporate for a steady four hours on the afternoon watch. If it rained—and around the "dry" Galapagos it rained for ten days—you couldn't get dry. Books mildewed; typewriters rusted; and the galley oven was filled with film packs instead of biscuit. In all weathers the temperature in the galley went to three figures. For ten months we used a spoon for our tinned butter and drank water at body heat. When we wanted a bath we waited till it rained or else oiled ourselves with sun tan lotion and polished off afterward with a Turkish towel. Below decks it was scrubby and crowded. With seven people eating and three people sleeping in one saloon (not to mention cockroaches increasing and multiplying and poking their antennas into everyone's affairs) the bluest upholstery and the whitest paneling will look a little haggard at the end of six months. So will the crew.

"You wait," people used to say. "You'll be at each other's throats before you're half way across the Pacific."

Anyone who has done much cruising as an amateur will admit the logic in that point of view. The wonder is, not that murders and mutinies do occur at sea, but that any long voyage ends in peace. Dire sea changes creep over all of us. It's a different life aboard ship, and it brings out a different side. A charming landsman can turn into a perfect brigand once he gets his hand on a halliard. A person who is usually the soul of tolerance will have things his way or no way aboard the lugger. Everyone gives himself nautical airs. Tempers shorten. Egos rage. The rough life is naively considered an excuse for being rough. In bad moments the ship has a way of dividing and redividing, like an amœba, into two unhappy camps: the maddening and the maddened, and no escape for either.

Weather, cramped quarters, nervous strains, water rations, cockroaches and ship's coffee—these, of course, are the routine drawbacks of a year-long voyage in a small yacht. The question is, What offsets them?

Fundamentally, the beauty and adventure of the life. The satisfaction of knowing that you've been averaging eight knots for a fortnight away from the nearest civilized shore. The restoring silence of great waters and the splendid harmonies of the spheres that bind a windy world from the horizon to the zenith. The sea and the ship. Like the Lord, they give you your peace of mind, as well as taking it away.

The next great asset is equipment. Such standard pieces as sail thread and biscuit will be taken for granted, and all the thought and labor and money that goes with them. They've been discussed a hundred times, and working lists can be found in the back of every amateur odyssey. I am noting here only certain "ruffles and flourishes" which may have escaped attention so far, and which I gratefully remember for having offset, in their small, specific ways, some of the discomforts and strains of a beautiful, adventurous life in a twenty-ton sailing ship at sea.

Ponchos: These were a last minute inspiration on the part of the owners. We were each provided with one and in the great rains off Galapagos they kept our bunks as dry as bones. While we slept peacefully under them the water streamed over us into puddles on the floor.

Records: The best part about music at sea is that it changes the direction of your thoughts. We had a portable victrola and we played our waltz medleys and Hungarian rhapsodies and Bing Crosbys till we knew every note and syllable by heart. The selection was made about two-thirds classical which turned out to be wise, since "Masterworks" gain by being played over and over. For our pleasure alone, victrola and records were worth the space they took up; more than once, too, they eased things pleasantly in lonely Pacific ports, when shy colonists and natives came aboard.

Books: I tremble to think of the rows that were silenced by the copy of Hoyle which Charles Crockett shrewdly supplied with Shakespeare and the Bible. We referred to it constantly. We also had the omnibus editions of Fielding and Jane Austen and Malory and the English poets. "All the things," as our librarian said, "that you've been meaning to read again after school and never had time for." Besides the classics, we had a few good moderns—Somerset Maugham's *Traveller's Library* among the best. For reference: a dictionary, an atlas, the *Columbia Encyclopaedia*, and we could have used an authoritative cook book, too. The Harvard *Traveller's Handbook* was useful, and so was *The Ship's Medicine Chest*. Even when you were well, that made splendid reading. It told you how to treat everything from measles to yaws, and the final chapter was headed, How to Dispose of the Dead Body at Sea.

Air Mattresses: Chiva set off with three of these. They were inflated at Panama and used thereafter, every day and night of the voyage.

Tea: "Thank God for tea," as Sidney Smith said. Somebody sent our ornithologist a hundred Earl Grey tea balls. They were as precious as a Napoleon brandy and on Earl Grey days one dripping little ball went from hand to hand like that eye the Furies shared between them. Even on ordinary days our black ship's tea spruced us up and made a break in the long afternoon and caused us to look more benignly, for an hour anyway, on the world and each other. A regular British teabasket with a thermos would be a practical piece of equipment on any cruise.

Chess: The wife of Ravan invented the game in the first age of the world to take her husband's mind off the siege of Ceylon. Ever since chess has been taking people's minds off their troubles and everything else, except a black and red field and 32 evenly matched fighting men. "You need never be dull as long as you have someone to play chess with," a planter in New Guinea once observed. Some talk of cribbage and dominoes—we had those old-fashioned games aboard too—but they just pass the time. Chess is the game for sea.

Dark Glasses: The Crocketts outfitted the whole crew with polaroid spectacles. More than one pair is needed for a person. When you want them, you want them, and you can't wait till the lost pair is found or do without because your only pair is broken.

Shoes: Rope soled shoes are much cooler than ordinary sneakers, safer on wet decks and more durable.

Mascots: Every ship needs one—a parrot or a turtle or a cat. Some dumb animal that can't answer back. Chiva had Edwardo, a Galapagos tortoise, who traveled from Wreck Bay to New Guinea without making a false step. We also had a mistake—Herma Humm the kinkajou, who was only thwarted in her design to tear us all to pieces by being put ashore in Tahiti. One mascot is plenty.

Stowing Gear: If you have a chance to look over your quarters beforehand and think you're going to be cramped, you can rig a hammock, like the ones they have in sleeping cars, on the carlins of your bunk. Ours were made out of ordinary fishnet. Bags and long baskets that you can sling from hooks also help the stowing problem and make the whole voyage more comfortable.

Sun-Tan Oil and Lavender: These items apply especially on long voyages. Lavender keeps linen fresher and absorbs dampness. An extra supply of sun-tan oil makes a fair substitute for a bath, finished off with witch-hazel. Witch-hazel you can use by the gallon for sun burn, etc.

Food: The simpler, the better. Jams and sweet chocolate are important on any ocean. Where all the ship's stores have to be preserved in one way or another, it is well to consider not only variety and quantity, but also proper vitamin content. Lemons and onions are essential from this point of view. So are dried fruits and unhusked rice. After you've made up a list, consult a doctor. Just like any other animals, ship's crews respond to a proper diet. The special of Chiva's galley was coffee. It was made by dripping boiling water through the grounds in a percolator top, and would have done credit to any cook ashore. Dripping seems to overcome the fatal effect of ship's water; perhaps the grounds act as a filter. Anyway, the result comes out clear and strong and tasting like coffee, instead of soup.

Not one of these suggestions would help to bring a ship into port. None of them are even necessities. But assuming the classic preparations, these extras are worth a little trouble.

One further asset, in conclusion, can be the attitude of the owners. Most yacht owners are as touchy as husbands in a French farce. You can't criticize their treasures. You can't even have any ideas about them. I understand that very well. No one beats my dog, either, and I run my house to suit myself.

But ours was a rare case. You could have said "Chiva's Crocketts" rather than "Crocketts' Chiva." They repressed any feeling of possession they may have had for their schooner, and their self-control and tact was well rewarded. The resulting freedom and naturalness aboard did a lot to tone down the sea changes mentioned above. If by some ghastly mistake we had all been members of one family and born in Chiva, we would hardly have been more at home in her. Swearing at her when she tumbled the soup and ketchup into our laps and dipped her beam ends under. Groaning about her in the flat nights off Galapagos, when she floundered in the winking phosphorescent swells with the dew dripping like cold sweat off her flabby sails. And after the most romantic South Sea islands, still being very glad to get back to her again where she rode at anchor, white and snug in the hot blue water, over sharks and coral heads and slimy *bêches-de-mer*.

Wherever we were, we were wonderfully free with advice and suggestions. If anyone thought the paint needed washing or the food was dull, they didn't hesitate to say so. We had the run of the galley at all times. Cigarettes were kept in tins on the saloon table; they were ship's stores and public property, just like the aspirin and the Lux toilet soap. In most houses and many boats you'd hesitate to have pets if you weren't the owner; or to fill all the mugs with botanical treasures. But not in Chiva. Off watch we did as we pleased, and to all intents and purposes she belonged to all of us. Only the credit was the Crocketts'.

Long yachting trips don't have to end in bust-ups or feuds or mutinies, but so many of them do, especially in the tropics. I remember a beautiful three-master out there with a full professional crew to handle her—but the owners couldn't bring her to port for fear the men would desert. And a pretty little sloop all the way down from 40 north latitude to 15 degrees under the equator: the minute her hook was overboard the crew of three hurried silently off in three different directions. And a young man forced ashore in a South Sea island off a schooner cruising for pleasure. In fact, the only other yacht we saw without serious internal dissensions was one belonging to a man who had sailed her single-handed around the Horn from Brittany to Tahiti.

I shan't pretend we didn't have our troubles aboard ship. When

George Adams took a sight off the New Guinea coast and announced, "Ten thousand miles this day. Ten thousand miles and never a harsh word," we could only laugh. But still we could laugh. And did. And arrived in New Guinea friends. Thanks less to sterling worth, I fear, than to the care and imagination that went into the planning of the expedition.

THROUGH THE GRENADINES

by COERT DU BOIS

JUNE, 1944

The pleasures of chartered cruising in the unfamiliar West Indies offer opportunities for yachtsmen who can fly to the Windward Islands almost as easily as they can now motor to Inland Waterway anchorages.

FOR THOSE who don't happen to know them the Grenadines are a string of thirty-odd islands, all small but some smaller, lying between twelve degrees and thirteen degrees north latitude and sixty-one degrees and sixty-two degrees west longitude. They belong to Great Britain and are part of the crown colony of the Windward Islands in the Caribbean Sea. The north half of the group, including Union Island, is under the administrator of St. Vincent resident at Kingstown, and the other half from Carriacou south is under the Grenada government with headquarters at St. George's. For this reason it is difficult to find a map of the whole group, and in sailing among them one has to have clearance from both island governments. Lying in a line roughly N.N.E. and S.S.W., they are in the track of the northeast trades and it is possible to sail from St. Vincent, their northern pier head, to Grenada on the south end of the string on a broad reach or even dead before the wind. Coming from Grenada north, it is a beat all the way.

I went south from Kingstown, St. Vincent, where I chartered the fifty-five foot, two topmast schooner Sea Queen for the voyage to

Grenada and call at any island en route at my option, ship manned and found by owner (ordinary seaman's grub specified). I wanted to get off early next morning so I got my gear and slept aboard that night in the four berth cabin. About midnight the crew, three blacks, came aboard noisily and smelling of rum and turned in on the fisherman's staysail which they spread out on the floor of the cabin. It rained hard in the night and the crew closed all ports, the cabin skylight and the companionway slide, and lit a lantern to make sure that no oxygen escaped being used up.

We got off at a good hour in the morning. Captain Hazell, master, Lloyd and Claudius, A.B.'s, Randolph, O.S. and the charterer, were cleared by the police and the security for St. George's via the Grenadines and ran over to Bequia, anchoring in Admiralty Bay off the town which used to be called simply The Harbor, but is now, in honor of the little crown princess, renamed Port Elizabeth.

A hundred foot schooner was building on the beach fifty yards from the water's edge. The hull was practically complete and she was to be launched in a few days. Since there were no ways, launching was to be done by "cutting down." It seems that in this process (how widespread the method is, I don't know) the ground is smoothed and rollers are set in place under one bilge—in this case the starboard. Two anchors are sunk and given time to bury themselves off the beach in four fathom water with a double three sheave block tackle on each. At the time appointed the master of ceremonies—in this case Old Man Tannis—swarms aboard and directs like an orchestra leader the six axmen stationed at the shores on the starboard side. These "cut down" the shores like repeatedly sharpening a lead pencil till the hull eases down onto the rollers. Then, with the women tailed onto one fall and the men on the other and with the yells, screams and songs rising high as the rum gets in its work, the blocks are hauled together and the schooner takes the water foot by foot till she rides on an even keel.

Over the hill in Friendship Bay on the windward side of Bequia is, I think, the only whaling station left in America. Here a few families, descendants of the harpooners of the New Bedford and Nantucket whalers of the '50s, carry on a whaling business complete with try-works, double ended boats with harpooner's platform, steering sweep, loggerhead, line tubs and lead lined bow and counter chocks. Mr. Fitz Roy Oliviere, one of the harpooners, showed me the bomb gun and the bomb lance which shoot a murderous contraption that looks like a foot-long copper twelve gauge cartridge with an Apache arrowhead in the forward end. It blows up inside the whale and tears a few cubic feet of him all to pieces. They allowed they got their equipment from New Bedford, from the Whaling Museum I reckoned. These boys station lookouts on the high peaks of the islands hereabouts—Battowia, Baliceau and Mustique—who signal with smoke (believe it or not!) when they sight a spout. If they sight one to windward they generally get him. If he gets down to leeward they can't tow him back even if they kill him. One whale a year is a good average.

We went north around Bequia, holding the starboard tack clear across the St. Vincent channel. Then close hauled on the port tack until the Bequia Bullet, a pointed rock off the northeast coast of Bequia, closes with the point of Sal Bay, when you can ease sheets and reach for Mustique. Directly opposite St. Vincent at the narrowest part of the channel there is a "hurricane hole" in the north coast of Bequia where a schooner may shelter in a blow. It might stand some yachtsman in hand to know it's there. We left Battowia and Baliceau (said to be a corruption of *belles oiseaux*) on our port hand and closed in past the Pillories on Mustique.

This island is stocked with cattle, horses and goats and raises corn and pigeon peas. There is a settlement on the north end with a population of about 400 people—cowhands and fishermen—who sail beef and fish in sprit sailed double enders to Kingstown. There is good water all the way close in along Mustique, Petit Mustique (pronounced petty) and Savan Island but a nasty shoal, named Montezuma on H. O. Chart 1640, about a mile off the leeward side of Mustique.

We squared away for Cannouan, leaving Petit Cannouan on our port hand. This is barren and uninhabited and its bluff shores did not invite exploration. Maho Bay in the extreme north end of Cannouan looks attractive, but the skipper said anything drawing over six feet better keep out of it because it is shoal with coral heads all over the place. We went around the northwest point and pulled into Charlestown Bay, shortened down to fore and staysail and anchored in three fathoms, 400 yards off the newly built wooden pier. There's a shoal a half mile out from the pier but easily discernible by the light green color of the water and there is plenty of room inside. We went ashore and found a rather poverty stricken community of about 300 raising corn and Marie Galante cotton. Old Man Alexander, who seemed by way of being the bull of the herd, accompanied us on a bit of a walk and was persuaded to lend us a hand casting net on payment of two shillings, supplied by Claudius, A.B., on promise that we leave it with Old Man Bullard, Clifton Bay, Union Island, at some indefinite time in the future. It seemed a dubious kind of a deal to me, but he was quite satisfied.

We shoved off about noon and had lunch aboard of cold fried fish (trigger fish, squirrel fish and snappers), avocados, boiled yams and coffee. We were headed for Tobago Cays. After rounding the southwest point of Cannouan Island one holds for Channel Rock and leaves it close on the port hand. After rounding the rock leave everything that breaks to port until the beaches on the two northern Tobago Cays (which are almost in line) bear southeast, then stand straight in. A three fathom channel will open up between them and there's where you drop your hook. No finer spot in the Caribbean.

As we rounded Channel Rock a noble great barracuda snagged onto the spoon we were trailing and when we got him aboard and quieted with a mahogany gob stick he weighed in at about forty-five pounds. Whether or not you eat a barracuda seems to depend on geography. Off Cuba you don't, unless the ship's cat has passed on it and given it the green light. In the Grenadines it seems there are no "copper banks," whatever they are, and so the barracuda feeds only on clean fish and is consequently good to eat. Our crew went ashore on Tobago Cay where there is a built in fireplace, cement ends and two iron bars, under the manchineel trees back of the beach. When their fire was a long row of coals they put on an iron pot with a bit of coconut oil and onion and garlic in it, then rice and enough water to steam it, then chunks of barracuda. Two breadfruit were next put on the irons to roast and when everything was ready an hour or so later here was the menu:

A hooker of rum and water, five hookers to the bottle
Barracuda stew and rice
Fried barracuda roe—homemade pepper sauce*
Roast breadfruit—Fried plantains—Boiled yams—Coffee

When we had partially recovered from this, about the time the full moon got up twenty degrees or so, the skipper took a rum bottle,

* that made Tabasco sauce taste like mother's milk.

filled it full of kerosene and twisted up a bit of sail cloth for a wick. With this as a flare and Claudius at the oars we eased along the rocks in the ship's boat and pretty soon Claudius whispered:

"O Jeedus! O Jeedus! Look at dat great gran'daddy ob all da crayfish!"—and Old Man Alexander's cast net went over him—wh-i-s-s-h!

And there in the bottom of the boat was an e-normous spiny lobster, seven pounds on the hoof at least. Pretty soon we caught his elder brother and went back to camp, built up the fire and when two buckets full of sea water were boiling, we

> "up with their heels and smothered their squeals in
> the scum of the boiling broth."

After eating a couple of twelve inch legs with a good-night hooker we shoved off to the ship and turned in.

My diary says of the next morning: "Crew got up at 6:30 and went ashore and warmed up last night's orgy and yelled for us at 7:30. I swam ashore and had breakfast."

These four little uninhabited cays with their brushy hills, their manchineel groves along the foreshores, their white sand beaches and the three to five fathom channels and anchorages between, all completely protected to windward by breaking coral reefs, Horseshoe, Egg and World's End, form a hideout hard to beat for a vacationist who wants to be listed as missing.

Reluctantly we filled away for Mayero Island to the westward, a high island a mile and a half on the long axis. At the head of the bay on the west side is a well built wooden pier and a yellow sand beach with good holding ground in three fathoms 200 yards off. The bottom is covered with "sea eggs," those gray, soft haired sea urchins that are said to be good to eat. The village on the hilltop with its pointed thatched roofs looks quite African, and is. The 200-odd inhabitants raise corn, cotton, pigeon peas, limes, chickens, pigs and goats. We acquired a bucketful of bait—silver sides and blue runners —with Old Man Alexander's cast net and put out in the ship's dinghy to a five fathom bank a mile or so to the northwestward of the anchorage and bottom-fished with three hooks on short wire leaders set a foot above a lead sinker on the extreme end of the hand line. We caught a mess of squirrel fish, butter fish and surgeon fish and a couple of nasty moray eels and a long nosed pipe fish. When you get one of these spotted moray eels on you think you're fast to the bottom, and then there's a crack and up comes a two foot branch of coral with one of these horrid poisonous slimy members tied into it with a rolling hitch.

Back at the ship we found Claudius had been performing on the lobsters and he had a dish ready with a sauce made out of the lobster fat, a bit of oil and lime juice, onions and garlic and a dash of his homemade hot sauce that I named "devil sweat" which, I may say, was something!

We ran around to the south side of Union Island, going between it and Prune Island. That is a foul channel and it is best to keep well over toward Prune where it is clear. This little island, by the way, appears to be uninhabited and has an excellent beach along its west coast. It needs exploring. We anchored in Clifton Bay, Union Island, and after an examination by the police conducted by shouting from pier to schooner, account the police didn't have any boat, we were permitted to land and turn over Old Man Alexander's cast net to Old Man Bullard, as per agreement. It had certainly earned its two shillings!

Union Island is thickly populated and very rugged with peculiar sharp peaks called *pitons* running up to 1,000 feet which, they say, are very sporting to climb for those addicted to mountain climbing. It is the frontier of the St. Vincent Grenadines and passports are necessary to go to Carriacou across a three and a half mile channel.

This is the big island of the group, six and a half miles long and 8,500 acres in extent. It is thickly populated and has several fair sized settlements, Hillsboro on Hillsboro Bay on the lee side being the largest and boasting a cotton gin and a lime oil mill. Marie Galante cotton is the chief crop though a changeover is taking place to Sea-island cotton of which parachutes are made. Mabouya Island in the entrance of Hillsboro Bay is reported to have a well of sweet water on it and looks like a fine place to camp while exploring the many bays and inlets around Carriacou that have such fascinating names as Great Carenage, Harvey Vale, Manchineel, Bretache, Grand and Watering Bay.

And, by the way, this manchineel tree is a low, spreading, round topped tree with whitish bark which grows in thick groves on the edge of beaches and never far from the sea. It has thick, shiny, dark green leaves like a rubber tree and in fact exudes a white latex when you break off a leaf or twig. It has the reputation of causing bad blisters if rainwater or dew drips from the foliage onto your bare skin and all Caribbean sailors are afraid of it and walk most gingerly among them, nor will they stop under a manchineel tree in a rainstorm.

South from Carriacou there are a whole slush of little islands we didn't have time to explore, Saline and Frigate, Les Tantes, Kickin' Jinny, Ronde and Isle de Caille, London Bridge, Sugar Loaf and Green; then you come to Grenada. Kickin' Jinny, named after any mean lady mule, is a 670 foot conical rock that stands on the edge of a mean current rip that sets to the west and works up a steep short sea even in good weather. Skipper Hazell said that in a northerly blow it is really bad and it is good to stand well out to the westward. The rock is a bird refuge and used as home by pelicans, boobies, cormorants and man-o'-war birds.

We slid down the leeward coast of Grenada close in, fascinated by the view of high jungle-covered mountains and deep gulches, lovely bays with black sand beaches, coconut groves with fishing villages at their heads and miles of light green cocoa plantations with the black-green fingered leaves of breadfruit poking up through, till we slid into the deep harbor of St. George's with the old French forts on the hill and the picturesque little red and white town dozing along its waterfront.

THE DEVIL'S BELT:

History in Long Island Sound

by THOMAS FLEMING DAY

MARCH, 1910

This sort of historical writing about familiar cruising grounds is favored by English yachtsmen. American cruisers, for the most part, seem to care little about the colorful past of the waters through which they sail. American rivers, lakes, states and many remote regions have had books written on their backgrounds, folk-lore, legends and historical curiosities. It's time that our coasts, bays, sounds and sea shores had their traditions recorded.

THE Devil's Belt; to whom does it owe this name; when was it bestowed? Those questions I for one cannot answer. All I can tell you is that it is called so on the old Sea Cards and in early books written to pilot our ancestors through its deeps and over its shallows. Why was it christened the Devil's Belt? Perhaps because it led out of Hell Gate, or more to the reason because it resembles in shape a belt of Wampum such as the Indians used in trading. But despite the name, the Devil had nothing to do with forming the Sound or in building up the Island that parcels it from the ocean. The one to be credited with this work is a personage of lesser note, but of far greater power, one who has been known to untold generations as Jack Frost. The Sound and its islands, its estuaries, its bays, its rivers, are all his work, being digged, piled up, scooped, and quarried by his henchmen, the ice. Thousands and thousands of years ago, just how many thousands Science refuses to state, the borean pole came down somewhere into what is now known as Canada, and the polar ice-cap extended its mighty glacier masses as far as what is now latitude forty degrees. Here the icy feet of the glaciers were thrust off the rock, and into the yellow sands and black oozes of the sea bottom, the gravel, clay, and mud was ploughed up and raised into a ridge upon which was dumped by the melting ice the boulders and gravel it had gathered, as it scraped and scooped the rocks of Canada and New England. But Jack Frost was not to have and to hold forever this foreshore his battalions had advanced and seized; the Sun, rallying all his power, came back to the attack, hurling against the icy bulwarks his constant restless fighters, the Wind and Sea. The first attacked the glaciers head and flank, the second roared, and bit at their bases, and inch by inch the frost forces were driven North again. Slowly the ice retreated, leaving behind, as a proud mark of its Southern conquest, a huge up-piling of sand, gravel, and boulders, and inside this moraine, lying like a line of dead where the last fierce onset had left the files of a desperate and final charge, spread a succession of drip pools or catch basins: The Devil's Belt is one of these.

Now I am not going to write you a set story, but am going to yarn to you, gathering and relating bits here and there of what I know about the Belt, first, because I love it and love to talk about it; and secondly, because you will enjoy it more if we just simply yarn. The Sound to me is of all the world's waters the most familiar, the most interesting and the most beautiful. I don't question but what there may be many more sounds, but this one we are talking of is my Sound, the one on which I learned first to master the sail, to race on, to cruise on, to live on; such being the case not in my hearing unrebuked shall any man set up against it aught which makes any other sound as a stretch of water interesting and beautiful.

This love for my Sound kept my ears open at all times to hear it talked about, and made me anxious to collect all stray bits of gossip regarding its history, and to learn of its vicissitudes. I waylaid and brought to conversation the old, who had seen and sailed upon it long years before I did, and listened eagerly to their half-remembered and half-imagined tales. I searched old books and pored over all charts. Much I have learned, but much more would I have gladly known. Something of what has come to me either by eye or ear I now tell to you.

Early Voyages

The first European who saw and sailed the Belt was one Juan Florens, a French Corsair, who came there in the reign of Francis I, about the year 1524. This searcher was also known as Giovanni da Verrazano. He was an Italian and like Hudson was looking for a short cut to Cathay. Home again, he or some of his crew drew a map calling the country visited New France, and on this chart 'tis said Long Island and the Sound are shown and many other points between what is now Virginia and Cape Cod. In this map the Sound is called Baia Hondo.

It is sure that after his time and before the coming of the Dutch the Sound was frequented by Biscayans and others, trading and fishing. But these fellows never printed their logs, and their tales of adventure never went beyond the fireside of tavern table, nor did they know except vaguely where they had touched and traversed. It is said some records of these early voyages are to be found gathering dust in the archives of the small fishing towns of France and the Channel Islands. If a fur trader found a place of good barter he kept it to himself, nothing was to be gained by spreading broadcast such news. So that no doubt the Sound was often visited before Block sailed it in his native-built Onrest.

Block built his vessel in 1614 at Manhattan Island. She was sloop rigged, of these dimensions: Over all 42½ feet, length of keel 38 feet, breadth 11½ feet, about 16 tons. He it was who, voyaging East, named Hell Gate after a branch of the River Sheldt in East Flanders between Axel and Hulst, I suppose because the run and roar of the tide reminded him of the Flemish passage. Saw and explored East Chester Creek, examined City Island and its sister spots, passed and named the De Kees Islands, now Stratford Shoal, called at the mouth of the Housatonic, named Falcon and Jan William Islands, called the Connecticut, Fresh River, and then sailed on and out through the Race to discover places beyond as far as the Vineyard.

Following Block, but on the other course from East to West, came Captain Thomas Dermer, a very worthy mariner in service of Sir Ferdinand Gorges. Dermer sailed from Maine to Virginia in a pinnace, being, so he says, piloted through the Sound by an Indian who drew a map of the route on the lid of sea-chest with chalk. He is the first Englishman who is known to have traversed its length. At the time of his voyage a terrible plague was killing off the Indians by tribes, and trade in consequence was dull.

Now came the Puritans with their Bibles and Blunderbuses. A Sachem from Connecticut visited the Plymouth Colony and invited the English to settle on the Fresh River. He offered corn and beaver-skins as tribute. His real object was to get the help of the white man to defeat and dethrone another Sachem named Pekoath. It puts one in mind of the fable of the sheep and the goat inviting the wolf to adjust their quarrel. Winthrop refused, but the eyes of the spoiler were opened and in 1633 the bark Blessing was sent by the Governor to spy on the Dutch and to forbid them building on the Connecticut River. What irony a bark named the Blessing, the first to bring to the home of the Connecticut savage the men who of all others disgraced with murder and rapine the name of Anglo-Saxon! How strange it seems that the very men who fled from their native land to escape the cruelties of the Star Chamber should have inflicted on the Indian such unnecessary and horrible barbarities. Without any apparent justifica-tion they rushed on these people, the rightful owners of the soil, and slew them, man, woman, and child, and like the Israelites of old, gloated over the dreadful deaths they had dealt out to a surprised and almost defenseless enemy. If ever blood cried for vengeance to Heaven it was the blood of the Connecticut savages, slain for no other crime than that of wanting to keep what God had given their fathers centuries and centuries before.

The Dutch had a fort on the Fresh River called Good Hope, but Captain Holmes, sent with a party to settle there from Plymouth, laughed at the Dutchman's guns and threats, and sailing past the place started a town some miles above it. This was the beginning of the end for the Dutch and Indians; the former were driven out and the latter killed off in the usual good old English style.

In 1636 John de Laete published a book in which is printed the following rather mixed description of the Belt:

"The river is thus named because it extends from the city of New Amsterdam. By some this river is held to be an arm of the sea or a bay, because it is very wide in some places, and because both ends of the same are connected with and empty into the ocean.

"This subtility notwithstanding, we adopt the common opinion and hold it to be a river. Be it then a river or bay, as men will please to name, it still is one of the best, most fit and most convenient places, and most advantageous accommodations which a country can possess or desire for the following reasons: Long Island, which is about forty (?) miles in length, makes this river. The river and most of the creeks, bays and inlets joining the same, are navigable in Winter and in

Summer without much danger. The river (Long Island Sound) also affords a safe and convenient passage at all seasons to those who desire to sail East or West; and the same is most used, because the outside passage is more dangerous. Most of the English who wish to go South to Virginia, to South River (Delaware Bay) or to other Southern places, pass through this river, which brings no small traffic and advantage to the City of New Amsterdam. This also causes the English to frequent our harbors, to which they are invited for safety. Lastly: this river is famous on account of its convenient bays, inlets, havens, rivers and creeks on both sides, to wit, on the side of Long Island and on the side of the fast or main land. In the Netherlands no such place is known.

"But let us return to the continent (South shore of New England). Here first a bay discloses itself (which some consider a river), called Nassau, six miles wide at its entrance, which is obstructed by islands, and about eight fathoms deep; afterwards it becomes narrower terminating as it were in a point with a depth of four, and five, and sometimes nine fathoms, except in the extreme recess where it is more shallow. It is surrounded by a pleasant and fertile country inhabited by sturdy barbarians, who are difficult of access, not being accustomed yet to intercourse with strangers. At the distance of twenty-one miles West of this bay, there is another bay, divided by an island (Rhode Island), at its entrance, so that it has two names; for the part on the East is called Anchor, and that on the West Sloope Bay. The savages who dwell around this bay are called Wapenokes (Wampenoags), though it is said by others that the Western side is inhabited by the Nalucans (Narragansetts). Twenty-four miles or thereabouts beyond we enter a very large bay (Long Island Sound), enclosed by land for a long distance, or rather by islands intersected by channels, of which there is a great number, until we reach the mouth of the great river. There are also numerous small islands, to which no particular names have been given; navigators take the liberty of changing them arbitrarily. Near the entrance of this bay, the main land forms a crooked prominence in the shape of a sickle (Stonington, Watch Hill), behind which an inlet receives a small stream, that flows from the East and has received its name from our people, 'Ooster Vievievtjen.'

"Another little river discharges on the same part of the coast, which derives its name from a chief of the natives, called Siccanamos

(Mystic or Noank). Here is a very convenient roadstead. Behind a small promontory there is another stream (The Thames), that is navigable for fifteen or eighteen miles; here salmon are taken. The native inhabitants are called Pequatoes, who are the enemies of the Wapenokes. From thence the coast turns a little to the South, and a small river is seen which our people called Frisius (Niantic), where a trade is carried on with the Mohicans. Next comes a river called by our countrymen De Versche Riviere, or Fresh River (Connecticut River), which is shallow and shoal at its mouth, so that it is difficult for small vessels to ascend it. Near the sea there are but few inhabitants, but within the interior of the country dwell the Sequins (Middletown Indians), at the distance of forty-five miles; the Nawes (Hartford Indians) are the next above; they cultivate the land and plant maize from which they bake cakes called by them leganic, Wa-ha-ha (corn cakes). In the year 1614 they were defended by a kind of palisade in the form of a camp against their enemies in latitude 41 degrees, 48 minutes, as I find it was observed by our people. Beyond live the Houkans, who are accustomed to descend this river in boats made of bark of trees sewed together.

"Another river meets us twenty-four miles West of this to which the name of Red Hills (New Haven) has been given; the Querepees inhabit its banks; many beaver are taken here, since a demand for our goods has stimulated the naturally slothful savages. Twelve miles West an island (Stratford Shoals) presents itself and soon after many more are seen, whence our people called this place Archipelago (Norwalk Islands). The bay is here twelve miles wide; on the main reside the Suwanoes (Stamford tribe of Indians), who are similar in dress and manners to the other savages.

"I have remarked that the large bay (Gardner and Peconic Bays) was enclosed by several islands, separated by one another only by small channels. These are inhabited by a race of savages who are devoted to fishing, and thus obtain their subsistence; they are called Matouwacks. The name of Fisher's Hook (Montauk Point) has thus been given to the Eastern cape of this island, which some consider the head of the bay. In the interior of this bay a branch of the great river (Harlem River) or another river as others consider it, discharges, which our people call Helle-gat, or the entrance to the infernal regions. The current of the sea setting from the East to the West, meets another current of the great river near an island which our countrymen called Nutten Island (Governors) from the great abundance of nuts which it produces."

CHARTS

Outside of Giovanni da Verrazano's and Block's map the earliest chart known to be in existence is one made by an English Naval Surveyor about 1720. This is in possession of the British Museum, but I have never seen a copy. It is said to extend from Boston to New York, and to contain many interesting details, including the Old Channel that formerly cut through Cape Cod just below Chatham. The Dutch Chart, published at Leyden by John de Laete, is evidently an elaboration of the Block map, an original copy of which is, I understand, on file at Albany among the State papers. De Laete was a noted geographer and traveler who published his work, a "History of the Dutch West Indies," in 1636. He claimed to have, and probably did sail, the Sound about that time, as he very clearly describes several localities and gives the correct distances and compass courses.

Just prior to the Revolution the Government had a survey made of the Province of New York, and a map prepared by one Claude Joseph Sauthier. The copy seen by me was printed in 1779 at Cornhill, London. Its general outline is correct but in detail full of considerable errors. In the Sound he shows Little Neck, Cow Bay and Oyster Bay, but completely omits Hampstead Harbor, the most prominent of all these indentations. Cow Bay he calls Musketo Cove. His outlines of Cow and Oyster Bay are sadly incorrect. With what we call Huntington Harbor he is much more successful, and Lloyds Harbor is almost exactly delineated. The portion back of Eatons Neck now comprising Northport Harbor he calls Cow Bay.

Sauthier evidently never visited the Sound, as he leaves out nearly all the islands in the West End. My favorite, Huckleberry, is nowhere to be seen, and Fox and Pea are also missing. He has the two Captains in under the title of Momissing Isles. His delineation of the East End of the Sound is much better; he gets in Falcon and Duck, Fishers and Gut Island, but puts these latter two in the wrong place. Fishers is shown very small and too far off the North Shore. Gardiners Bay, Shelter Island Sound and Peconic Bay are very well done.

It seems strange that Sauthier should have made these mistakes, as in a work printed by order of the British Government during the Revolution, containing a number of charts and drawings of different localities, the islands and bays are clearly shown and in their proper places. In this work are two charts, one of the East River to Whitestone and the other from Frogs Neck to a few miles beyond the Executioners. In these City Island, Heart, Fox and Huckleberry are shown and named. Execution Reef is shown, and also the spot North Northeast of it we call the Middle Ground, but the Stepping Stones are omitted. There is a line of soundings up the Channel.

There are also a number of hand-made maps covering the operations of the British Army while in pursuit of Washington after the defeat on Long Island and the evacuation of New York. These cover the land from New York to Rye and are not badly done. In these Davenports Neck is called Myers Point, and is shown as the place where General Knyphausen landed with his Hessians and Waldeckers and took possession of New Rochelle. He came very near cutting off the Americans, who were retiring before Howe's main force, that had landed on Pells Point. The Americans fought a skirmish on what is now City Island Road, and another in New Rochelle just about the junction of Cedar Road with Drakes Lane. The wounded were carried into a house now standing on Cedar Road, just East of Drakes Lane. In this map Hunters Island is called Hunts Island. Echo Bay is shown but not of the right shape, being made much too wide. In the earliest maps, the neck between Cow Bay and Hampstead Bay is called Cow Neck, the neck between Hampstead and Oyster Bay, Hog Neck, and Lloyds Neck, Horse Neck. This is said to be the Horse Neck upon which the Dutch attacked and defeated a tribe of Indians. These British army maps were evidently made by men on the spot, but Sauthier's map is likely compounded largely of hearsay. The first modern charting of the Sound was done between 1830 and 1840, and was carefully and properly executed, and in these charts most of the localities bear the same names they do to-day.

Why the early names should have been changed I cannot say; it certainly would have been better to have kept the ancient orignial designations. What sense is there in substituting Faulkners for Falcon, or Gull for Gut Island, or Execution for Executioners? Jan William is certainly a more desirable name than Goose Island, which means nothing, whereas the original name was given by Block and recalls a historical event. How much better it would have been to have kept the name DeKees for the Stratford Shoal or Middle Ground. The same with Marthas Vineyard, a name that in its present sense means nothing, whereas the original Indian name does. Long Island is another chestnut; there are hundreds of Long Islands. The original Indian name of Metoac is distinctive and descriptive, and would add a charm to a charming piece of land.

The English settlers, I suppose, through patriotism or contempt· for the Indian names, plastered the whole coast with names borrowed from the old country. From Cape Cod to Narragansett Bay they covered the land with towns labeled after the cities and villages they left in Somerset and Devon. The Netherlanders were not more wise or euphonious in their selections, and repeated the names of Flemish and Dutch towns at every opportunity.

REVOLUTIONARY WAR

During the Revolutionary War the Sound was the scene of considerable martial movement, but not being the field of the main operation after the campaign of 1776, its battles and sieges have been ignored by the historian. Outside of the expedition that followed the battle of Long Island, the British left the Eastern country alone, except for some punitive campaigns, during which they bombarded and burned several of the towns, and destroyed considerable rebel property. The majority of the residents of Long Island were loyalists, or else pretended to be, as the British trade carried on through the commissary department was extremely lucrative, and as the Red Coats paid in negotiable paper or gold for what they wanted, the thrifty farmers of Kings, Queens, and Suffolk, rather leaned towards the banner of St. George. Much of the supply of food and fodder used by the garrison at New York and the army in the field was gathered in Long Island, and the British had fortified posts to protect this trade scattered throughout the island. One of the principal posts was sited on the top of Lloyds Bluff, and though several times attacked by the Continentals, was never taken. The object of this post was to further and protect the London Trade, a forbidden traffic in British goods which was carried on between the producers of Old England and the consumers of New England. The goods were stored at Lloyds Bluff and at favorable opportunities loaded into sloops and whaleboats, run across the Sound, and on the Connecticut shore delivered into the hands of smart Yankee merchants who ran them into the upper colonies. One landing place was Stamford, where the contraband was taken overland through Westchester to the Hudson, and then sent up state on that river.

This London trade was one of the sorest thorns in the sore side of Washington, and he endeavored in various ways to check and suppress it, but it was so popular and lucrative that not only were the New England merchants engaged in it, but even members of Congress and officers high in the army shared in the spoils. What we now call graft was rampant on both sides in the Revolution and this select trade formed one of the chief sources. Several officers who were sent to suppress the trade joined in, and it is said that one Connecticut general, a man held high in esteem as a patriot leader, was caught red-handed by Washington assisting in the running of this contraband. Among those sent by the Commander-in-Chief to stop the London Trade was Col. Benjamin Tallmadge, an officer in the Dragoons and a native of Setauket, Long Island. He was a brave and honest officer, and the following is an account of an adventure that happened to him while carrying out his orders.

"The campaign having now closed, I took my old station upon the shores of the Sound. Through my private emissaries, I obtained much information respecting the illicit trade carried on to Long Island, etc., and many of these trading boats fell into our hands. One venture I must relate, from the singular circumstances which accompanied it. In the course of the Winter, I was informed that one of our public armed vessels, which was appointed to cruise in the Sound to protect our commerce and to prevent the illicit trade (technically called the London Trade), was actually engaged in carrying it on. She was a large sloop called the Shudham, armed and equipped, and commanded, I think, by Capt. Hoyt. I hardly knew how to suspect him, but having been minutely informed of the invoice of her goods, and that she would be at Norwalk on a given day, I felt in duty bound, under my orders, to watch her. I repaired to Norwalk with a few dragoons, and finding said sloop coming upon the harbor, I took out a warrant, got a constable, and when she anchored below at the Old Wells, I got a boat and went on board. After due salutations were passed, I took the Captain into the cabin and informed him of my suspicions and errand. He flew into a great passion, and first threatened to throw me overboard. I endeavored to satisfy him of the futility of such threats, and ordered him, by virtue of my superior military rank, to obey my commands. He immediately ordered the anchor to be weighed and the sails hoisted, and stood out to sea with a smart wind at North-west. I ordered him to put back, but he refused, and swore most vehemently that he would throw me overboard, when I assured him if he made any such attempt, I would certainly take him along with me. My Captain continued his course towards Lloyd's Neck, where the enemy's fleet lay until we had reached about the middle of the Sound. I inquired of him where he was going, when he informed me, with an oath, that he would carry me over to the enemy. I informed him that for such an offense, by our martial law, he exposed himself to the punishment of death.

"He professed to care nothing for the consequences, and swore he would do it. I maintained my former course, and very sternly ordered him to put about his vessel and return to Norwalk, assuring him that if he executed his threat, I would have him hanged as high as Haman hung, if I ever returned, as I did not doubt I should. The time now became critical, for we were rapidly approaching the enemy, when I again demanded that he should put about his ship and return. He now began to hesitate, and in a few minutes he ordered his men to their posts, and put his vessel about and steered directly back into Norwalk Harbor. As soon as he came to anchor down at Old Wells, so called, the Captain went ashore in his boat, and I never saw him again. I now found myself in the peaceable possession of the vessel and its cargo. On taking up the scuttle in the cabin, I found the assortment of English goods agreeably to my invoice, which I had duly libeled and condemned. Thus ended my hazardous contest with the Captain of the Shudham who must have been a man of void principle, and wholly unworthy the commission he held.

"On the 20th of January, 1783, we captured several boats with goods, etc., both foreign and domestic.

"Having noticed one of the enemy's armed vessels frequently passing across the Sound, and taking her station under Stratford Point, and learning that her special business was to bring over goods, and take back produce in return, as well as to annoy our commerce from East to West through the Sound, I began to entertain hopes that we might capture or destroy her. To this end, I rode over to Bridgeport to find some suitable vessel for the purpose. Capt. Hubbel had the very thing I wanted, and moreover wished to have the Sound freed from such a nuisance, as he wished to prosecute his accustomed voyages to Boston, etc. We finally came to the following agreement, viz.:

Capt. Hubbel engaged so to manage and navigate his vessel as that he would absolutely come in contact with the enemy's sloop-of-war; which being done, I engaged to take or pay him for his vessel, which must of course fall into the enemy's hands. I accordingly ordered forty-five men from my detachment, under the immediate orders of Lieuts. Rhea and Stanley, of the Legion, together with Capt. Brewster's boat's crew of Continental troops, to be held ready for service. On the 20th of February, 1783, the same vessel was discovered under Stratford Point. The troops were immediately embarked—the whole to be commanded by Capt. Brewster—with particular orders not to appear on deck until they should be needed. Capt. Amos Hubbel, who commanded our vessel, left his anchorage at about two o'clock, and at 4 P.M. the vessels were within speaking distance. The enemy immediately commenced a full discharge of their cannon and swivels, which crippled Capt. Hubbel's vessel in her hull, mast, and rigging very considerably. He, however, stood at the helm himself, and although a shot had passed through his mast, yet he brought his bow directly across the side of the British ship.

"When within a few yards of each other, the order was given for the troops to appear on deck, when the command to fire immediately followed, and in a moment the two vessels came in contact, when the whole detachment boarded the enemy's ship with fixed bayonets, and she was captured as in a moment. Nearly every man on board was either killed or wounded, while not a man of our detachment was hurt.

"In a few hours both vessels were snugly moored at Blackrock Harbor, and all was again quiet. I reported this affair to the Commander-in-Chief, who returned his thanks in his letter dated February 26, 1783, and gave an order of condemnation of the prize, the avails of which were duly distributed to the troops.

"After this event we captured several boats, some belonging to the British and some to our side, for we served all that we found carrying on this illicit trade pretty much alike."

OTHER WARS

The Sound suffered somewhat in the 1812 War, but nothing like as severely as the Chesapeake. During the years 1813 and 1814, it was closely blockaded, and the trade and traffic brought nearly to a standstill. Owing to the New England States having opposed the declaration of war, the British Admirals were instructed by their Government to treat the inhabitants with leniency, but to enforce a strict blockade. At the same time fire and sword was ordered carried into the Chesapeake region, those States having fomented and voted the declaration, and their towns and shipping were harried and destroyed. Admiral Warren, who was in charge of the fleet blockading the Eastern States, was a kind-hearted man, and, like most of the British officers of his day, exceedingly averse to murdering people who came of the same blood and spoke the same language, so he entered into agreements with some of the towns to the effect that if the inhabitants did not attempt to molest the ships and boats while in discharge of their duties, the ships and boats would not molest them. It was the breaking of this agreement by the people of Stonington that led to the bombardment of that place.

Owing to the American frigates having taken refuge in the Thames River, the British maintained close watch off that place. The main fleet lay in Gardiners Bay, but La Hoque, the flagship, with some smaller vessels, anchored off New London. On La Hoque at that time, serving as midshipman, was Edward Parry, afterwards famous as an Arctic explorer, and the man who discovered Etah and the tribe of Eskimos from whom Cook and Peary hired their drivers and dogs. Parry tells of the days spent on the blockade and of several adventures in which he took part.

An attempt was made to blow up La Hoque with a torpedo, but it failed to do any damage except to thoroughly wet about a half-dozen hands. At the moment of the explosion a boat was detected by the Maidstone containing one man, who, being captured, pretended he had come off to sell provisions and had nothing to do with the torpedo. This man was put in irons and the sailors dubbed him Torpedo Jack. After a few days' imprisonment, though still protesting his innocence of the explosion, Torpedo Jack offered in exchange for his liberty to pilot the boats of the squadron up to Pettipaque Point in the Connecticut River, where a number of privateers were lying and building. This expedition of 120 men, commanded by Captain Coote, burned about $300,000 worth of shipping.

The most curious thing is the good understanding that existed between the naval officers on both sides, which would be inexplicable if we did not recall that fighting was a business with them, and they looked upon the destruction of private property as part of the game, which in no way damaged their personal fortunes. But it was a different story to the civilian owner, who was paying for the candle. Letters and papers were exchanged between the blockaders and blockaded, and when any European news of importance was received in New London it was sent off to the Admiral's ship. Several times British officers visited the American ships and dined and talked over another duel, like the one between Chesapeake and Shannon. When a captured sloop was blown up by an infernal machine, and a lieutenant and several sailors killed, the American Commodore at once sent off word disclaiming any connections with the outrage and laying the blame for it on some New York civilians who, it seems, had contrived and rigged the machine. Naval officers at that time had not become hardened to the cowardly warfare of torpedoes and mines, and to use such weapons was considered derogatory to the profession. The two vessels that did most damage in the Sound were the Maidstone and Borer; one was a ship-rigged sloop and the other a brig-rigged sloop. They haunted and worried the coast from Cape Cod to Throgs Neck; and traditions regarding them lived long among the Rubes, but, curiously enough, they were supposed to have wrought their havoc during the Revolution. It was Maidstone that burned the vessels in Buzzards Bay at Wareham, and who held up and destroyed the trade in Vineyard Sound. One of these vessels fought an action with two privateers off New Rochelle, of which there is no account in any history.

An old sloop skipper of Greenwich, Conn., told me that when a boy a vessel he was in was brought-to by a British man-of-war near Sands Point, and that having no cargo they were let go, and given a pass to show to any other vessel that might detain them.

The next and last war that had for its field the Sound was the steamboat rate war that broke out in the Thirties. This was hotly contested, and one of the vessels engaged in it was rammed and sunk, but it is a story that will do for telling some other time.

TRADE AND TRAFFIC

Historians as a class ignore the principal and most interesting phases of Colonial life, and scorn to descend to relating anything of less importance than the operations of an army. They will waste pages discussing some trivial skirmish between a handful of men, but are totally silent on the operations of trade carried on over the waterways during the years of peace. You may search American history through and through and will find nothing relative to commerce on the Sound, and its bearing on the prosperity and growth of the Colonies bordering on that stretch of water. Here and there is a state paper left to gather dust, which partly covers this point, but to the average historian it is of no interest and is cast on one side and ignored in his search for facts to distort and suppress or relate as he sees best. The majority of our historians are worse than worthless. Many have deliberately falsified, and much that is of interest is suppressed by them because it is supposed to be derogatory to the character of the men concerned or to the cause which the historian sets out to glorify. Letters dealing with things of importance are edited and changed, and in some cases wholly suppressed, or so altered as to convey a meaning altogether different from that intended by the writer.

In regard to Colonial commerce, histories are for the most part silent, and in consequence a general belief has grown up that there was little inter-colonial water traffic and the Colonies possessed few vessels. We are led to believe that stretches of water like the Sound were but little used and that a sail traversing those channels was a rare sight. An investigation shows that this was not so, nor was the country bordering on the Sound sparsely populated in the eighteenth century. There were many fairly large towns, and these towns carried on a constant and considerable commerce both with the other Colonial towns and with the home country and the West Indies. In 1756 New Haven had a population of 5,000, New London 3,000, and Stonington 2,900. The Colony of Connecticut at the same date owned 100 vessels, with a total tonnage of 3,202. These were mostly sloops, but she had a few ships, schooners and brigantines. There was a large fleet of sloops engaged in trade between Boston and New York, that passed through the Sound, and every village had one or two vessels making regular passages to New York or Newport, which was at that time one of the considerable ports of the country. The roads were so bad that traffic over them for goods for any distance was costly if not impossible. These sloops averaged about 30 tons burden and were in rig and build like the market sloops so common on the Sound and Hudson fifty years ago. It was a practice of these old mariners to seek shelter each night and come to anchor, and the bays on the South Side were favorite places for resting in. They made a business of working the tides, not being much on the wind, and this and fear of night voyaging probably accounts for the long passages. I read of one passage that took over thirty days from Boston to New Haven.

All along the Sound, wherever sufficient fall could be found, were tide mills, and to their back doors came the sloops either loaded with grain to go between the stones or empty to take away a cargo of flour. This flour was conveyed to New York, Newport and New London, where it was transferred to seagoing craft that took it to the West Indies to be traded for sugar, rum and molasses. Much of this rum was consumed in the country, but a deal of it went to Africa to be bartered for negroes who were taken to be sold in slavery in the southern colonies, Jamaica, Cuba and Hayti. The interdict of this African rum traffic by the government was one of the grievances that led to the Revolution. The people of New London and Stonington were deep in this slave trade, and one of the favorite fitting-out spots was Little Narragansett Bay.

While the sloop traders of the Sound may have been, as they were in later days, a cautious and patient set of voyagers, their deep-water brethren seem to have been the opposite. A more daring, devil-may-care set of mariners never hauled on a fall or cuddled a tiller. In their small vessels they sailed everywhere, and traded as they pleased, without much respect for the laws of man or the rights of nations. In those days the colonies of Spain were closed to other vessels than her own, but the American colonists seem to have had as much fear of the Dons and respect for their ordinances as did Drake and his companions, and they haunted the Antilles and Main in their barques and made good traffic everywhere, despite the vigilance of the Guarda Costa. The West India trade was the great trade in those days, and it moved South with flour, pork and fish, and North with sugar, rum and molasses.

No doubt the Sound trade was the breeding and training place of those mariners for whom in after years the world grew too small. We can imagine their trepidation when making the first voyage around Cape Cod, or the Hatteras; places famous in coaster traditions like the Hope and Horn in the annals of the deep-water man. In my early days I knew old sloop skippers who after long lives of voyaging confessed that they had never been beyond the Race, and one I met who had as boy and man sailed between New York and Greenwich for sixty years, and whose boast was that he had once voyaged to

Bridgeport. Another old fellow who sailed out of Eastchester Creek had never passed East of Eatons Neck, and who looked upon the waters beyond as a fearful place. Yet he was a splendid Hell Gate pilot, and many a day I have seen him take his sloop through that strait of whirlpools and cross-sets and rocks in a dead calm or a heavy breeze in a way that showed he was past master of his profession. We dread the unknown only because it is unknown. I met another skipper who had ventured for the first time in his life out of the Hudson into the Sound with a schooner load of brick. When I overhauled him off Duck Island he was lost and in a terrible fright, and swore that never again would he be caught voyaging East of the Battery. What frightened him most was that, it being hazy, he could not see the South Shore, and had an idea that he must have sailed past the end of Long Island in the night and was out to sea. This good man had never seen a chart. I led him back to Branford and we parted, he very grateful and me full of boyish wonder that a real captain of a real schooner could be so ignorant. But I have since thought how like that man must have been the old mariners who first ventured into unknown waters, and have since read of a Nova Scotia Skipper who started on a voyage to Barbadoes without chart or anything to guide him except the order "go to Barbadoes." He set off determined to get there by asking the way, and he did. One can imagine the faces of the captains of the big square-riggers when he held them up and in response to their hail, inquired "What's the course to Barbadoes?" Nor is this timidity and ignorance confined to professional skippers. I have known yachtsmen who sailed the West End of the Sound all their lives and never ventured beyond Captains Island or Matinicock Point. And to-day there are many who have never been out of the Belt, and when voyaging from point to point hang lovingly to the shore. The long-distance races have done much to remove this timidity and many venture further and further every year.

HARBORS

The harbors of the Belt are many, and no better anchorages than some of them are to be found in the world, that is for small craft, such as yachtsmen voyage in. The best harbors are on the Long Island side, being deep, narrow bays, surrounded by lofty sand-bluffs and having a good holding bottom of clay and stiff mud. They are not only perfect anchorages, but they are beautiful spots, clear, lakelike basins, framed in rich sandy browns and yellows, and backed by a vivid setting of green. They were also, until lately, homes in a wilderness, but alas, this charm will soon be lost, as man is invading their shores, with his glaring, ugly structures, and is cutting and clearing away the beautiful woods. One of his examples of bad taste is the desire to cover the sand slopes with grass, destroying at once the most noted feature in giving the rich warmth to the island landscape.

The first of these harbors from the West is Cow or Manhasset Bay, a deep indentation about three miles East of Throgs Neck, or Frogs, as it is called in the old charts. This was anciently a famous anchorage for coasters, but to-day is seldom used, as the average coaster is too big and clumsy to enter it. I have seen as many as thirty vessels riding out a Northeaster in that bay. The next is Hampstead Bay, a noble sheet of water but a poor anchorage, as it is open to a Northerly wind and an Easterly sea. It runs far up into the island, a narrow and shallow arm, that is surrounded by the highest of the Long Island hills.

The next bay is Oyster, a deep, narrow indentation that splits into two arms, the one penetrating South being known as Cold Spring Harbor. It is a perfect anchorage for small craft. The next is the premier bay of the whole, its entrance being between Lloyds and Eatons Neck, a deep, open channel that leads in until there branches off several harbors which swing back behind the bluffs for a mile or more. The favorite of these is Lloyds Harbor, a choice rendezvous for yachtsmen, completely landlocked and surrounded by wild woods that shut out all sight of man and his noises. Beyond Eatons Neck is a large bay, nearly ten miles from horn to horn, but which has no good anchorage. This is known as Smith Town Bay, from a town inhabited by an ancient family of that name. In the early charts at the head of this bay is shown what is called Three Sisters Bay, but no such bay to my knowledge now exists. Beyond Cranes Neck the Easterly point of Smith Town Bay is a lagoon-bay known as Port Jefferson Harbor. It is a fine anchorage, but its entrance is through a narrow, jetted channel, through which a very swift tidal current flows. This is the last harbor on the South Side of the Belt; thence on there is no opening of importance until Plum Gut at the Eastern end of the island is reached.

There are many bays on the North Side, but they are all small, rocky, and muddy, and while safe anchorages, are not to be compared with those on the South Side. The North Shore is also more densely populated, and is divested of its woodlands. Most of the yacht clubs harbor on the North Shore, because that is where the yachtsmen live. Pelham Bay, Leroys Bay, Echo Bay, Larchmont Harbor, Indian Harbor, Stamford Harbor, Black Rock, Morris Cove, and Sachems Head are all yachting holds. This latter is a very small but pretty nook in the rocks at the end of a granite point, a mere basin, capable of holding perhaps a dozen yachts. In the old days it was a favorite hole for coasting sloops. The place got its name from the murder of some captured Indian sachems by the colonists, who it is said at this spot decapitated several chiefs. Behind it are huge granite quarries, from which thousands of tons of rock have been taken to build the breakwaters along the Sound and at Point Judith. Beyond Sachems Head until Black Point is reached the harbors are very rocky and not to be commended. Niantic Bay is a fine sheet of water, but open to wind and sea, and not a good place for small craft. New London has a fine river harbor with a wide, deep entrance.

But the harbors I love most on the Sound are the ones into which in my boyhood cruising days I crept at nightfall and tied up snugly. Harbors where no other craft came to disturb our night watches. These were behind islands, up narrow, winding creeks, and even in old mill-races. I recall one of these at a place called Green Farms, which we invariably sought when in that vicinity; it was the race of an abandoned tide mill. Here we lay snugly berthed and laughed at storms from all quarters. Here the Rubes of the neighborhood after milking time, came down and sat on the stones and chatted and asked questions, and told us their family troubles. In return for our company, they brought gifts of milk, onions, corn, and potatoes, and sometimes a loaf of fresh bread or a cake. After a year or two we became like the circus, a yearly expectation, and were welcomed like a budget of good news. Another favorite spot was in back of Leets Island, one of the Thimbles, a pretty group of rocks about ten miles East of New Haven, and a famous ground for sand sharks, which we hunted and harpooned like whales. Oh, for those happy, devil-may-care days again, when we slept in the open cockpit and lived off coffee, hardtack, and what we could beg or plunder! In those times we were regular Wallensteins and Tillys and the Palatinate never suffered deeper depredations from those famous plunderers than did the shores of Connecticut when we elected to voyage along them.

ISLANDS

The Belt is not prolific of islands, and none of them except Fishers are large. I suppose there might be one hundred all together, including rocks with bushes on them. At the West End are City Island, once called the Isle of Man, and in old charts New Citty Island; Heart Island, Fox Island, now called Davids, Pea Island and Huckleberry. There are also several inner islands, separated from the mainland by narrow, muddy channels. On the Long Island side there are no islands until Plum Gut is reached. The principal islands along the Connecticut shore are the two Captains, off Greenwich, the Norwalk group, Falcon, or Faulkners as it is now called, and Duck. Near Faulkners is a small island called Goose, which was the Jan William of Block's map. Duck Island is famous in story as being the site of a British fort during the Revolution, placed there to protect the London Trade. The well on the island was dug by the soldiers. All these islands are wasting rapidly away, and no doubt most of them were originally connected with each other and the mainland.

The soft parts between the rocks are washed out by rain and sea and two bays form one on each side, these indentations work slowly in, making an isthmus, then this isthmus is swept away and two islands made out of one. Davids and Huckleberry once made one island and so did the two Captains. The Norfolk Islands were also at one time a solid body. Fishers Island was connected with Watch Hill, and Duck Island with the point of land to which a bar now runs. Faulkners and Goose Islands are rapidly wasting away. On the former in Revolutionary days there was a fine spring of water, but it now issues under the sea, the land that held its opening having disappeared. There was years ago a fine spring on the South side of Huckleberry, but at present the tide rises into its opening.

In Block's day what is now Stratford Shoal was two islands with trees on them. He called them the DeKees Islands. In 1800 they were still above water, and an old sea captain resident in Port Jefferson could remember going there to cut rushes for candle-wicks at the beginning of the last century. A very old gentleman who was living in New Rochelle in 1875 told me that when he was a boy what is known as Upper Green Flats, between Pine Islands and Huckleberry, had trees on it. I can remember when this shoal was always above water at high tide.

The land bordering the West End of the Sound is unquestionably sinking very rapidly; in the last thirty years the rocks have gone down a foot or more. There are now deep channels in the same places where in my early days a boat could not pass except at high water. A few hundred years more and all the islands of the Sound, with the exception of the largest and highest, will have disappeared.

LIGHTS

The lights on the Sound are numerous; in fact, they are so many it is like going up a street with gas lamps on each side. Several of them could be dispensed with, as owing to the shore being well lighted, especially on the North Side, they are no longer necessary. The oldest light is that at the entrance to the Thames River; this was built in 1789. Eatons is the next in age, being first lighted in 1799; it is also the tallest of the Sound towers, being 143 feet above high water. Faulkners, which looks higher, is only 94 feet; this tower was built in 1802. Sand Point is the oldest light at the West End; its beams first flashed forth in 1809. Execution was built in 1850, and put a stop to those rocks gathering in every year a harvest of wrecks. Stepping Stones was built some time in the Seventies after the steamer Elm City was smashed on one of the boulders. The oldest of the two lightships in the Sound is Bartletts Reef, first anchored in 1835.

The Sound is well buoyed as well as lighted, and navigation for moderate-sized craft is easy and safe.

FLORIDA'S INDIAN KEY

by VINCENT GILPIN

OCTOBER, 1935

Many innocent-looking coastal islands and coves have dramatic stories in their pasts. Digging them out can be a fascinating game, adding zest to coastwise cruising.

What memories the mere names of Florida's Indian Key, or New Hampshire's Smutty Nose, evoke in historically minded yachtsmen!

THE Florida Keys form a sweeping chain of islands, two hundred miles long, palm-fringed, remote and lovely. Beginning at Miami on the southeast coast, they swing south and west, past Key West, to the Dry Tortugas, far out in the Gulf of Mexico. They define the Florida Straits, and form the left bank of the mighty Gulf Stream, being protected from it by the great barrier reef of limestone and coral. Incidentally, that steaming current from the Caribbean brings them the nearest approach to tropical climate in the United States.

They are familiar to travelers as the foundation of the "Oversea Highway" to Key West, and to sportsmen as bases for the pursuit of tarpon, tuna, sailfish and other monsters of the deep which frequent the reef. Their pre-railroad history is largely forgotten; most of those who see them assume that they were just worthless bits of wilderness, without human interest. The flood of visitors and the mounting tide of new residents which came with the highway immediately and overwhelmingly outnumbered their predecessors, so that the interests and troubles of the old days have faded into the mists of the past, and now linger like ghosts of the long-ago in the minds of the few who knew the region before the automobile came.

Nevertheless, the islands had their history, in spite of their loneliness—perhaps the richer thereby. Previous to Florida's cession to the United States in 1819 it was isolation which gave them their chief value as pirate strongholds. In this remote labyrinth of islands sea raiders were well-hidden, and further protected by the dangers of navigation on the reef and in the intricate shoal waters between them and the mainland, which were neither charted nor marked.

But soon after we took over the peninsula a bold and ingenious man saw the chance of more legitimate profit in the region, because of these same difficulties of navigation, which made the Florida Straits more fruitful in wrecks than any other part of our coast. Jacob Houseman, of Staten Island, bought Indian Key, a small rocky island to seaward of the head of Lower Matecumbe, with a fair anchorage, and close to a good channel into Florida Bay. It was about halfway down the reef and so within a day's sail of all the wrecks in the Straits. It lies a mile off the present highway embankment which joins the Matecumbes, and probably not one traveler in a hundred even sees the tiny scrap of land against the blue-green waters of the Hawk Channel, as he goes by. Even the trim cruisers which lie off it between raids on the fish of Alligator Reef think of it as just another island. Yet a century ago Indian Key supported the largest town within hundreds of miles, and a little later it was the scene of a dramatic tragedy.

Houseman was a man of action, and shortly after his purchase he had established on the key a wrecking community which crowded its ten acres with buildings and brought affluence to his family in Staten Island. This was the first town on the Keys, and for twenty years the only one of consequence. As to the ethics of Houseman's business there would seem to have been some question, since his neighbors on Staten Island were not taken fully into his confidence. They knew he carried on the business of salvage, and the comforts and luxuries of the family were evidence that he was successful. But there were further stories, long current, of mysterious vessels slipping into Arthur Kill at night and disappearing before morning, which coincided with sudden accessions of rich and varied merchandise.

Wrecking, of course, has always lent itself to the diversion of choice bits of cargo or equipment from the legal channels of salvage to the possession of those who saw them first, without benefit of customhouse. On the great reef, where authorities were far to seek, and where ships driven ashore promptly went to pieces with the loss of most of their contents, and little chance of checking up on what had been removed, it is evident that the temptation to this procedure was great. Certainly the keen rivalry of the wreckers can scarcely be explained by the salvor's share of the meager proceeds of wreck auctions, where unsuitable goods must be thrown on a limited market.

At all events, Indian Key became headquarters for a good-sized fleet of smart sail-craft, many of them North River sloops; it is said that sixty such vessels scoured the reef, with lookouts at every masthead, and all was fish which came to their net. There were plenty of wrecks to keep them busy, for the navigation of the Straits even now is a chancy business. The racing current of the Gulf Stream forces southbound traffic to edge in as near the reef as possible to escape its greatest strength; the reef itself is extremely irregular, and the crystal-clear water is deceptive, tempting pilots to run by sight, while cross-tides make on and off the rocks in unexpected places, but little understood. In view of the steamers which still go aground on the reef, in fine weather and by daylight, in spite of many lighthouses and other marks, it is obvious that the small sailing ships of 1825, feeling their way into this unsurveyed thicket of dangers, must have run a very high risk of loss.

So Jacob Houseman and his associates prospered exceedingly until 1840, when the story of Indian Key came to a violent end, for which it is now chiefly remembered. The name most closely linked with this tragedy is not Houseman's, but that of a visitor, Henry Perrine, physician and botanist, one of the first men to recognize the tropic features of south Florida.

Dr. Perrine had been ten years consul at Campeche, Yucatan, where an important part of his duties was to obtain tropical seeds and plants, against the opposition of the Spanish authorities, who were not minded to share their flora with the United States. By befriending the Indians, however, he made a large collection, and brought it back with him in 1837. He was offered a tract of land in Louisiana as an experiment station, but had evidently made a study of climates, and probably recognized the importance of the Gulf Stream, since he selected southeastern Florida for his work, and was granted a township on lower Biscayne Bay.

The Seminole war, however, was in an active phase, and he could not take possession. The next best thing was to proceed to Indian Key, considered too far from the mainland to be in danger, and there await settled conditions. This he did, by the brigantine Lucinda, landing with his family on Christmas Day, 1838. The story is told by his son,

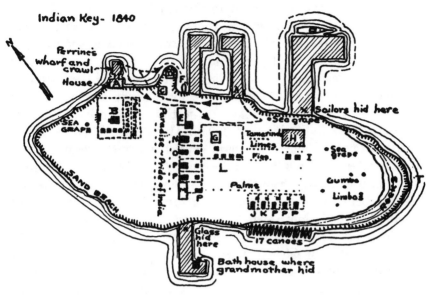

PLAN OF INDIAN KEY

A. *Perrine house.*

B. *Howe's.*

C. *Carpenter shop.*

D. *Blacksmith shop.*

E. *Store, which 6 Indians were plundering when Perrines took boat at F.*

G. *Houseman's.*

H. *Warehouse, with cistern under in which two men and boy hid.*

I. *Senator English's.*

J.-K. *Houses of Glass and Beiglet, who gave alarm.*

L. *Indians when discovered by Glass.*

M. *Tropical Hotel.*

N. *Mott's house.*

O. *Mrs. Smith and Mrs. Sturdy.*

P.P. *Vacant houses.*

T. *Where Mrs. Smith, Mrs. Sturdy and baby hid in rocks.*

——*From "A True Story of Some Eventful Years in Grandpa's Life," by Henry E. Perrine, 1885.*

Henry E., then twelve years old, in a book of reminiscences published half a century later, in which the eager joy of the lad in such adventures is clearly reflected. One may guess that his elders looked upon this removal to the wilderness with far more question and anxiety.

Only the scattered "forts" of the Seminole war and the lighthouse at Cape Florida broke the wilds, save for a newly established naval station and hospital on Teatable Key, nearby, which may be regarded as a part of the Indian Key settlement. The voyage down the Straits and the Hawk Channel, the warm crystal water, the beauty of the densely forested islands beneath the golden sun, were marvels to them all. Indian Key was then covered by large trees, both native and planted, between which peeped some forty buildings, for the little island was a close-knit town.

Houseman's mansion stood in the center, and northwest of it (inshore) was that of Charles Howe, trader, postmaster and customs officer, each surrounded by well-planted grounds, with rows of slave-quarters. Between was Howe's store, and nearby on the northeast shore were carpenter and blacksmith shops, with three large wharves to seaward, and behind the latter a large warehouse. On the same shore, farthest from the sea, was the house assigned to the Perrines, on a stone foundation over the water, with its own wharf and verandahs overlooking the sea.

Scattered over the key were several rows of small houses. The ends of the key were shaded by large gumbo-limbo and sea-grape trees, while in the center were avenues of palms, Paradise and Pride of India trees, with orchards of limes, tamarinds, mulberries and figs. The observer must picture much finer trees than any left today, since the island was almost swept clean by the hurricane of 1906.

Here the Perrines settled down comfortably to await peace. The community felt itself amply protected by the twenty miles of water between it and the mainland. Occasional echoes of the war reached them, as when General Harney sailed past after his defeat on the Caloosahatchie, but it all seemed very far away and meaningless compared to the thrill of the new life in this entrancing climate. One may imagine what it meant to young Henry, who learned to shoot and swim and sail, and made many excursions over reef and channel and bay, all full of marvels. His sister started a school for the children of the key. Dr. Perrine explored the region and planted many seeds, especially on Indian Key and its neighbor in Florida Bay, Lignum

Vitae Key, which is larger than Indian Key, with richer soil, and was the garden of the community.

So passed a year and a half of busy, happy life, warm winter merging into breezy summer with scarcely a change of temperature or weather. It was a true paradise, and we may imagine that none of the doctor's family regretted the continuance of sufficient activity among the Indians to forbid exchanging the comfortable home and pleasant friendships of Indian Key for the lonely struggles of their unlocated wilderness township on the mainland. The days were full of life and color, with many a white sail gleaming on the blue water, and the clear air filled with the ring of blacksmiths' hammers and caulking mallets. Loitering darkies gossiped at each other's doors, women planned their housekeeping and discussed domestic problems, and children turned reluctantly from the charms of this adventurous fairyland to the monotony of the three R's. Never was quieter or more settled life, and never did disaster seem farther away than in August of 1840—but on the seventh of that month it came.

Two carpenters, Glass and Beiglet, living in the houses nearest to Matecumbe, were roused at two in the morning by some slight noise, and saw with horror seventeen Indian dugout canoes drawn up on the beach. The Indians had come! They hurried out to warn the community, but it was too late. The Indians were already at their posts, awaiting dawn, and on seeing the two whites they opened the attack at once. The sleeping town was aroused by a sudden burst of yells and rifle shots, and the busy, happy life of Indian Key was at an end.

Pandemonium followed. Utterly surprised, with enemies at every door, the whites made no resistance, but fled and hid as best they might, each household for itself. There was no thought of protecting property. The Indians made it clear that anyone interfering with them would be killed without a word. The night echoed with shouts and screams and the crash of glass and woodwork, with shots and groans and curses, and soon it was lurid with the glare of burning buildings.

Glass and Beiglet dodged into an empty house and hid in the attic until the looting was over at daylight, when it was fired, and they dashed through the flames and escaped. The Mott family, father, mother, grandmother and two children, caught the worst of the opening attack, rushing to hide in an outhouse, whence they were at once dragged forth. The parents saw the children clubbed to death and the baby's body cast into the sea, and then were themselves killed in each other's arms and the clothing burned from their bodies. Meanwhile, the grandmother had slipped off into a bathhouse on a wharf, where she escaped notice until the raid was over.

The Howes reached a boat, rowed off to their small schooner, and sailed to Teatable without opposition. Otis, a carpenter, was shot in the first attack, but managed to reach a boat and push off; he then fainted from loss of blood, and floated about until noon next day, when he was picked up and revived. A Mrs. Sturdy, her daughter, Mrs. Smith, and a grandchild, reached the broken rocky shore at the seaward end of the island, and hid until morning. Henry Goodyear, later of rubber fame, was on the island, and hid in a cupola until daylight, when he rushed forth prepared to fight, but was not molested. The Houseman family alone attempted to reach their guns (which were on the ground floor) but found the Indians already in possession. They escaped in the rear and rushed into the sea, followed by their dogs, barking, and stopped long enough to drown them; then, stripping off their too-visible white night clothes, they swam to the nearest boat and made off to Teatable. Several men hid in the basement of the warehouse and came through safe, but a boy with them was suffocated by the smoke.

The Perrines endured the most trying adventures of all. At the first alarm the doctor ordered them all to the basement, which was open to tidewater, and was called the bathroom. Here in their night clothes they huddled in the water, while the doctor barricaded the trapdoor entrance behind them, and went to talk with the Indians, thinking that his profession and his command of Spanish would protect him. At first they seemed amenable and retired, and apparently the doctor retreated to the attic to watch developments. The shivering family then passed several terrible hours of suspense, unable to leave the "bathroom" and without means of knowing what happened above—a trying time, hardest on Sarah, the older daughter, who had been ill for a fortnight and was near exhaustion. They found their way to a concealed passage under the wharf, originally designed to hold a boat in which to escape just such an attack, but now barred by piling which formed a turtle-crawl under the end of the wharf. From the crawl a trapdoor opened to the wharf above.

Once in this nerve-wracking time two heavy guns were heard near by, and the trembling watchers were assured of rescue by an expedition from the naval station on Teatable Key. Nothing further happened, however, and their fresh hopes slowly died as the night wore on. The fact was that invalided seamen hastily armed a small sloop with two little cannon, sailed for Indian Key, and went aground; they then trained the guns and fired them, only to have the recoil carry them both overboard into the mud, whence they were recovered thirty-five years later!

Before daylight the Indians returned to Perrine's, now drunk, and broke into the house, yelling and calling for "the old man." There were confused sounds of conflict and ravage, and then the dread crackle of flames. Nothing more was ever known of the doctor's fate, but he must have been killed in this attack.

One may imagine the state of the helpless family below. As the house burned the bathroom became untenable, and they retreated to the wharf-passage, near the turtle-crawl piling. Eventually the planking above them was fired, and they were scorched as they lay in the water, now shallow with the lower tide, plastering their heads with wet marl from the bottom. Fiercely they dug at the base of a partly loosened pile that they might escape into the turtle-crawl, but it was spiked above, and could not be removed.

Thus dawn found them. As it broke they were nearly betrayed by the turtles, which woke and splashed about their enclosure. An Indian posted on the wharf heard them, raised the trapdoor into the crawl, and peered down, but saw only the turtles, though the family, close against the piling in white garments, might well have been discovered. It was at all events fortunate that they could not move the pile, since if they had they would certainly have been in the crawl now, helpless under the eye of the Indian guard.

As daylight grew many of the raiders departed, their boats deep-laden with the loot of houses and stores. At the same time the flames drew nearer and nearer to the trapped family, until destruction seemed inevitable. Finally the boy, screaming that he would rather be killed by Indians than burned to death, squeezed his slim body past the loose pile. Giving up his family for lost, he waded past the turtles in the crawl and climbed through the trapdoor onto the wharf, expecting instant death.

He found himself alone! Not an Indian was in sight, and the dazed lad waded ashore by the embers of his home and wandered aimlessly down the island, past the store, to another wharf, and then back toward the crawl again, noticing an empty skiff on the beach opposite the store. Then, to his utter amazement, his mother and sisters emerged unharmed from the crawl. They had at last dug out the foot of the loosened pile.

The lad remembered the skiff, led them to it, launched it and started to Teatable, rejoicing in his ability to scull it with the single oar remaining. Scarcely had they made an offing when there were yells behind them, and six Indians rushed from Howe's store, where they had been collecting goods to load that same skiff, so absorbed that the wandering boy and the fleeing family were alike unnoticed. No other boats were near, and the Indians could only watch their escape.

So they reached safety at Teatable, stunned with grief and terror, wet, cold and exhausted, with only their night clothes left from the rich and well-appointed life of a few hours before. They received every kindness, were clothed after a fashion (at first in sheets!) and a fund was raised for them. Boats were sent to the ruined key and picked up a number of survivors. They also found in the ashes of the Perrine house a few charred bones, supposed to be those of Dr. Perrine, which were buried on Matecumbe.

The Perrines went back to their New Jersey friends with no further thought of the township on the mainland. It lay neglected until 1876, when the son Henry spent a winter in a futile attempt to make good the family's title, which was conditional on placing a settler on each of its thirty-six square miles. After that it was once more forgotten until 1906, when the Key West railroad traversed it, and the family name was revived and perpetuated in Perrine station, sixty-five years after the doctor's death.

Such was the end of the first and most picturesque settlement on the Florida Keys. The island was not again occupied until the railroad came, save by government engineers for a brief time when Alligator Reef Lighthouse was built. Houseman survived less than a year, to die in an altercation over a cargo of goods taken from a wreck. On the sea side of the island, just above high water, lies a fine marble tombstone, not mounted, but lying askew on its back, as it was landed, with the following inscription:

> Here lyeth the body of Capt. Jacob Houseman, formerly of Staten Island, State of New York, Proprietor of this island, who died by accident May 1st, 1841, aged 41 years 11 months.

To his friends he was sincere, to his enemies he was kind, to all men faithful.

This monument is erected by his most disconsolate tho affectionate wife, Elizabeth Ann Houseman.

Sic Transit Gloria Mundi.

Nearly all of the old foundations and cisterns and some of the smaller buildings remain, and can still be identified on the plan of the town given in young Henry's book. Tamarinds and other trees set out by the doctor are in their prime, and prickly poppies, stray cotton bushes and other plants are descended from those of 1840. The beach at the Perrine house has been washed away and its foundations are gone, but through the shoal clear water, mingled with the sand, are to be seen thousands of bits of glass and china with the quaint design and sprigged decoration of the period. Many are blackened and partly fused by the fire which destroyed the house nearly a century ago.

To stumble on such intimate relics of that dreadful night, while the peaceful sun sparkles on the blue Hawk Channel, and crowded traffic thunders to Key West over the nearby road, is to go back in one heart-stirring step to the pioneer days of exploration and adventure. There, in the midst of holiday sport, we may hear again the blood-curdling war whoop, the vicious crack of rifles and the screams of the wounded, and see the billowing, flame-reddened smoke cloud roll away over the quiet waters.

A VIKING SHIP

by FREDERICK K. LORD

JANUARY, 1913

The Gogstad ship, the best preserved of the Viking skutas, is a maritime museum in itself. Revealingly described by Mr. Lord, this beautiful hull shows the genius of the early Norse shipbuilders.

IN THE year 1880, at Gogstad, near Sandefjord, at the entrance to the Fjord of Christiania, there was unearthed the finest specimen to date of a Viking ship.

Unfortunately the literature of the North is very meager in reference to details and dimensions of vessels. In no case is the dimension of a ship mentioned in the Sagas which have come down to us, and only once is the length of a boat partially given.

The size of a boat was usually expressed by the number of rooms or rowers' benches, and was a simple method which gave the people of that time a very good idea of the size and dimensions of the boat, without going into detailed measurements. This scarcity of dimensions has been a great drawback in determining the size and construction of the Norse ships; and were it not for the beautiful custom of burying dead warriors in their vessels we should have little information regarding them. There were three methods of burial: cremation and interment on land; putting the deceased aboard his boat, with sail set, then applying the torch; and burying the ship on the shore with the body in the vessel. It is this latter custom which has enabled us to glean something of the actual construction of the boats.

Towards the latter part of the 19th Century systematic diggings were begun, which resulted in the unearthing of several of the old ship tombs. These finds added much information to the subject. But by far the greatest find of them all was the discovery of a ship at Gogstad.

The Sagas, rock tracings and tapestries, indicated the external characteristics of ships, but it was not until the discovery of the tombs that an opportunity arose to obtain definite knowledge of the size and structure in detail. Aside from the ships, their grave mounds contained many things of great value and interest, as it was the custom to bury with the deceased his accoutrements, horses, animal pets, and other personal effects. The Gogstad ship was found in a mound 150 feet long and 15 feet high, situated 500 feet from and 18 feet above the sea. The boat was placed with her bow towards the water, as if ready for a voyage again. Owing to the fact that the vessel was buried in blue clay the hull is in a remarkable state of preservation. The only parts rotted away were the extreme tip of the bow and stern. As the clay strata reached only up to this point it is supposed that the soil above caused the tips to decay. It seems likely, however, that such was not the case. The ends of many ships were carried high up into a figurehead. In order to bury these heads it would be necessary to dig a grave twice as deep as would be sufficient to inter the hull. As the digging of a hole big enough for the ship must have been a heavy task, it seems improbable that the work would be doubled in order to get the figureheads interred. As these heads were highly ornate and often covered with beaten gold it seems reasonable to suppose that they were chopped off at the gunwale and removed, or else used as tombstone or memorial.

Just abaft the mast the dead warrior was placed, and a wooden tent erected over him. With the body a pea fowl and very small dog were found, while the skeletons of a dozen horses and several dogs were scattered throughout the mound. Many objects of interest were unearthed in the hull, such as ornaments, jewelry, implements, weapons, cooking utensils, and many pieces of carved wood. Several beds were found. They were low and wide, being held together by fids, in order that they could be readily taken apart and stowed. Two carved pieces of wood, with bronze animal heads on the arms, formed part of the seat of the chief. There were bailing scoops, larger in capacity and better in shape than those used today. There was an oak gang plank, 24 feet long, 10 inches wide and 2 ¾ inches thick, ornamentally carved in a manner affording a hold for the feet.

Many of the wooden fragments were carved in a beautiful and artistic manner, and it is unfortunate that the purpose of many of them is not known; but future discoveries may make it clear. The

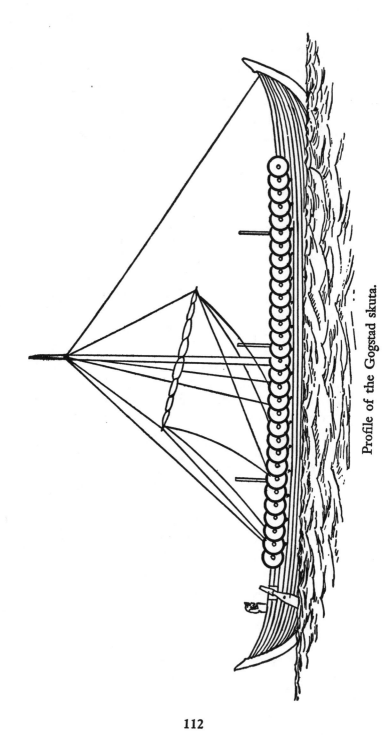

Profile of the Gogstad skuta.

112

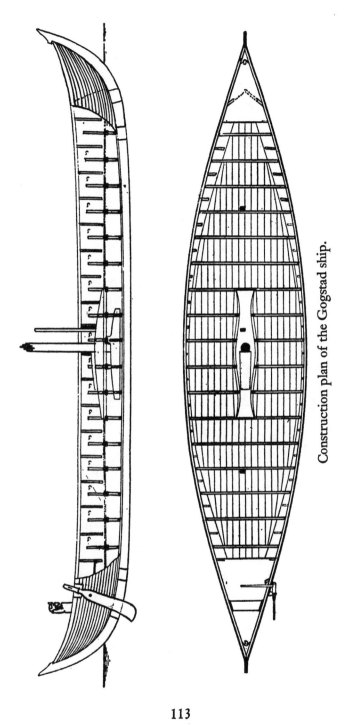

Construction plan of the Gogstad ship.

remains of a sledge were found, and also fragments of three oak boats. Oarlocks were made from a natural oak crotch, and let in and riveted to the gunwale. A leather thong passed through a hole in the throat and was tied to the oar. This construction is superior to the thole pins and metal rowlocks of the present day. It afforded a good grip on the gunwale; the pins being natural crook and thick at the root was well nigh indestructible; the wood was easier on the oar, and the leather thong held the latter so that it would be free from back-lash and impossible to unship or fall overboard. Three small boats were in such bad shape that restoration was impossible, and the only accurate measurements obtained were the lengths of their keels, which are as follows: 23.6, 18.4 and 13.8 feet. Assuming that their ends had the same amount of overhang as the big ship, and breadth in propor-tion, then their length over all and breadth would be 30.6 by 6.1, 23.8 by 4.8, and 18 feet by 3.6 feet breadth respectively. A ship the size of the Gogstad one would ordinarily carry only two boats, and as the 30-foot boat would be a pretty large one to carry, being 1/19 the size of the ship, there is some doubt as to its belonging to the outfit.

This vessel belongs to the class known as a *skuta*, a type of small warship often mentioned in the Sagas. She was the smallest seagoing vessel, and built for speed. Such a craft must have been very much used, being light, swift and handy, for short voyages and general pur-poses. Due to the decayed ends, her length could not be accurately ascertained, but it is close to 80 feet between rabbets and about 70 feet on the water line, excluding stem pieces. The breadth is about 16½ feet. The date in which the boat was built is unknown, but antiquarians place her between the 8th and 11th centuries, A.D. Con-sidering the date and art of shipbuilding in other countries, a glance at the lines shows her to be a wonder. This vessel may be considered the connecting link between ancient and mediæval types of ships. Her proportions and scantlings prove that her builders had large experi-ence of shipbuilding, and that they understood the art, which was subsequently lost, to be revived only in modern times, of shaping the underwater portion of the hull so as to reduce the resistance to the passage of the vessel through the water.

It is the opinion of experts in naval architecture that for model and workmanship this vessel is a masterpiece, nor for beauty of lines and symmetrical proportions could she be surpassed today by any man connected with the art of designing or building ships. Certainly a strong statement, in view of the fact that we have a thousand years' more experience, but nevertheless true. It is doubtful if there are in this country today a score of men with enough innate ability to design a boat, for the purpose intended, equal to this one in appearance, seaworthiness and speed. With regards the two latter qualities, she is worthy of careful study.

The lines of the ship were taken off by Mr. Colin Archer, and along with other data embodied in a paper read before the Institute of Naval Architects in 1881. It is to this very interesting account that the writer wishes to acknowledge his indebtedness for the plans and much information. Acknowledgment is also due to Du Chaillu's extremely interesting work on the Viking age.

THE MODEL

Turning now to the lines, let us consider some of the features of the design, viewed in the light of modern architecture, and see how well they agree with the practice and theory of today.

CALCULATIONS ON FORM

Length between stem rabbets .... 79 feet 0 inches
Length l. w. l. over stems .... 74 " 0 "
Length l. w. l. faired into stems .... 71 " 0 "
Length l. w. l. between rabbets .... 69 " 6 "
Extreme breadth .... 16 " 8 "
Load water line, breadth .... 15 " 4 "
Draught to rabbet .... 2 " 9 "
Draught, extreme .... 3 " 8 "
Depth from rabbet to gunwale .... 6 " 0 "
Displacement at 2 ft. 9 in. draught .... 63700 lb
Area of midsection .... 25.74 square feet
Wetted surface of hull 760+95 for laps .... 850 " "
Wetted surface of keel .... 190 " "
Wetted surface, total .... 1040 " "
Center of buoyancy, from O station 50%
Center of midsection, from O station 50%
Center of gravity l. w. l. plane, from O station ... 50%
Area of l. w. l. .... 695 square feet
Breadth to length ratio at l. w. l. 4.83

VIKING SHIP
DATE 900 A.D.
FOUND AT GOGSTAD 1880

Lines of the Gogstad ship.

Breadth to length ratio at gunwale	4.74
Pounds per inch immersion	3700 lb
Coefficient fineness, l. w. l.	64 %
Coefficient fineness, midsection	61.2%
Block coefficient	33.3%
Prismatic coefficient	54.5%
Sectional area curve, a versed sine	
Shell expansion	1375 square feet
Lateral area, hull	111 " "
Lateral area, keel	79 " "
Lateral area, total	190 " "
Area rudder	7 " "
C. L. R. keel and hull	50%
Least freeboard	3 feet 6 inches
Mean freeboard over l. w. l.	3 " 7 "
Approx. freeboard at ends	5 " 7 "
Position of mast	48%
Diameter	12.5 inches

The most striking feature of the model is the extraordinary beauty and fineness of the lines. Considering the forms of contemporaneous ships, it seems almost incredible that a vessel so far ahead of its time could be produced. The boats of Norway are today almost exactly like this old ship, and such an instance of persistence of type is without parallel in the history of shipbuilding and affords indisputable proof of the skill and knowledge of the Norsemen in designing and building ships. Considering the leading dimensions and type, what designer today would undertake to improve the lines of this boat? Could he produce a fairer set of water-lines, buttocks and diagonals?

The boat has a long floor, and the distribution of her displacement is good for a boat of her purpose and speed. Referring to her sectional area curve it will be seen that it is a double versed sine, filled out a little at the ends; exactly as used by the best designers of today. The centers of buoyancy, midsection, and load water-line plane are all exactly amidships. The center of lateral resistance is also amidships, and the mast was stepped about 8 inches forward. Considering the fact that these boats sailed at times with wind abeam, the arrangement of centers is excellent. The coefficient of fineness of the load water-line, block and prismatic coefficients, all check up with modern practice in vessels of this type.

The Construction

The construction of the ship is extremely interesting. Restricted as they were in tools and materials, the Vikings nevertheless produced boats that show great ingenuity and practical knowledge of boat-building. Oak was the only wood used in the hull. The fastenings were oak trenails and small iron rivets in the planking, knees and keel scarfs. The axe was the main tool. There is not a real bolt in the boat, or indication of a saw being used.

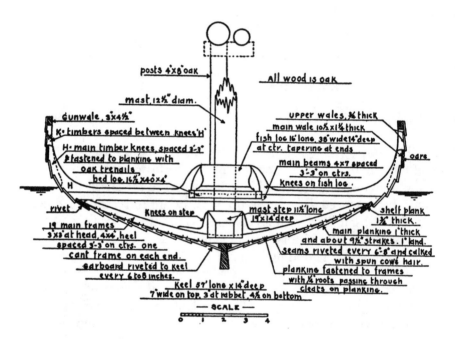

A glance at the plans shows that the method of construction was different from present-day practice. Instead of a multitude of frames there were only nineteen of them, spaced 3 feet 3 inches apart. They are 4 inches at keel and 3 inches at head, and of natural crook to correspond to the deadrise. The frames are not fastened to the keel, and there are no floors at all. The frames extended nearly up to the water-line where their heads are riveted to an extra heavy planking strake. Running athwartships on top of the heads are main beams or thwarts 7 inches wide and 4 inches deep. From the underside of the thwarts to the top of the keel, stanchions are placed, thus making a

triangular bridge construction of the framing system, which is extremely light and strong. Landed on top of the thwarts were heavy
knees running up to within two strakes of the gunwale and secured
with iron nails. Midway between these main knees were intercostal
ones running from the water-line up to the gunwale. This method of
construction is unusual but apparently served well.

The boat may be considered as made up of two distinct sections,
each serving a special function.

The portion above the main beams is the working part of the ship,
and probably held the crew and everything she carried, and consequently was comparatively strong. The portion below was to give
form to the boat and float the crew and its load above. Looking at it
this way the construction seems well adapted to its purpose. The
keel is 14 inches deep, 7 inches broad at the top, and 4½ inches at
bottom. It is tapered in to 3 inches at the rabbet, to form a backing
for the garboard. The keel proper is in one piece, 57 feet long. The
stem and the keel are joined by a heel piece with vertical scarfs,
fastened with two rows of rivets. The planking of the boat is of the
lap-strake type. There are sixteen strakes to a side, and they vary in
thickness. The first nine planks, beginning at the keel, are one inch
thick; the next, or shelf plank, is 1¾ inches; then come three more
one inch; the next, 1¼ inches, is the strake pierced for oars, and the
two remaining wales are ¾ inch. The planks run about 9½ inches
wide with one-inch laps. They are riveted about every 6 or 8 inches
along the lap and calked with cow's hair spun into a cord. The interesting part of the planking is the method used in fastening it to the
frames. The planks were worked out so as to leave a raised cleat where
it touched a frame. Holes were bored in the cleat and in the lower
edge of the frame, through these was passed a tough root about ¼
inch thick and formed the only connection between frame and
planking. The frames were shaped in section and were very light
compared with the other scantling. There can be little doubt that the
boat must have worked considerably in a seaway. Her real safety
probably lay in a tough and elastic skin, which would be strained less
if allowed to work somewhat rather than be held rigid in spots. As
the cargo was live weight the strain on the hull was light.

The ends of the vessel are rotted away, so it is impossible to tell
just how they terminated. It is probable that the stern heads were
finished plain, the ship being rather small to be decorated with figure-

heads. The indications are that several of the upper strakes did not run into the stems, but finished at the under side of the gunwale. The mast is a big stick, 12½ inches in diameter, and its method of stepping is unusual. The step proper is 11½ feet long, 19 inches deep, 14 inches wide, and jogged over the frames and fastened thereto with knees. On

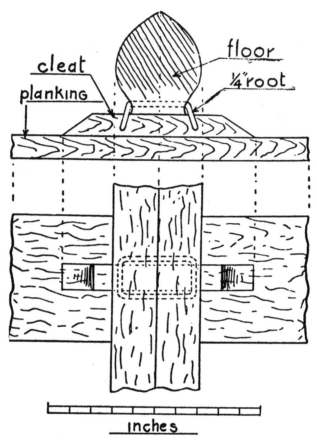

Viking method of fastening planking.

top of the main thwart frames is a slab 16½ feet long, 4 inches thick, and 40 inches wide, jogged in. On this is mounted a huge block of oak, 16 feet long, called the fish, and braced with heavy knees to the thwarts. There is a slot 6 feet long just abaft the mast hole. This provides room for the mast to be lowered aft. When the latter was stepped a large block of wood was jammed in the slot to hold it up. In order to prevent undue thrust on the keel the step was provided with a raised portion connecting it with the fish.

The weights given in the appended list are carefully calculated from the dimensions, assuming the weight of oak to be 50 lb. per cubic foot. They are interesting as showing how the strength is distributed rather than an expression of actual weight.

CALCULATIONS ON WEIGHTS
All wood is oak. Wt. taken at 50 lb. per cu. ft.

	Pounds
Planking	6200
Keel and stems	2400
Frames	810
Floor boards	2500
Main thwart beams	1800
Main knees on thwart beams	1400
Intercostal wale timbers	400
Gunwale	750
Knees on mast step and fish log	175
Mast step	750
Fish log	1250
Fish log bed	900
Stanchions under deck beams	95
Three spar stanchions	270
Rudder and tiller	300
Allowance for all other wood	2000
Total wood in hull	22000
5000 iron fastenings	350
12½ inch mast and yard	1000
Sail and rigging	650
24-ft. gangplank 10x2¾ inches	220
32 oars at 18 lb	570
64 shields 3-ft. diameter at 15 lb.	910
Wt. of boat as above	25700
100 men with accoutrements	22000
Ship's outfit, provisions, dunnage, spare arms, etc.	16000
Total	63700

The ship was steered on the starboard side with a vertical rudder. It is mounted at the end of a conical piece of wood projecting far enough beyond the side to allow the rudder to hang vertical. Through a hole in this and the rudder a rope was rove. It had a knot on the outside and was fastened inside. This made a sort of universal joint. The post was strapped near the gunwale to keep the rudder from swinging out of place. A small rope running down to the keel provided means for unshipping. The rudder post is 7 inches thick and the blade about 22 inches wide. The tiller worked athwartships, and the chief sat in an ornamental seat. The length of the spars is not known. The mast has been estimated at 40 feet. The yard was 8½ inches at center, 3 inches at ends, and estimated 35 feet long. Assuming these dimensions then the sail area would be somewhere around 900 square feet. The ropes were of bast made from the bark of trees. The sail was of woolen approximately square or slightly wider at the foot and probably was particolored. It is known that red, white, blue and green were used and designs embroidered or painted on sails.

There were three upright posts upon which the mast and yard rested when down. Over this at night a tent was stretched, under which the crew slept, each man in a leather sleeping bag, when the weather was cold. They generally slept ashore, however. No cooking was done on board. The flooring of the ship was composed of short pieces fitted in between the thwart knees. The oars were about 16 or 18 feet long and two men served each oar, rowing by turns. An interesting detail is the slot in the oar holes, allowing them to be pushed through from the inside. When the oars were not in use a sliding shutter closed the holes and kept the water out.

The shields were often hung on the gunwale overlapping, thereby taking up less room and helping to keep out spray. They were painted alternately orange and black. The crew is estimated at not less than eighty men. The workmanship on the boat is excellent, being executed with care and neatness throughout. Many parts are decorated with ornamental tracings and carvings and the whole bespeaks the conscientious care with which these Viking boats were built. Driving down the wind with swelling sail, shields on gunwale and crowded with a crew of lion-hearted men dressed in barbaric splendor, the whole a mass of color—what a sight it must have been!

LESSONS FROM A CHINESE SAMPAN

by C. ANDRADE, JR.

JULY, 1917

One day, Mr. Andrade came across an accurate model of a Chinese sampan. Being an inventor, patent engineer and a designer of original yachts (as well as a champion of the uncluttered cabin) he started to study it. This is the result of his analysis of the model. The lines and sail plan were drawn by George B. Douglas.

THE accompanying lines and sail plan illustrate a very interesting model of Chinese sampan. The model from which this was taken is an authentic piece of work, evidently made by a Chinese shipbuilder, as it contains all the peculiarities of design and construction that belong to the Chinese system of naval architecture. It is a fact not generally known that the Chinese are, and for many centuries have been, very successful sailors, and the model shown herewith is a good illustration of their ability as designers. It will be noted that the lines embody many of the refinements which are found in the most up-to-date boats in the United States. For example, the wetted surface of this model is reduced almost to the theoretical minimum for the displacement shown. There is not a single square inch of surface wasted in any projecting keel or skeg or deadwood.

The sheer line of the bottom of the boat also illustrates a peculiarity which naval architects in this country have just begun to appreciate, and that is, that the run can be carried out quite full, almost to the stern, and then come up, with a sharp turn, without hurting the boat's speed in any way. This fact has been known for a number of years to the torpedo-boat builders of England, who carry their displacement curve very full, almost to the stern. The same thing is shown on the Herreshoff small steamers of the type of the Mirage,

123

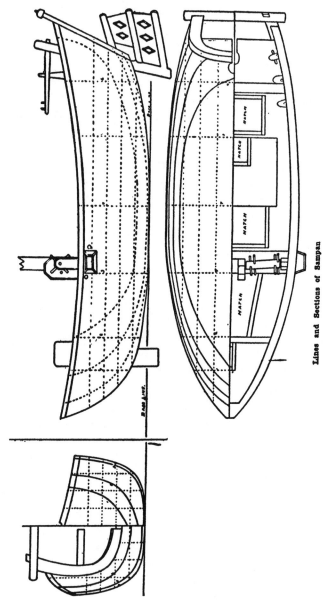

Lines and Sections of Sampan

Lines and sections of Chinese sampan taken from model.

and other boats of that class, where the keel line is carried out with an easy curve, about to the point where the shaft leaves the hull, and then turns up rather sharply to the stern. This same feature accounts for the very short overhang, with strong upturned buttock lines that are found in some designs of the Herreshoff sailing yachts.

There is quite a marked flat portion on the bottom of the hull, so that she can go aground and rest at low tide without heeling over. Indeed, the whole boat appears to be designed for this contingency, because it will be noted that she depends for lateral plane on two features; first, a dagger-board forward, which can be lifted, and, second, a very large rudder aft, which also can be housed entirely within the hull, when not in use. It will be observed that the dagger-board contains the great essential which is necessary in a member of this type, i. e., narrow width with great depth. It is well known that the former edge of the keel, or centerboard, is what does most of the work, and the Chinese apparently have grasped this fundamental principle. Therefore, while the dagger-board seems to have a very small lateral area, it will be noted that its area is of very high efficiency, particularly as the board is located right under the fore-foot, where it works in solid water, which is undisturbed by any portion of the hull, and which is not affected by any lateral movement that would be gathered by the hull further aft. This dagger-board has two different holes and a stop, so there are three different adjustments at which it could be carried, thus changing the balance of the boat very materially, as desired.

The rudder, as is common with Chinese rudders, has five diamond-shaped holes in the blade, and the blade itself is of very thin wood. The purpose of these diamond-shaped holes is undoubtedly to permit dead water to run through to the back of the rudder blade and prevent the accumulation of dead water along the after edge of the rudder. As already stated, the rudder can be completely housed in the hull, simply by setting it straight fore-and-aft, and then drawing it up through a slot, which is cut for the purpose in the deck. This construction is shown in detail at the stern of the hull in the sail plan.

There is no planking across the stern of the boat, but there is a big open space somewhat like a well all the way from the transom to the heavy after bulkhead, which is shown in the sail plan and also in one of the photographs. I have known of this peculiarity of Chinese construction for many years, but only recently have I been able to evolve any theory which would account for it. This method of construction must have some great advantage, or the Chinese would not have adopted it originally, or having adopted it, would not have adhered to it for centuries, as they have. It is my belief that the purpose of this stern construction is this:

It will be observed that the stern of this model is very full. The half-breadth plan shows that the water-lines are carried out to their full beam, almost to the transom. This, of course, gives the model great stability, and also great ease in driving, but it has the disadvantage of making a stern with too great buoyancy, that is to say, if this boat were planked solid across the transom, and were driven off in a heavy following sea, the enormous surplus bouyancy of the stern would make her pitch to a dangerous degree, and would tend to bury her head. It is at this point that the reason for the peculiar stern construction becomes apparent, for it is obvious that if this boat is running off with a heavy following sea, the instant that a wave strikes her stern, a very large volume of water will be momentarily held in the space between the stern proper and the after bulkhead. In a large boat, this weight of water would probably amount to a ton or more, and the weight of this water momentarily holds down the stern and prevents it from lifting unduly on a following sea. The effect is just exactly as though a very large weight of ballast were placed in the stern of the boat. Everyone knows that this is the only proper and safe way to trim a small boat when running off in a heavy following sea. But the Chinese stern has this advantage over the permanent ballast, and that is, that the moment the sea has passed the water runs out of the space at the stern, and the boat is left light and free to travel with much greater speed than if she were loaded down with a ton or so of ballast at the stern.

It will be observed, on reference to the buttock lines, that the boat carries a long and very efficient floor practically from station No. 2 to the very stern of the boat. This feature will, of course, make the boat very fast on a reach, and will make her very easy to drive.

It is quite apparent from a glance at the body plan that the boat will have to be weighted with a generous amount of inside ballast before she will acquire much stability, but as she is built for carrying weight, that feature is really an excellent one.

The anchor is an interesting detail, as it will be noted that it is quite large, in comparison with the rest of the boat, and is made entirely of wood, the only metal being on the single fluke. It will also be noted that the stock is placed at the end of the anchor, next to the fluke, and not at the cable end. As soon as the anchor strikes the bottom, the weight of the metal fluke brings it down, and as soon as it takes hold, the stock lies flush with the bottom, and makes an anti-fouling anchor.

There are a couple of little hand windlasses of primitive type, one on each side of the mast, as shown in the half-deck plan. The mast is set in a tabernacle, so that it can be lowered when going under bridges, etc.

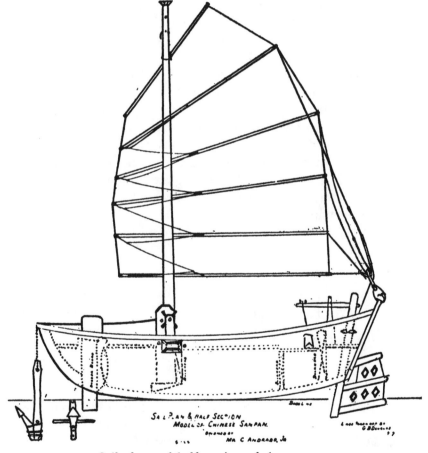

Sail plan and half-section of the sampan.

It will be noted that the rig is very simple, and very efficient. The mainsheet rigging is quite interesting, consisting of a single length of sheet, which is rove in an unusual manner, as will be noted from the sail plan. The wooden block through which all the parts of the sheet run has a little becket at its lower end, and this becket runs along the wooden traveler on the extreme stern.

I believe that a boat built exactly on these lines, including the un-usual stern construction, would make a very comfortable and useful small boat for cruising. I can see no objection to building such a small cruiser with a jib set on a stay running to the stem-head, and a mainsail which might hang over the stern a foot or so, so as to be easily reefed.

As the lines are drawn, it shows the stern a little higher than the bow. This is a peculiarity of Chinese construction, and is a feature that was common on all old types of sailing ships, as it will be recalled that Columbus's ships, and the Half Moon, and all the sailing vessels of that time had the stern considerably higher than the bow. Many theories have been advanced for this, but modern practice, of course, has gone the other way. I suppose one reason for making the stern higher was so as to give the steersman a better view; second, so that the vessel would ride head to the wind, in case she was left to drift in a gale; and, third, to avoid the danger of being swamped by over-taking waves in a heavy sea. With this high stern, and the daggerboard down all the way, this sampan should lie head to the wind in any kind of a gale, without any sail at all.

HOW I CRUISE

by CHARLES M. BLACKFORD

AUGUST, 1940

I HAD a shock the other day. I was asked how I went about preparing for a cruise. I looked at the guy a moment. I don't know just what he expected but whatever it was I didn't give it to him.

"Prepare?" I said, "all I do is buy a few cans of stuff, a couple of loaves of bread, fill the water jug, throw in some cooking pots, a few extra clothes and go."

He opened his mouth a couple of times. "Don't you have lists?" he asked.

"Sure I have a list," I answered, "but I can carry it in my head: beans, spaghetti, canned stew and such stuff plus some salt, pepper and sugar swiped from the kitchen at home. If the guy along with me must have it, some coffee, but that's really complicating life. I'm really a sort of a finicky person about food. A couple of boys in the club started out for a week-end with a couple of dozen buns from a bakery day-old stock, a can of beans and two cans of peas. They returned in time for school Monday none the worse for it."

"But butter, fresh meats and things like that?" the guy asked.

"When I go cruising I go for fun," I answered. "I don't intend to play valet to an ice box or chef to a five course dinner. One old carton carries the chow, another the cooking and eating gear. All you have to do is pull them out into the light and dig. No hunting about under berths or in dark lockers."

My questioner seemed somewhat shaken, but his eyes lit up again. "Now when you plan a cruise . . ." he came back hopefully.

"I don't plan," I answered. "I may think about going a certain place five or six years, then when the combination of circumstances seems just right, I collect someone to go along, chuck my gear into the cabin and start. Generally I don't get there. Quite often I find myself headed in the opposite direction, the wind being what it is. I have places where I want to go in all directions and all distances so it doesn't really matter. But when I do get started I run day and night as long as the wind is fair. If it heads me before I get to my destination I don't argue but run into the nearest hole the wind allows me to make. Generally I find it quite as interesting as the place for which I was heading (I'm always disappointed in my destination if I accidentally happen to arrive there). Coming back I take it easy, duck from pothole to pothole with a couple of days tucked up my sleeve for bad weather. If I don't use them up I spend them in a short run from home just lazing around and finishing up the grub so we won't have much to lug off the boat. I cruise for fun, not as a self-imposed endurance contest."

Evidently I'd shattered the poor fellow's fondest illusions as he went his way a saddened man.

But it wasn't baloney I'd been feeding him. There are a number of things that need a little elaboration, though. Take the matter of food. Why make a ceremony of cooking when one can buy very good meals in cans needing only a little warming? Potatoes and onions and fruit in small quantities, yes. If you want steaks and chops it won't kill you to wait until you get in port and can run up to the store, buy the stuff and bring it right back and throw it in the pan. By having several destinations in mind I'm never bothered by the head wind problem. I figure, and it frequently works out, that by the time I'm ready to come home, the wind will have shifted about so as to give me a decent slant back. The fast run down to the limit of my cruise comes while I and my crew are fresh from ashore and in the frame of mind to get a kick out of it and by starting home in plenty of time one can drop into most of those places you want to visit and make it in short, lazy hops. My routine is to start early, about the break of dawn, and get in in the early afternoon in plenty of time for a swim, a visit around and an unhurried meal before dark. That way one has the advantage of the land breeze going out and the sea breeze coming in. Early to rise makes for early to bed which solves the light and mosquito problems. We get under way as soon as we get up. One of us cooks and eats then the other eats and washes up. As we alternate in cooking the one who cooks has to use things he washed up and put away which cuts out one grand field for argument.

Arguments bring to mind the question of shipmates and the quality and quantity of shipmates is one thing many of these earnest planners of voyages leave entirely up to chance. They frequently bluster around at the last moment asking everyone they know and a few they don't if they'll fill out the berthing capacity of their boat, for that's what it amounts to. Whether they're compatible or combatable it never enters their heads to discover beforehand. The older, and greyer you become in this business of selecting shipmates the more you are inclined to do one of two things: have a vessel large enough to have a paid crew or one small enough to be sailed by yourself in a pinch. A newcomer in the game wonders how many persons he can pile aboard and an old-timer wonders what is the least possible crew for his craft without making killing work for all hands. If you're the kind that likes a crowd don't cruise. Just run down the coast twenty-five miles, drop the hook and break out the booze.

About the only things a group of men will have in common is a taste for women and likker, and they will share the likker . . .

So, first of all, your shipmate must be compatible and to be compatible he must have the following qualifications:

1. He must like, or not mind, the way you live aboard your boat. 2. He must be willing to eat the things you eat. 3. He must like to cruise in the same fashion you do (of course all this applies to a she or an it).

Once you get them eliminated through the above there is another thing to take into consideration: a. Does he know as much (or more) about sailing as you? b. Does he know a little and thinks he knows all the answers? c. Is he plum green and knows it?

The "a" type is the ideal but extremely elusive, the "c" kind are my second choice because they generally will do what you tell them but the "b's" have to be approached with caution and trepidation. They always know all the alternatives. They always know how the other fellow did things and always tell you about it when seconds count. Your course is either too far out or too far in and you never carry sail as long as the other guy. His confidence is as awesome as his ignorance and you wonder all the time if you ever were like that. You don't dare lie down without fear of the course being changed and you can't stay awake without hearing how the other guy ran things. A green hand is generally sufficiently humble and grateful to do what you say without question and willing to do all the dirty work. It is a good idea to try a chap out on a couple of week-ends. On the first one he's on his "company manners" but on the second he drops his front. If he passes you can file him away as future cruise crew material. From the above you can see that it is difficult enough to get one good shipmate much less a boatload, so keep that in mind when you buy your boat.

I'm not an offshore cruiser. I don't revel in rolling over, and sometimes under, blue water. Steering by compass for watch and watch carries no thrill. I was being paid to do that in my 'teens. Making a landfall on the nose doesn't interest me as the exception is generally the other way around. But if I ever did go deep water on my own I'd set my course, try to keep as near to it as possible until I thought I was somewhere near my landfall then (if I remembered what day it was) take a sight as a sort of a general check up. It is surprising what you can do on just compass and log. If I could afford it I'd have a radio direction finder and forget what little navigation I do remember.

Having spent fifteen or more years deep water I get my kick out of browsing in and out of pot holes. Cruising is a time of relaxation to me, not a desperate race against time and wind. I've gone out for days, had a good time and never been twenty miles from my mooring.

FACING FACTS
ABOUT SMALL CRUISERS

by STANTON G. TIFFANY

MARCH, 1933

SMALL cruisers in this article refer to those up to 35 feet in length although there are many larger boats to which my remarks would apply.

A man will spend considerable money for a cabin cruiser and often virtually pays money for unnecessary inconvenience and discomfort. If he wants a boat for day use with a place to hover in sudden storm he may as well buy a day cruiser and not lug around a big cabin which is not arranged to be any more comfortable than a day cruiser.

Sleeping on a board bunk with a cushion on it is not restful and is not necessary. Berths should be equipped with springs and lee-rails or with canvas on pipes. The latter while not as expensive or as pretty to look at make mighty comfortable berths. As one does not have to pace around a cabin for exercise, floor space is not as important as it is generally imagined to be. A 2 foot berth is not wide enough for restful sleeping and it will be found much better to narrow the cabin floor and make the berths wider. Avoid upper berths if possible on a small boat.

The writer was aboard a cruiser this summer which had uppers and lowers and there wasn't one good night's sleep in the whole four bunks. The uppers were merely jokes when it came to good sleeping. Personally, I would prefer a hammock in the cockpit.

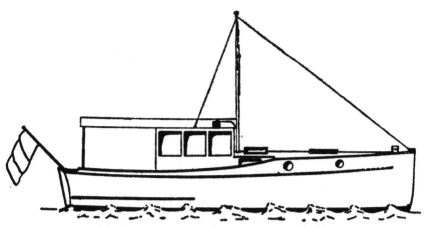

Profile of Mr. Tiffany's 32 ft. cruiser.

This particular 30-footer was laid out in miniature to encompass the accommodation of a 40-footer.

A berth just six feet long is too short, and while it may suit the present 5 foot 6 inch owner it is too short to give a taller man a good rest. In planning the layout arrange for 6 foot 6 inch berths. If not needed at present these few inches may affect sale-ability later.

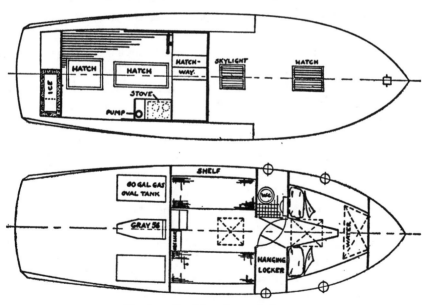

Deck and cabin plans of above.

Generally, cruisers lack stowage and hanging space. That the boat is small is not reason for having to keep your clothing and personal effects in a duffel bag. A full length locker makes for comfort and some drawers (that will slide) keep the small articles where they can be found when wanted.

It is not necessary for the stove to be in the cabin. The old argument about drying out and warming up the cabin is a fallacy when it comes to having to use the cook stove to do it. Proper ventilation will dry it and a very small heater will warm it. There are several of these available. There are far more times when it would be preferable to cool the cabin than heat it.

If you have ever gone to bed in a cabin which has been made red hot by the sun all day, then the cook stove at supper time, with the cooking odors thrown in free, and have tossed and gasped for a little pure cool air, I shall not have to say more.

Regardless of type, locate the stove outside the cabin, where you have some elbow room and where the cook can still be one of the party.

Dispense with the small sink. You must heat dishwater to put in the sink, and then must wash the sink, so heat the water in a good deep pan on the stove, leave it where it is to wash the dishes. Without effort the dishwater can be emptied over the side. You save the expense of fittings, have one less hole through the boat, one less pipe to clog and have the means of doing a good quick job on the dishes with a lot of cabin space made available for other fixtures.

The owner of a small power cruiser, regardless of how he or anyone else believes, is not a deep-sea, 'round-the-world, he-sailorman. He boats mostly in summer, and selects fine weather to the best of his ability. In other words he enjoys fine weather and likes to be out in it. By the same reasoning, he enjoys his meals outdoors, in the cockpit. Many more meals will be served on deck than below. It is practical therefore to have the stove and the ice-chest near the scene of action. In rough weather, cooking and serving on a small cruiser is unsatisfactory and little is usually done, so that the added height of the stove above the center of buoyancy need not be considered a deterrent to this plan.

The accompanying plan shows how the ideas herein set forth are simply and serviceably embodied on a thirty-two-footer. This boat has an ideal layout for comfort. She affords the privacy of two staterooms, good ventilation, plenty of locker, drawer, shelf and hanging space, plus real cooking facilities. When not in use the stove is completely housed in, the top making a convenient chart table. The dishpan stows below the stove.

The refrigerator common to many small cruisers is inadequate in many respects. There is no use in attempting to be high-brow by saying you have a refrigerator if it is not a utility. It will be found far more useful and convenient to have a well-insulated ice-chest that will keep some amount of food with room for a generous-sized

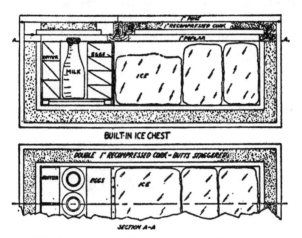

The ice-chest under the after cockpit seat.

piece of ice. The place for this is under the after cockpit seat as shown, where it can be easily iced and frequently aired and cleaned. The latter is important. An ice-chest as shown under a standing top and under a seat with a cushion on it will keep ice regardless of the sun.

The drawing shows that in a space 11 inches by 12 inches by 12 inches there can be stored six pounds of butter, three quart bottles of milk and four dozen eggs. An ice-chest 11 inches by 12 inches by 36 inches inside, will store the above, plus a quantity of cheese, meat, salad ingredients and other foods, on the ice, in its compartment. Those not assisting with the meal can sit elsewhere about the boat at that time.

With thought and planning and a small outlay of money, the average cruiser can be fitted with a standing top over the cockpit together with a shelter at its fore end. Add to this cockpit side curtains with good-sized lights and your cruiser becomes a veritable little houseboat; snug, warm and roomy. The curtains can roll up and strap to the top and can be had reasonably from a canvas goods house or can be enjoyably made by the owner by following a few simple instructions.

With the above thoughts in mind, look your little vessel over; see how a neat, simple forward shelter and standing top will improve her appearance. Arrange the stove and ice-chest space. Then go below and see how you can best utilize the newly-acquired cabin space for a dresser, hanging space or bigger, better berths. It is assumed you have a good lavatory and toilet and plenty of fresh water tank capacity. Talk to your boat builder. If he gets your order early you'll get a good job at a good price and when spring comes along you'll go overboard ready to enjoy comforts that you never knew the old ship could give you.

BREAKING 100 ON WATER

by GAR WOOD

SEPTEMBER, 1935

DURING THE YEAR OF 1885 I received my first taste of boat racing. I was two years old then, and the Wood family had moved to Lake Osakis, Minnesota, where my father operated a clumsy old wood-burning steamboat, the Manitoba, as a ferry across the lake. There was another ferry on the lake owned by a Wesley Mann, and named for him, and considerable rivalry existed between the two boats. Whenever we met, an informal race took place; the speeds were low but the excitement was terrific.

When I was eight the race to end all races and decide for all time the championship of Lake Osakis was held. One day, when the Manitoba was plying over the lake in the course of her daily duties, the Mann appeared from behind going full speed. My father was at the wheel of the Manitoba and my brother and I (the entire crew) were looking after the fires and doing odd jobs around the deck. As soon as the Mann came abreast of us, we crowded on all steam and the race of the century began. Our old boat slowly but surely drew ahead, then, when we still had a mile or more to go, we discovered that we didn't have enough fuel to finish at top speed.

"Break up the furniture," yelled my father, so we set to with axes smashing every available piece of woodwork and feeding it to the furnace. We won the race but there wasn't a table or chair left on board when we got to shore. As nearly as I can remember we averaged eight miles an hour.

Some years later, after father had moved the family to Duluth, Minnesota, when I was nearly out of high school, three motor boats were bought and put in service in the harbor by the Government Engineering Department. I was intensely interested in them and when an expert from the boat factory came down to put the engines in shape I tagged him all around and succeeded in landing a part-time job working around the boats.

My first real job, which influenced my whole life, was partly due to a red-headed girl. The army major in charge of the boats was in love with the girl and wanted to take her on picnics across the lake. He needed someone to run the engine for him so I was appointed, after demonstrating I could run the engines. The picnics were a decided success. The major made marvelous headway and I learned a lot about marine engines and boats.

I worked on those boats several years, at a salary of 45 dollars a month. The boats were used principally to carry engineering inspectors from one job to another. In the day's travel they often met and invariably a race would be on from which we got almost as much thrill as we do now from a major race. In those days there was no carburetion system in gasoline engines. We used high-test gasoline and air valves. The power would drop as the engines were used and usually after a few hours they were pretty weak. You would have to keep the air valve closed; if you opened it, there was a backfire. I decided that if I could get gasoline into the engine in conjunction with the air I could keep up power, so I experimented with a squirt can. I would open the air valves and squirt in gasoline; thus I had the crude equivalent of a modern carburetor. Those old-type engines had their spark device fixed. Advanced spark had not yet been invented but by a system of trial and error I discovered that sticking a screwdriver between the spark cam and the roller advanced the spark and increased the power of the engine and made the boat run faster. With a squirt can and a screw-driver our engine was speeded up and we invariably won. We kept the secret.

As we cruised over those Minnesota waters at eight or ten miles an hour I used to dream of myself building and driving the fastest boat in the world and winning important trophies. Little did I know that this ambition would be realized. But later events made them possible and I humbly thank the red-headed girl and hope that she and the major lived happily ever after.

When I stopped running the Government motor boats, automobiles were coming into general use and I decided to work as an automobile mechanic. Later I moved to St. Paul, Minnesota, where I was married, and started selling the new automobiles Henry Ford was putting on the market. While I was in St. Paul a friend asked me if I would like to go on a cruise down the Mississippi with him in a new boat he had built. He wanted me to do the navigating and I was delighted to go on a vacation.

We took our wives along and arrived in Dubuque on the morning some motor boat races were being held. As we were going alongside the dock I saw a man tinkering with the engine of a racing boat called the Leading Lady. When we ran past her I asked the man in the boat if I could be of any help. He asked me aboard and, after a little while, we had the engine running nicely and took her down the river in a race. The banks of the river seemed to fly past me; I had never gone so fast in my life. When we got back, whistles were blowing and people were cheering and we suddenly found ourselves in the middle of an excited crowd. "You did that ten-mile run at 30 miles an hour," someone said. "You've broken the world's record!" The thrill of breaking a world's record has never left me.

When I returned to St. Paul I built my first real speed boat. She was a single-step hydroplane similar to our present Miss America, but crude and small, The Little Leading Lady. Her hull cost me 40 dollars and the engine was the same one used in the Leading Lady which had made 30 miles an hour. The Little Leading Lady made 34 miles an hour and won every race in which she was entered.

One day I saw a truck driver dumping a five-ton load of coal by hand and got the idea which supplied me with money to do the things I had always wanted to do—boat racing and building. It took that truck driver nearly half an hour of hard work to tip the truck body to dump the coal. Why, I thought, isn't there some mechanical contrivance operated by the engine to do all that work for him? I studied this problem for a time—in fact, I thought of little else. What I needed was something simple and foolproof that could be operated by simply pulling a lever or pushing a button. Then I remembered the hydraulic cylinder on the old Manitoba which my father had used in reversing his engines. It was built on the general lines that I wanted, but I had to have something to pump high oil pressure with.

I sent for details and catalogues of every gear pump made. None seemed to answer the exact purpose—the pressure and power were too low—but I tried one out and found the manufacturer had underestimated the qualities of his own product. The first hoist I made cost me every cent I had, 200 dollars, and I sold it for the same amount. The idea was accepted by truck manufacturers; my business prospered and ran into millions.

After the hoist—a definite time mark in my life—I built boat after boat and drove them in every available race. Miss Detroit II won the Gold Cup in 1916 and the one mile trials at a speed of 54 miles an hour; next year she raised the world's record to 61.7. Miss Detroit III came next. Powered with a Curtiss airplane engine, the first aircraft engine to be put in a boat, she made 73 miles an hour.

The war stopped motor boat racing all over the world. We were busy turning out truck hoists and dump bodies for the Government and it kept me well occupied, but I managed to devote my spare time to the development of faster boats. The end of the war seemed the proper time to attempt to bring the Harmsworth Trophy, then held by England, back to the United States. Two boats were built for the purpose, Miss America I and Miss Detroit IV, the latter a big, heavy boat for use in rough water. These two boats really started my boat-building factory. Both boats were powered with Liberty engines. Miss America developed a speed of 79 miles an hour and Miss Detroit IV 70 miles an hour. Both boats were taken to England in 1920 and Miss America won the Harmsworth Trophy from Sir Mackay Edgar's Maple Leaf VI. In 1921 Sir Mackay challenged but his boat sank during the race. From then on the series of Miss Americas turned back all contenders.

During all this time the British were developing faster and faster boats and produced really serious opposition for water speed supremacy. Major H. O. D. Seagrave and Miss Marion Carstairs built boats which started knocking records into the discard. A speed of 100 miles an hour seemed an imminent possibility and I was determined to be the first man to do it.

When England challenged in 1928, we built Miss America VI. She cost around 75 thousand dollars, and carried engines of 2,200 horsepower. On her second trial she suddenly broke into pieces and sank, carrying her crew down with her. We immediately designed and built Miss America VII and had her ready for the race in exactly 14 days—and successfully defended the Harmsworth Trophy against the British, raising the world mark to 92.8 miles an hour. In March, 1929, we were beaten in the Biscayne Bay Regatta by Major Seagrave on account of a steering gear giving way but a few days later we went out and boosted the world mark again, this time to 93.1 miles an hour. In 1930, Major Seagrave drove his big Miss England II over Lake Windemere, England, at a speed of 98.7 miles an hour but struck a log just after finishing the course and was fatally injured.

In 1931, I realized my dream and drove Miss America IX at 102 miles an hour. This record didn't last long, however. Kaye Don, in Major Seagrave's old boat, which had been raised and rebuilt, pushed the speed mark up by degrees to 110.2. Then followed the 1931 Harmsworth Race. Don took the first heat but next day he cracked up on a turn and the trophy remained in America.

In 1931 and 1932 Miss England III, built for Lord Northcliffe and driven by Kaye Don, raised the mile record to 119.8 and a challenge was again made for the Harmsworth Trophy. Miss America IX was too slow for that kind of competition; so in 1932 we built the tenth of the series, a 38 foot boat with 6,400 horsepower. In the Harmsworth Race, Miss England ran into bad luck when her engines failed in both heats; so the trophy was retained in the United States without any great trouble. Following the Harmsworth Races that year, with Miss America X, we again brought the world's record on water back to the United States, averaging 124.86 miles an hour, which still stands at the time of writing.

In 1933, Hubert Scott-Paine brought over his radically designed Miss Britain III for another British attempt to raise the trophy. She was a sweet little boat but didn't have enough speed to worry Miss America X. However, she finished both heats in good order, something no other British challenger had been able to do, and we knew we had been in a race.

Although no Harmsworth Races were held in 1934 or 1935, we were not idle and kept experimenting with Miss America X. By the use of extra super-chargers and new fuels the horsepower has been raised to 7,600 and we were seeking to increase the world's speed mark once again.

Many people have asked me what, in my opinion, is the maximum speed obtainable on water. That is a hard question to answer but I think I am safe in saying that 150 miles an hour is highly probable within the next few years and that 200 miles an hour is not beyond the realm of possibility in the future. Of course, engines will have to be much more powerful and we'll need further perfection in hull design before that day dawns.

ON SEA GOING BOATS

by THOMAS FLEMING DAY

JULY, 1899

THE first and absolute necessity of a seagoing boat is freeboard; the second is a complete deck and water-tight openings. Given these two things and you have an almost safe craft. There is no question of capsizing a well-designed yacht of to-day by power of the wind. Our outside ballasted boats cannot be kept wrong side up, so long as the water is kept out of them. They may be hove-down on their sides and fill and sink, but they cannot be turned completely over so long as they retain their buoyancy. I have been in one of them, a boat carrying only about half the usual weight of lead for a vessel of her size, that was laid on her side in a squall with both mainsail and jib in the water; she remained in this position for nearly two minutes, and then righted when the force of the squall was spent. Her lead kept her from turning right over, and her large freeboard kept her from edging down. She simply made a bottom of her side and floated on it. That is one advantage of freeboard. Had she been a narrow-sided boat she would have been forced between the pressure of lead and wind deeper into the water, but as it was her displacement, owing to the bearing up of the sail and mast, was probably less when in that position than when standing upright.

Again, freeboard increases the range of heel. This is of enormous advantage when sailing in a sea way with a strong breeze. The tripping power of the wave is exhausted before the rail is brought down, and the boat not receiving a load of water on her lee deck rights so much quicker. A low-sided boat when canted by a beam sea edges her rail under and shovels the water up on her deck as she recovers. For this reason seagoing craft should have their upper freeboard slightly tumbled home. Bulwarks and high rails are bad things, and combings should be kept well inboard, while raised cabin houses if fitted should not be carried too close to the waterways. Rails and bulwarks as far aft as the rigging can be raised to an advantage, as they prevent the water from coming in and not passing out. Water in breaking on board will always follow along anything like the side of a house, and when reaching a break spread in. This is how cockpits are so easily filled. The height is suddenly cut down from house to combing, and the sea having become crowded up to the height of the house in its passage aft, when it comes to the low place rushes into the cockpit. If the combing is carried up to the height of the house the water will pass along and go out over the stern.

Ballasted boats should never go into rough water unless they have water-tight cockpits and water-tight companions and openings. But a water-tight cockpit, unless it is well-scuppered and really self-bailing, is of little use. In eight out of ten small yachts the cockpits are not, although they pretend to be, self-bailing. They will bail perfectly when at anchor. In order to bail quickly the floor must be at least 10 inches above the load water line. Here again freeboard comes in. Again, the placing of the scuppers in the forward end of the cockpit and their outboard openings under the bilge is decidedly wrong. In the first place it keeps the water at all times in the forward end of the standing room against the cabin, just where you move about; in the second every drop that goes out through the lee pipe has to force its way against a pressure. This pressure is also constantly driving the water up and into the boat. The place for the scuppers is aft with the openings under the stern. Here there is constant suction so long as the boat is moving ahead, no matter to which side or how far she heels. Again, if the floor is sloped aft, whatever water is on the standing room will run aft and be out of the way, a measure of comfort that those who sail in rough water can appreciate. It is not generally known but a boat going at speed of four knots and over will, if equipped with proper scuppers, siphon, i. e., suck the water out.

Another bad practice of builders is to put stationary seats around a cockpit with lockers beneath them. This never should be done. You cannot keep them tight, the wood being constantly subject to water and sun. Never put lockers of any kind in a boat with outboard openings. Another bad practice is that of putting in low companion thresholds. The threshold of the companion should be as high or higher than the side of the boat, and should on no account, no matter how high the cockpit floor is, be on a level with it. The usual manner of constructing companion doors is also open to objection. The new method in which the door slides down into a recess through a rubber-packed joint is far better than the old way of closing. Such a door can be made absolutely water-tight, and can be opened partially under way. This enables you to see into the cabin or out of it without running the slide back or risking getting a wash below by opening the doors. These may seem trivial details, but it is the neglect of such to whose account the loss of the majority of seagoing vessels must be placed. Poor hatches and low, badly protected engine room skylights are responsible for nearly all the steamships that go to sea, and are never heard of again. Keep the water out and you can live out anything in the way of sea or wind. Let it get in and everything that before made your craft seaworthy will be an aid to your ending. Your ballast will be a weight to sink you, and the empty space that gave you buoyancy so much room to quickly fill with water.

After this, look to your pump. Where is it? In most yachts directly amidships, drawing out of a well over the lowest part of the keel. Where should it be? In the place where it can be used when most wanted—the bilge. You must have a means of drawing from the center, so you can pump out when at anchor or sailing upright. But all pumps should have a bilge intake. It would be a very simple matter to make such a connection with a cock to cut off the other intakes. How often, when he least wants to, has a man to let his boat up, so as to get the water amidships for the purpose of pumping it out. If he could pump from the bilges this coming up would be unnecessary. To kill a boat's way in a heavy beam or head sea, so as to get her on her keel, is a dangerous artifice; but it must be done with the pump amidships, if you want to get the water out, and keep a dry cabin. Every seagoing small yacht should have at least two fixed pumps, and a movable one. The fixed pumps should be constantly looked to, and the limbers kept clean. Never stow inside weight along side of or over the intake, and never allow rubbish to be swept into the spaces between the floors. With a good pump a man can keep down all the water that will work into a tight boat through her bottom, topsides and deck.

All seagoing yachts should have the rudder post boxed up and carried well above the water line. The neglect of this is the cause of much leakage. She should also have in her rudder blade a boring or rod in which to make fast emergency lines or chains. In craft that have their rudders well under them a rod must be used, but in shallow boats with broad blades a hole bored through the outer edge will do. These lines are extremely useful when anchored in a sea way; by hauling them taut over either quarter you can relieve the strain on the head of the post and gear attached to it. In case of a breakdown of the quadrant, wheel or post head, you can at once take control of the rudder and keep the boat under command.

No boat should go into rough water for a long run unless she have ringbolts aft for the purpose of passing boom lashings, and also a fixed boom crotch, or at least one that can be made immovable. There is no other way of keeping a boom steady when the sail is lowered down. You cannot by any possible means do so with lashings, unless you can horn it in a crotch. A loose boom is a constant menace. Provision also should be made for the trysail sheets, and for body lashings for the crew, and lashings for the boat, even if you have davits. The principal weak spot in the rigging of a boat that is to be driven in heavy water is the bobstay. That piece of rigging is often carried away in a sea than any other, and usually it is the bolt that goes. Look to it, and look to it well; for if it parts, most likely you will lose your mast. The only safeguard lies in rigging a preventer stay that will set up with a tackle, the fall leading inboard. The stay should be of wire rope properly and strongly secured to the stem. Use either a gun-tackle or luff-tackle—the latter is preferable—and be sure to give it plenty of drift. When in use, set it up just scant of the strain, so that if the bobstay parts it will catch the strain before the spar gets a good spring. In boats that have a forestay set up to the stem head there is less likelihood of this accident happening; but it is always best to have a preventer fitted. Make the fall fast around the bitts or mast where you can readily get at it, and hold a turn to set it up. Seagoing boats should have two shrouds on a side and set up with lanyards in preference to rigging screws. If you fit the latter, have them about twice the size of those ordinarily put on by riggers. She should also have a heavy set of masthead runners and duplicate eyes to set them up to, one pair being placed well aft. Our modern full-bowed boats are very hard on their rigging and spars when in a sea way, and need to be heavily ironed.

Outside of her ordinary sails a seagoing yacht needs a trysail, a small square-sail, and a small jib or staysail, all made of heavy canvas. Particular attention should be paid to the roping and clews of these sails. It is of no use using heavy canvas if the clew irons are frail and the rope light. A gaff-headed trysail is better than a jib-headed, but it is more bother to set. Care should be taken to see that the cleat or ringbolt for the trysail sheet is in such a position as will allow the sail to be properly sheeted, for a trysail when used for riding must set flat, or else it will bang itself to pieces.

In seagoing craft looks don't count, and therefore be not afraid to make all your rigging heavy and strong, and wherever possible have a fitting or tackle that can be instantly made to take the place of one that carries away. Always when in rough water or in heavy weather keep a vang or downhaul on the peak of the gaff. It is sometimes the only thing that will bring the sail down, and it gives you command of the spar, especially when the yacht is rolling heavily. The chafing of gear when in a sea way is constant and ruinous. To prevent it a close watch must be kept on all ropes where they pass through blocks or lie against spars or other ropes. If your halyards and sheet remain long in one place they must be canvased or armored with some sort of chafing stuff.

ON NIGHT SAILING

by THOMAS FLEMING DAY

JANUARY, 1900

THERE are not many yachtsmen who sail at night, but there are numbers who are afraid to. The majority of those who do are men who are forced to stay out, and would, if they could get there, rather be in port snug at anchor and enjoying a good sleep. But outside of these there are a few who, like myself, enjoy night sailing, and will take a dose of it every chance they get.

To the man who has never navigated in the dark it appears a dangerous pastime, but in fact it is many times less difficult to lead your vessel from port to port at night than it is in the day. But certainly to the ordinary dangers there are added a few peculiar to darkness, the principal of these being the other vessel. It is this that makes night sailing more dangerous than day sailing, and it is a peril that cannot be ignored, for its end, where a small and a large vessel is concerned, as is most frequently the case, is generally fatal. But this danger is one that can be readily guarded against by the use of good lights and a constant and lively lookout.

In well-charted and well-lighted waters there is little risk of running ashore or of striking reefs or shoals, as the lead and the compass tell the same story by lamplight as they do when the sun is up, and it is one of the advantages of night voyaging that the yachtsman is obliged to depend on these instruments, and therefore learns their proper use. Both compass and lead are too much neglected, the ignorance of the former instrument being more common than is generally supposed. Very few yachtsmen can correct a compass course either for deviation or variation, or know how to allow for drift or leeway.

The great advantage of night-sailing is that it increases the confidence in yourself as skipper. After a passage through the darkness, when by use of your knowledge you have safely brought your clipper into harbor, you know that you *do* know something about navigating.

146

Sailing in the daytime, you are constantly able to correct your course by eye, and the compass becomes a mere auxiliary upon which little value is placed as a guide, but at night it is at times your sole dependence, and must be watched and followed implicitly. Having once followed the needle, and finding that it leads you truly to your port, you will have a strong confidence in its guideship, and a firmer and better opinion of your own ability to use its directive powers.

To sail at night—that is with comfort—you need a good second man—a man upon whose skill and judgment you can place an implicit reliance. There is no fun in sitting up all night unless you have slept the whole day before, but in taking two watches of four hours there is but little to either worry or weary you. The handy crew for night sailing is one of four, giving two to sleep and two to work.

The first watch goes on at eight, one man going to the helm and the other to the lookout. I find it better to shift tricks every hour, as a man who has only one hour at the helm will pay more attention to his steering. To watch a compass sixty minutes under the poor light of our binnacles is all that a green hand wants to do, as it is extremely wearying to untrained eyes. While the helmsman pays rapt attention to his card and course, the lookout must keep watch ahead, see that the lights are burning, stand by to trim sail, and keep tab on the chart of the distance sailed.

The chart should be laid out by the skipper where the watch can get a quick look at it, and the course should be marked out upon it with pencil. It is also a good idea to have a slate or a paper alongside the binnacle, with the compass course marked on it, and also to have the watch enter there the wind, distances, lights passed, etc.

When the second watch comes on at 12 o'clock the one in charge of the first watch must show him the yacht's position on the chart, and give him a brief summary of what has passed during the four hours, being careful to inform him of any changes in the wind or weather. The helmsman on giving up the helm must give the new man the course, and the new man must repeat it after him in the hearing of both officers. These are details, but such as should be carefully attended to, as they prevent mistakes and possible disasters.

The watch whose watch is below should keep it there, and not stay on deck. If called on deck for the purpose of shortening or making sail they should come at once. The skipper should not, unless it is necessary, interfere with the man he places in charge when his own watch is below. By doing so you teach that man not to depend on his own judgment and knowledge. If he is a man you can trust, trust him, or else don't let him have charge.

One thing in night sailing: Remember, that it takes about three times as long to make or shorten sail in the dark as it does in the day. Therefore, if you have to get in canvas give the men plenty of time. Never parley with squalls at night; take in sail until you find out just what the blow is going to amount to.

Always carry a lead in the cockpit close at hand, and if lining a shore have a cast taken every fifteen minutes. When going into a harbor at night or through narrow fairways keep a good lookout ahead, astern and all sides of you.

In order to be comfortable and to keep your crew in a good humor, each watch when it goes on or off duty should be given a bite to eat and a warm drink. If you have a cook or steward he can attend to this; or, if all amateurs, the odd man, if there is one on hand. If you don't carry either a spare hand or cook then the watch below should get something ready for themselves and for those coming off before going on deck. A big pot of coffee or cocoa, that can be warmed up, is the best thing. A well-fed and warm crew is a willing and good-tempered crew. If you let your men get cold, wet and hungry, they will soon degenerate into a set of growlers and spoil your night sail.

ON SINKING SHIPS

ANOTHER widespread fiction even held by many seamen: that there is a tremendous suction when a vessel sinks. There is nothing of the kind. As a vessel goes under the surface there is an inrush to close up the vacancy, but there is no suction after the sinking body is under the surface. If a vessel was drawn down by force there would be a suction; but a sinking form cannot sink faster than the water is displaced by its weight, and therefore, water being a dense medium the fluid must close in behind simultaneously with its displacement before. I have stood on the deck of a sinking craft and gone under with it, and instead of a suction there is just the opposite—an upward rush that makes it impossible to sink with a vessel unless you cling to her. A lifeboat on the deck of a vessel would float clear if the ship sank under her, so would a cask or a man or anything floatable.

T.F.D.

ON THE SIMPLE LIFE

THE fire is well burned down, the end of the last log is sticking out of the gray ash, smoking and smoldering like an old love affair, and there is no more fuel in the locker. Let her go out, say I, for I'm sick of this armchair life and want to get outdoors, where a man doesn't have to breathe the same air twice over in order to get a good lung full of oxygen. I'm tired, boys; tired as a dog that has hunted rabbits all day. The only difference the dog runs his quarry to earth, while mine take to the water.

I was just thinking, what's the use of all this—this living, this working, this worrying, this fretting and fussing? Isn't the negro who sits in the shade of the plantain, content that he has a shirt to his back and a meal in his belly, the more sensible fellow? You and I at the end of it will get no more than he will—six feet of mother earth. To the devil with your fifty years of dress shirt existence, trousers with pockets, and houses with doors, and all the rest of the paraphernalia that goes to make up civilization. When are we happiest? The day we throw this all off, and, clad in our worst, play savage on some lonely shore, dragging a meal out of the water as our ancestors did before some misguided idiots invented money, markets, and manners.

To-day I have a thousand-fold the knowledge possessed by the most learned and brilliant of the ancients, but am I any happier? Not a bit. You and I are being dragged at the wheels of the thing we call Progress, and those who ride, cry out to join in a song of triumph. For what? Look in your hands. Is what you have succeeded in grasping worth any more than a fistful of yon gray ash in whose crumbling heap the last sparks are flickering and passing away?

T.F.D.

ON YACHT CLUB VISITORS

IF YOU invite a man to visit your house, you would be astonished and perhaps indignant if he opened the door, walked in, made himself disagreeably at home without first knocking and announcing his arrival.

A strange yacht clubhouse is, so far as you, a visitor, are concerned, the same as a private residence, and you have no more right to walk in there and make yourself at home without announcing your arrival than you would at a private dwelling. The fact that courtesy of the club has been extended to your club does not entitle you to the privilege of dispensing with the usual expression of good manners.

Whenever you visit a strange club, no matter if you are only going to stay for a meal or to embark a friend, always before going to the bar or the dining room, find one of the officers and request permission to partake of the club's hospitality. Do the same if using their anchorage or float. If you don't do this how are the members of the club visited to know you are a member of a club to whom the privileges have been extended? It is very disagreeable for an officer to have to walk up to a man and ask who he is and what club he is a member of, yet I have seen this done fifty times. Many unannounced visitors have the extra bad manners to resent these inquiries. Here are two cases that point: The owner of a large yacht used for a whole season the float of a small club; he did not want to join the club, and had nothing whatever to do with the members, and went off in the Fall without even thanking the officers for the use of the float. Another man, the owner of a steam yacht belonging to a large club, anchored off the same small club for several weeks; once while his yacht was out he accepted the shelter of the clubhouse for himself and friends while waiting the vessel's return, and was conveyed aboard in the club's launch. Before leaving the anchorage he invited the officers and members of the small club aboard, entertained them, and on leaving asked the Commodore to accept as a slight appreciation of his club's courtesy a cup for the next regatta. I will leave it to the reader to decide which of these men to imitate.   T.F.D.

150

ON THE BERMUDA RACE

The Bermuda Race is certainly notable for the great number of entries, if for nothing else. Pleasant weather, and little sleep lost, and a good time for all. But I really think you gentlemen of the East might restrain your back-patting a little. Being a Floridan, no one can accuse me of prejudice in favor of California. Frankly, I'm damned if I can see why anyone wants to live on that barren coast. But my sympathies are all with the Westerners when they laugh at the spectacle of the Easterners fancying themselves such brave, bold sailors because they dare the week-end jaunt to Bermuda. The California-Hawaii ocean race is the blue ribbon event of all deepwater yachting, and the East might as well admit it, because all the rest of the world knows it. Mere number of starters does not make the greatness of a race. I've seen sixty start in an outboard motor race. A hundred might as well have gone to Bermuda, considering the race originated at the center of by far the biggest yacht fleet in the world. Now really, boys, isn't it about time to turn over the Bermuda course to the small fellows, craft 35 feet and under, and the rest of you draw your finish line at the Azores? Not until you do that will you be able to look any blessed Californian in the eye and tell him where to go. True, the Azores have no Chamber of Commerce, no government tourist promotion bureau, no big hotels, and the simple natives, warmhearted and sincere though their hospitality is, have none of the skill of our beloved Bermuda cousins in raising whoopee with the visiting firemen. But these things are not *really* essentials of seamanship and navigation, are they? The whole globe has no more beautiful and interesting mountain peaks to visit than these Islands of the Hawks. I have been urging an Azores race for years, and I intend to keep right on until somebody starts it, to shut me up if for no better reason.

JOHN G. HANNA

ON SPRAY

Since the Suicide Squad has been for many years building exact copies of *Spray*, and will continue doing so for many years more unless restrained, perhaps I can save a life or two by explaining, as simply as possible, the basic reason (skipping many other good reasons) why *Spray* is the worst possible boat for anyone, and especially anyone lacking the experience and resourcefulness of Slocum, to take off soundings. It is for the same reason that the Cape Cod cat and the inland lake racing scow are not suitable for ocean going. Everyone who has handled these types knows that, though they are extremely stiff initially, if they are ever heeled beyond a critical point, they flop right over as inevitably as a soup plate, which they resemble. What a boat does in a coastal chop has no bearing on what it will do in the great waves of the deep sea. A big lurching cross sea, that would scarcely disturb a properly designed hull, can—especially if it coincides, as it often does, with an extra-savage puff of a squall—flip over a *Spray* hull just as you would a poker chip. The capsizing of one *Spray* duplicate, off the coast of South America, was recorded in The Rudder many years ago. Many duplicates trying to duplicate the circumnavigation have disappeared without trace, just as the original *Spray* and Slocum did. Others have been wrecked, with part or all of crew saved in various ways. Of the great fleet that has tried in all these years, but one *Spray* duplicate ever completed the circuit—Roger Strout's *Igdrasil*. And his published accounts of his voyage indicate that throughout the greater part of it he met generally favorable weather; also that he carried an immense fuel supply (in relation to the size of his engine) and ran every possible mile under power. Moreover, in letters to this writer, he has stated that on at least two occasions his vessel was flipped up to the very point of the last roll-over, and for a second or two it seemed she would never come back on her bottom. After such experience, it is understandable that he says, if building again for such a trip, he would willingly sacrifice the much-loved comfort of broad decks and great initial stability for more of that *final* stability which infallibly rights a well-designed yacht

152

even if knocked down with her masts in the water. I trust a little sober reflection on these facts will cause a ray of light to dawn in the minds of another generation of would-be *Spray* duplicators. The famous old ship had her good points, and no one admires them more than I; but not enough to overcome some almost certainly fatal faults.

J.G.H.

ON CAPT. JOSHUA SLOCUM

ONE of my readers has written in asking why we call *Spray* a sloop when the pictures show the boat yawlrigged. We call it a sloop because Captain Slocum always did, and because she was really a sloop, the after-sail being an after-thought put on by the Captain when his mainsail went bad. Captain Slocum never had a very high opinion of that jigger, and in his heart, I think, was a bit ashamed of it. Before his last voyage, he told me that he was going up the Orinoco River, and through the Rio Negro into the Amazon and home that way, and that he expected to be away for about two years. But there was no news that he ever made the river or any port.

I expect the old sloop spewed a plank; she was getting considerably dozy the last time I looked her over. Even in the early days of her rejuvenation she was not of the strongest, being built out of whatever came to hand and cost least. That she lived as long as she did and stood the straining and racking of those voyages is another argument in support of my assertion that small craft are more seaworthy than large.

Captain Slocum was what we may call an uncommon man. He was extremely intelligent, and in his love of roaming and adventure reminded me of the celebrated Moorish traveler, Ibn Batuta, who wandered from Cape Spartel to the Yellow Sea, making friends with white, black and yellow; always observing, making men and manners his study, and living by the gifts of those whose ears he tickled with his tales of travel and adventure. Slocum, like Batuta, was a friend-maker, and everywhere he went the best of the land welcomed him, bid him to the board, and gave attention, while in his inimitable way he spun yarns of his voyages. At Gibraltar he was the guest of the

Admiral; at Montevideo the Royal Mail Company repaired his sloop without charge; in Australia and New Zealand they gave him sails and stores; at Cape Town the Government passed him over its railway lines; and even old Kruger handed him a cup of coffee. From port to port he voyaged everywhere welcomed and entertained, and it was not until he reached this country and anchored in the port of New York that a welcome was refused and his efforts belittled and ridiculed. The American newspapers, when they deigned to notice his voyage, made fun of his boat and himself, and several more than intimated the story of his single-handed world-circling voyage was a lie. Captain Slocum felt this derision keenly, and frequently spoke of it. At this time THE RUDDER was a small struggling affair, but it at once recognized the worth of the Captain's story and came out in strong support of it, publishing a picture of *Spray* and a short account of the voyage. Captain Slocum never forgot this, and he always had a good word for THE RUDDER and its crew.

One day he came into the office with the story of his voyage and asked me if we could publish it. I saw at once that the story was worth more than we could afford to pay, and suggested that he take it to one of the large general magazines. He did, and *The Century* bought and published it. Afterwards he brought in the model of *Spray* and Mr. Mower took the lines off as they appear in his book. Slocum's story is a remarkable one; I do not mean as the story of a voyage but as a piece of writing. It is written in a pure narrative style, absolutely devoid of any disfigurements betraying effort, and flows from page to page like a wind-favored tide. It is worthy to be placed beside any narrative writing in our language, even beside the work of the great master of that style, De Foe. Posterity will give this book a place, and your great-grandchildren will be advised to read Slocum's Voyage, as a specimen of clean, pure narrative, just as to-day they read Robinson Crusoe or the Voyage of the Beagle. Peace to Captain Slocum wherever he may sleep, for he deserves at least one whispered tribute of prayer from every sailorman for what he did to rob the sea of its bad name; and for such a man, who loved every cranny of her dear old blue heart, who for years made her wind-swept stretches his home and highway, what is more fitting than an ocean burial?

Not in old bannered abbeys are her children laid to rest,
  With the trophies of the chisel and the bronzes of the wall;

She takes them from their cradles to lie within her breast,
   To rest unchanged forever in that vast and lightless hall.

The loftiest of temples, the stateliest of domes,
   Where the master-minds of nations are laid with pomp and pride,
Are but low and spaceless fabrics beside the Fane of Foams,
   Whose nave no man has put to rule, whose floors are oceans wide.

It mocks in its magnificence the sepulchre of kings;
   The glory of the purple and the splendor of the bier,
And all the brass and marble are but mean and gaudy things
   Beside the splendid trappings that the dead inherit here.

T.F.D.

THE DREAM SHIPS

Of thousands of yacht designs that have appeared in THE
RUDDER *during the past sixty-odd years, these selections, at
least, may indicate variety.*

W. M. Birck

WEE PUP, A 7½ FT. TENDER

Designed by WINFIELD M. THOMPSON

JANUARY, 1906

THE portable, stable tender is not easily come by. Winfield M. Thompson, a brilliant contributor to THE RUDDER in its early years, modeled this one after a Monhegan fisherman's punt: 7 ½ feet long and weighing only 65 pounds, it carried up to four persons, or 700 pounds, safely and towed well.

It became very popular in those days when the pram dinghy was unfamiliar. B. B. Crowninshield and W. Starling Burgess, the famous yacht designers, had copies built for their own use—a flattering gesture to any amateur's first boat design.

Her dimensions are:

Length on top, 7 feet 6 inches.
Length on bottom, 6 feet 4 inches.
Width of ends: Top, 26 inches; bottom, 18 inches.
Width amidships: Top, 39 inches; bottom, 29 inches.
Freeboard at ends (from base line): Bow, 20 inches; stern, 19 inches.
Freeboard, amidships, 15½ inches.

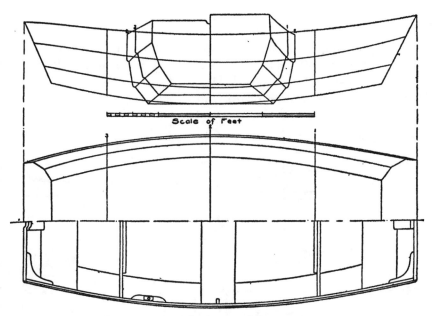

Scale of Feet

Wee Pup, the Monhegan fisherman's punt.

159

FINE LINES AND ROOM AFT
IN 12 FT.

Designed by BROR TAMM

SEPTEMBER, 1938

ONE solution to the problem of building a simple, flat-bottomed skiff with easy lines, by the famous boat and canoe builder.

Dimensions: L.O.A. 12 ft.; L.W.L. 9 ft. 5 in.; Beam 3 ft. 7 in.; Draft, with two persons on board, 4 in.

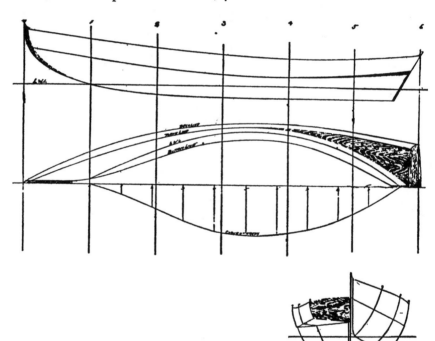

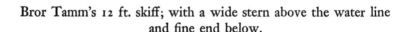

Bror Tamm's 12 ft. skiff; with a wide stern above the water line and fine end below.

SEA WREN, A 14-FOOT CATBOAT

Designed by EDSON B. SCHOCK

DECEMBER, 1907

AN EARLY RUDDER Design is shown on the following pages. The popular How-To-Build plans that appeared through the years brought into being thousands of small yachts all over the world.

Introducing this handy cat, her designer Edson B. Schock wrote: "In this design the main idea was to produce a boat that would be simple and easily built, one that would appeal to the novice who had little or no knowledge of the art or science of boat-building, but who could handle tools in a fair way. The boat was made only fourteen feet long so that should any one start to build and find he could not complete her, he would have very little money tied up, and the cost of having her completed by a regular boat-builder would be comparatively little."

As the boat was intended to be used as a school, so to speak, for the education of the boy, she was made as small as possible, her dimensions being:

Length o. a.	14	feet	o inches
Length w. l.	13	"	o "
Breadth, extreme	6	"	9½ "
Breadth, w. l.	6	"	2 "
Draught, rabbet	o	"	10¾ "
Draught, extreme	1	"	3 "
Overhang, forward	o	"	9 "
Overhang, aft	o	"	3 "
Freeboard, bow	2	"	3½ "
Freeboard, least	1	"	3½ "
Freeboard, stern	1	"	5 "
Sail area	224	square	feet

161

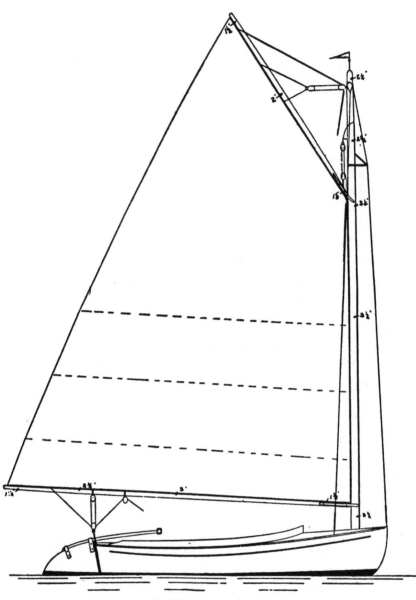

Sea Wren, a 14 ft. cat.

162

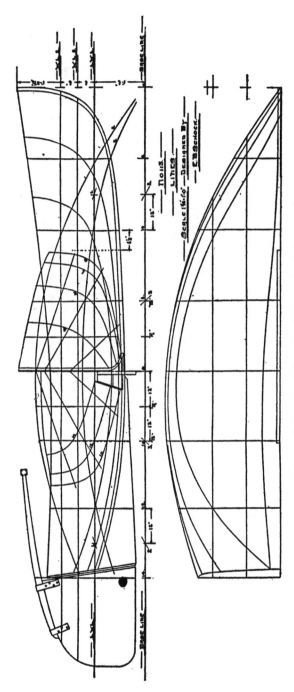

Lines of the *Sea Wren* by Edson B. Schock.

AN OUTBOARD RUNABOUT, 14 FT.

Designed by PHILIP L. RHODES

MAY, 1932

THE smart little outboard runabout shown here was designed by P. L. Rhodes of New York for use as a yacht tender. She is 14 feet overall, beam (over fenders) 50 inches, draft of hull 5½ inches and draft with motor about 18 inches. She exhibits beautiful form and has made speeds as high as 30 miles with the larger sizes of outboard motors. The motor is housed aft and all danger of overheating has been avoided by the use of louvres. The beam of the boat has been restricted slightly so as to stow on deck without taking up too much room athwartships. The weight of the boat complete without motor is 340 pounds. Steering is from the after cockpit, and the boat would be handled from there by a member of the crew while the owner is forward.

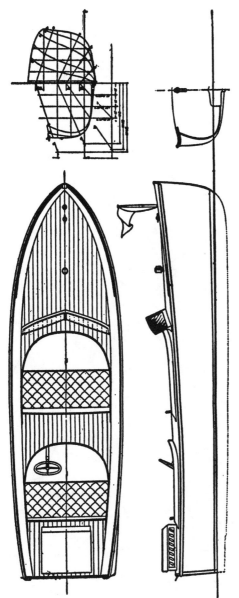

The Phil Rhodes 14 ft. outboard runabout.

AN INSTRUCTIVE TOY.
COCKLE, A 16 FT. CUTTER
Designed by J. R. PURDON

MARCH, 1915

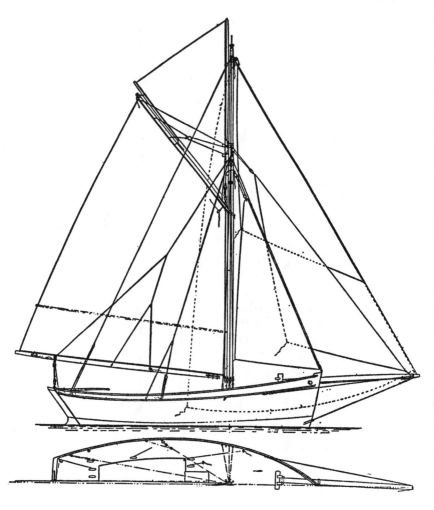

Deck and sail plan of *Cockle*.

How lucky were the two boys for whom this little jewel of a cutter was built! Her designer, J. R. Purdon, reported:

"Cockle was designed to give two lads experience with as much of the sails and rigging of the cutter type as it seemed reasonable to put on a very small boat, and with all of the seafaring and adventure that could be had on any boat—what might be called an Instructive Toy. She was to be very safe, easily handled, roomy enough to house two below in case they were caught out over night, and as small as possible to give these qualities with good sailing abilities. These requirements appear to have been met satisfactorily. Some cushions stuffed with cork shavings, to serve as life-preservers in case of need, are fitted to the floor of the self-bailing cockpit, making a very comfortable lounge for day sailing and a fine bunk at night with a shelter tent stretched over the boom to keep off the dew. Two portable pipe-and-canvas bunks make it possible to sleep below if the weather is bad. Of course "housekeeping" accommodations and conveniences are very limited—one has to go ashore now and then to get a full meal, but still the little boat has many possibilities for comfortable cruising on one-night stands. She is intended for sailing in deep waters, but for not very far at a time.

"A small club topsail is used altogether, in place of a working topsail, being easier to set and stow, more practical than a jib-headed topsail set flying and not too large to manage single-handed. The little boat is stiff and carries all sail easily in anything but the heaviest weather. Lying to in a "breeze o' wind" is her special forte; she will stay put as long as you choose to leave her, riding as light and dry as a gull. Her balance is nicely adjusted under various combinations of sails and even works out well with only foresail and reefed mainsail. This makes her very comfortable to handle and as a matter of fact she has been sailed practically single-handed under all conditions through the year, with much pleasure, ease and benefit to her "crew."

"In all sorts of weather, Winter and Summer, she has shown the most satisfactory capabilities. Her odd appearance and rather extreme proportions might lead one to suppose that her gait would be a disappointment, but the little boat has shown quite unexpected speed for one of her size and type. She has gone out into heavy Easterly weather off Marblehead, when none but the saltiest salts cared to try the "dust" and has sailed into it like the little ship she is, as dry as the

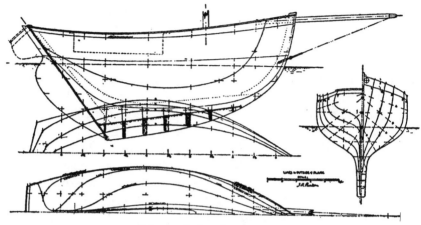

Lines of the tiny cutter.

proverbial bottle afloat with the cork in. Of course, to windward, in a sharp sea of her own length, she does a rather abandoned rocking horse act, but off a little and with a longer sea, she climbs up and down the watery hills like a roller coaster. In smooth water, she slides along as well as anyone could ask."

Cockle's dimensions are:

Length o. a.	18 feet	9 inches	=	5.715 meters
Length l. w. l.	15 "	11 "	=	4.890 "
Breadth, extreme	6 "	3 "	=	1.905 "
Draught	5 "	1 "	=	1.548 "
Sail area	330 square feet		=	30.657 sq. m.
Displacement	5,470 lb			
Lead on keel	2,850 "			

A SKIFF FOR TOM DAY, 18 FT.

Designed by T. W. MARTIN

JUNE, 1890

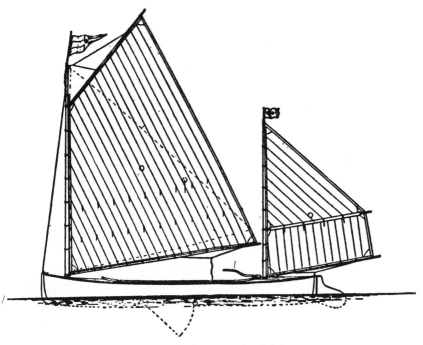

Sail plan of Tom Day's *Adelanta*.

THE second design to appear in THE RUDDER was that of a sailing skiff or canoe, which Tom Day had built for his own use.

Dimensions: L.O.A. 18 ft.; L.W.L. 18 ft.; Beam 46 in.; Draft 7 in.; Sail Area 140 sq. ft.

Adelanta, as she was called, was framed with oak, planked with cedar and decked with mahogany.

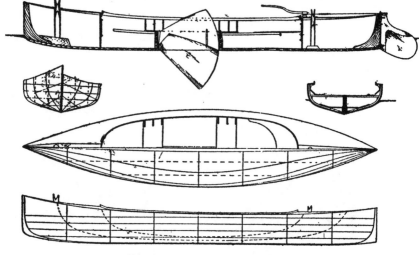

Lines and plan of *Adelanta*.

THE FIRST DESIGN, *SOLITUDE*

Designed by w. c. LEIBER

JUNE, 1890

IN THE June, 1890 issue appeared the first boat lines to be printed in RUDDER. It was this wholesome single-hander, *Solitude*.

Framed with oak, planked with cedar, decked with pine and with an iron keel, her cockpit was 18 in. deep and 10 ft. long, with storage lockers forward.

Dimensions:

	Feet	Inches
Length over all	20	—
" L. W. L.	17	—
Beam	5	10
Draught	2	7½
Least freeboard	1	3
Ballast outside		300 lbs.
" inside		600 lbs.
Displacement		1.5 short tons.

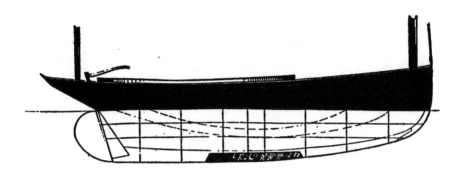

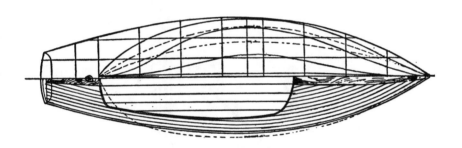

Lines and plan of *Solitude*. This was the first plan to appear
in The Rudder.

AN OPEN WATER AUXILIARY, 18 FT.

Designed by MURRAY G. PETERSON

DECEMBER, 1934

IF YOU have an eye for small craft, no further comment on this miniature motor sailer is necessary.

Dimensions: L.O.A. 18 ft.; Beam 6 ft. 3 in.; Draft 2 ft. 6 in. Sail Area, 142 sq. ft. Power: 1 cylinder, 2-cycle Lathrop, 5 h.p. for about 7 m.p.h.

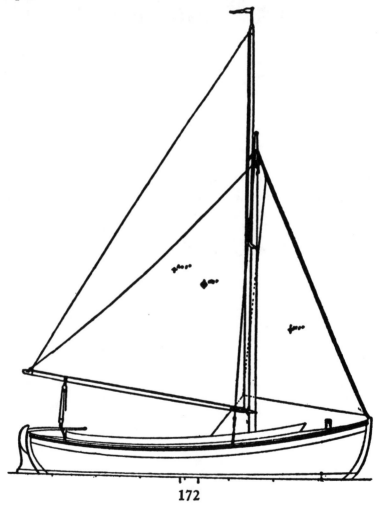

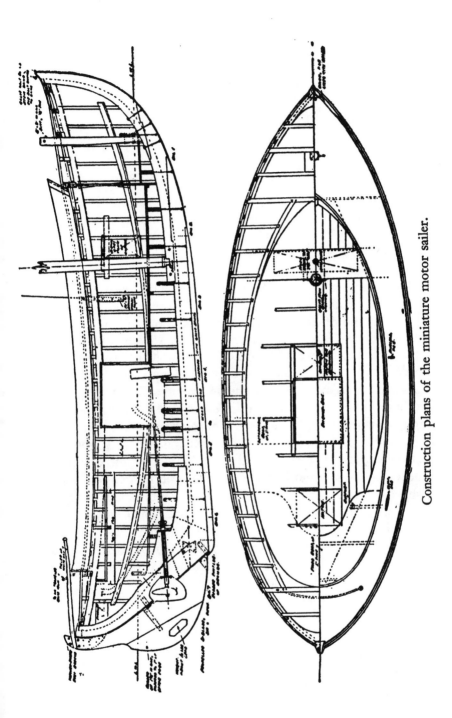

Construction plans of the miniature motor sailer.

173

A TABLOID CRUISER, 21 FT.

Designed by JOHN ALDEN

JULY, 1933

FOR several summers past a little 21 foot sloop roamed New England waters manned by father and son, sometimes by father, sometimes just son. Nova Scotia has proved not too far away and her cabin is usually full at Cruising Club rendezvous. She is a good little boat, and has helped to show that a good little boat can do about what her owner wants.

The drawings herewith show an improved little boat for the same purpose, i.e., a summer's fun for two with a fair degree of comfort and a minimum of expense. The new boat, now building for a Chicago yachtsman, is 21 feet 2 inches overall, 18 feet 6 inches on the water, 8 feet beam and 3 feet 7 inches draft. She has 1,850 pounds of outside iron and 311 square feet in her working sails.

A five horsepower Falcon engine provides the auxiliary power. The lines show a stiff and able little vessel that should be smart in average going. Reverse frames are eliminated and other simplifications have been made for economical construction. There is good sitting headroom over the transoms and the cabin has all the cruising convenience of many larger boats. The galley and lockers—an ingenious arrangement of the owner's—are particularly interesting, and give unusual facilities in a craft of this size. The stove, which stows under the sink, swings on a hinged platform over the transom and a table is formed by the horizontally hinged locker door. A useful ice box, as in many of the smaller Alden designs, forms the companion step or a seat in the midst of the galley.

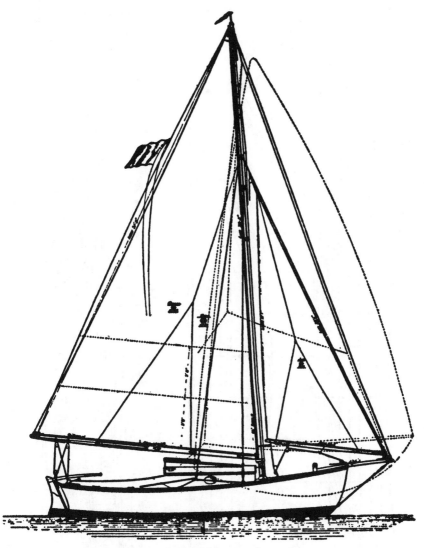

Sail plan of the Alden 21 ft. cruiser.

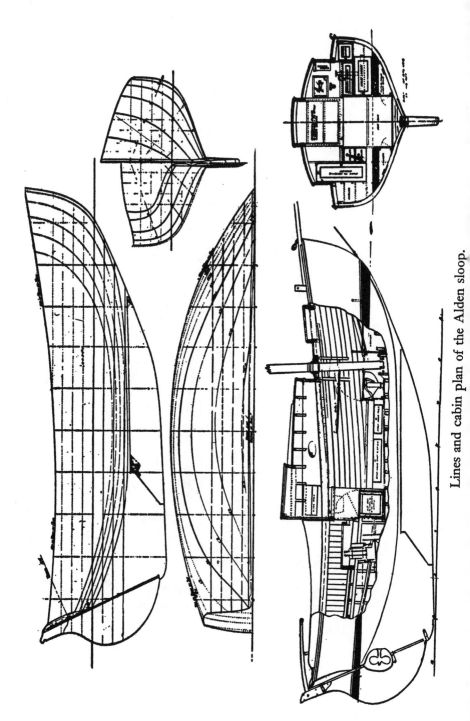

Lines and cabin plan of the Alden sloop.

A SINGLE-HANDER
FOR OPEN WATER, 24 FT.

Designed by FENWICK C. WILLIAMS

MARCH, 1933

MR. WILLIAMS describes his little dream ship: "It is always of great interest to see on paper the designer's idea of the most suitable craft for some specific purpose, planned without concession to any owner's ideas, good as these may sometimes be. This little boat was drawn as the designer's conception of a single-hander for open water cruising. Many of her features are borrowed from the experience of others; one or two may be original. The plans show a rugged double-ender of about 8,000 pounds displacement with a lead keel weighing 2,500 pounds, yawl rigged with overlapping jib, high peaked gaff mainsail and jib headed mizzen.

"The seven foot pram dinghy is stowed bottom up on deck forward of the house, as on Slade Dale's ocean going cruiser Postscript. On the forward deck there is a stout bitt, and nothing else.

"The steering gear, as far as I know, is original. Many doubts have been expressed concerning the practicability of this invention, if such it be, but as I have used a gear working on exactly the same principle on a different type of boat, I am confident that it is a thoroughly practical proposition. At any rate, it consists essentially of a shaft extending from the wheelbox to the rudder through the mizzen mast and sternpost. The after end of this shaft is sharply bent to an angle of about 45 degrees, and works in a well re-inforced, metal-lined slot in the rudder head. Thus the rudder is moved from hard over to hard over by a half revolution of the shaft. The steering wheel is geared to this shaft by a small and a large pinion to give the proper ratio and the customary direction of rotation.

"The cabin layout is simple and conventional, and their would be no plumbing in my deep sea cruiser. The construction would be very

177

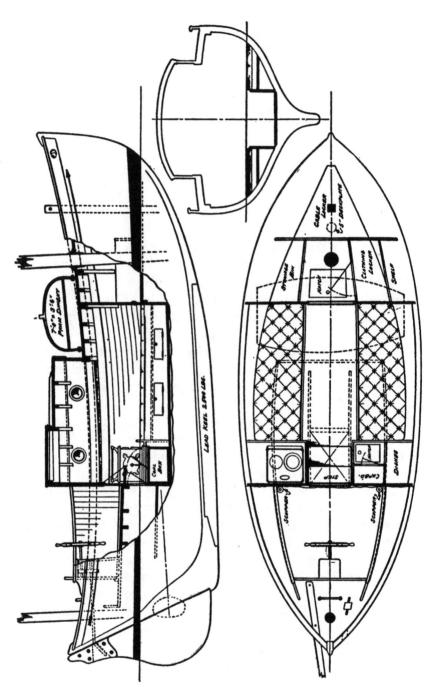

Cabin plan of the Williams' yawl.

178

strong but by no means massive. The dimensions of the hull are: l.o.a. 24 feet, l.w.l. 21 feet 6 inches, beam 8 feet 8 inches, draft 3 feet 9 inches. The bilges are moderate with the displacement well spread out, and a good run."

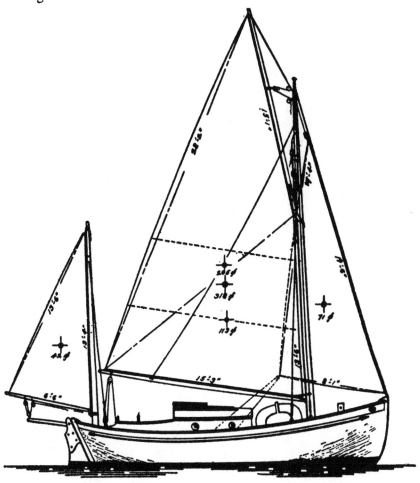

Profile of the Williams' 24 ft. single hander.

A KEEL CAT, 24 FT.

Designed by WINTHROP L. WARNER

APRIL, 1951

THE keel cat is not seen as frequently, nowadays, as its center-board sister.

This Winthrop L. Warner design offers six foot headroom in a hull only 24 feet overall. The deck and sail plans reveal a shapely and spacious little ship intended for both New England and Florida cruising.

Her dimensions: 24' l.o.a; 22' 6" l.w.l; 11' 6" beam; 3' 10" draft. Displacement, 11,200 pounds. Sail area, 432 square feet. Power, Gray 4-112 Lugger with 2:1 reduction gear.

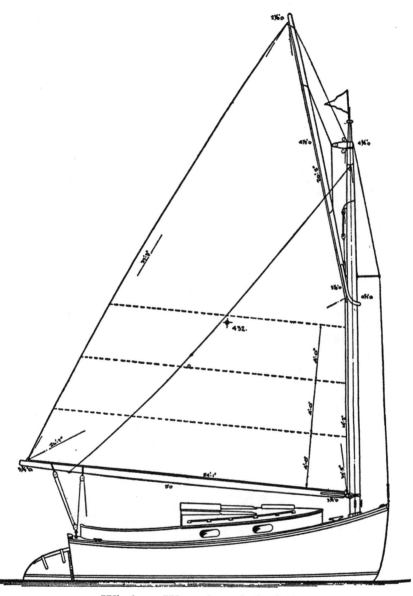

Winthrop Warner's 24 ft. keel cat.

Cabin plan of the Warner cat.

SEA HOUND, A CROSBY CAT, 25 FT.

Designed by CHARLES CROSBY

APRIL, 1912

THE Crosby brothers of Osterville, Massachusetts have become legendary as the developers and builders of seaworthy catboats. About the year 1857, C. W. and H. S. Crosby began building boats and in 1872, the sons of C. W. Crosby started in the business. H. S. Crosby had four sons—Herbert, Wilton, Joseph and Manly—and they became catboat builders, too. Daniel Crosby, the son of C. W. was the first to alter the accepted dimensions of the cat by increasing the proportion of beam, building a boat 25 ft. long with a beam of 11 ft., 3 in. So much for history.

Sea Hound is a true Cape cat in every respect; no views of the owner being allowed to alter in the slightest degree her form. She has the square broad stern, with the underbody kept well down, and the "barndoor rudder" as found in all cats in the waters around the Cape, and while a very full-bodied boat, her lines are all long and easy, giving wonderful qualities of seaworthiness, speed and room.

Her length was fixed at 25 feet water-line, in the belief that such size is about the limit of practicability in the type, and this appears to be well borne out in such cats as have been built to greater size, although *Sea Hound* herself gives no hint that such is the case.

The form of *Sea Hound* was determined from a model prepared by her builder, and her general arrangement is based upon plans prepared by the owner. It will be noted from the plans that much care has been taken to preserve harmony of line and to ensure simplicity in every detail. The cabin provides accommodations for four, in well-lighted and ventilated quarters, with every convenience for cruising. Stove space, food lockers, dish-racks, ice-box, etc., are all concentrated at one point and most simple and convenient, while all odors from cooking are at once carried off through the companion hatch. Unlike most centerboard cats the board is not in the way, as it is kept low and there is sufficient floor space forward to walk around same. Toilet is located forward and curtained off from rest of cabin, with

183

ventilation through hatch in cabin roof. The cockpit is very large and will easily seat twelve people without crowding, making the boat exceptionally desirable for day or party sailing.

Construction is heavy throughout, consisting of oak log keel sided 7 by 9 inches, frames oak 2 by 3 inches, planking selected cypress finished one inch thick and fastened with galvanized nails, all butt joints being made in between frames on butt blocks. Deck is of first quality white pine strips 1 by 1¼ inch laid on edge and finished bright. Cockpit and cabin are finished in cypress and hard pine with oak trim; all finished natural. All metal work is of brass and Merriman blocks are used throughout.

The general dimensions of the boat are as follows:

Length o. a.	25 feet	9 inches
Length w. l.	25 "	0 "
Breadth	11 "	6 "
Draught	2 "	8 "
Height at bow	4 "	6 "
Height at stern	2 "	2½ "
Freeboard, least	2 "	9½ "
Headroom	5 "	4 "
Sail area	725 square feet	

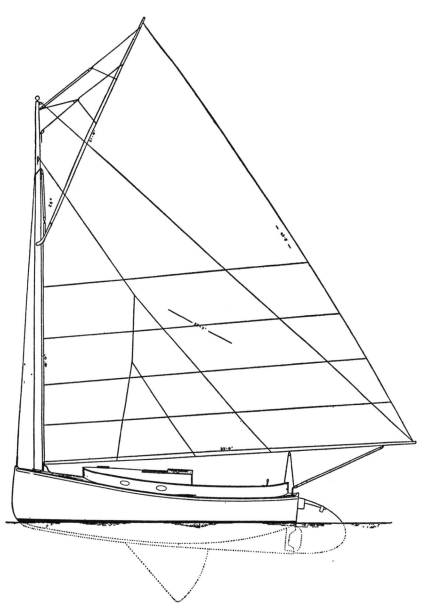

The *Sea Hound's* sail plan.

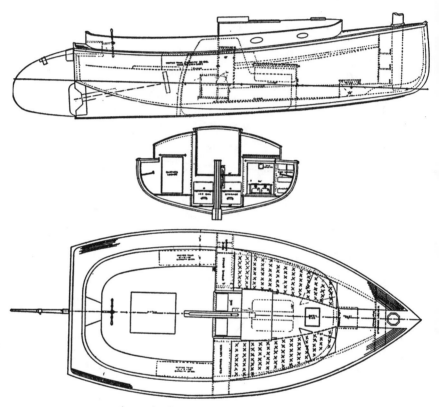

A typical Crosby cat cabin plan.

AN OUTBOARD CRUISER, 25 FT.

Designed by WILLIAM J. DEED

APRIL, 1933

THOUGH this style of cabin arrangement has been adopted somewhat for day cruisers and similar craft it has much to recommend it. Aside from putting the best part of the boat—forward—at the owner's disposal, it also allows one to get away from the motor, a feature not present in many outboard cruisers.

On an overall length of 25 feet she offers a lot of accommodation. She has 7 feet 6 inches beam and draws 2 feet to the bottom of the keel. The forward cockpit is 6 feet 6 inches long and full headroom is available throughout all the covered part of the hull. The cabin boasts four berths, counting uppers, and small galley space and w.c. separate. The after cockpit is only large enough to accommodate two men fishing and to allow access to the motor.

She is exceptional in having full headroom, but with this cabin arrangement it is possible to get this valuable feature without having her look like the Empire State Building. The covering over the forward cockpit has a hatch cut in either side to allow getting in from the deck.

The form is vee-bottomed and should make her easy to drive and easy to build. She is especially well adapted to amateur construction, though she was not gotten up with this primarily in mind.

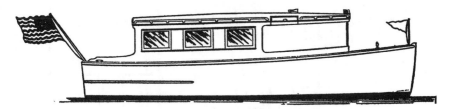

Profile of the Deed outboard cruiser.

187

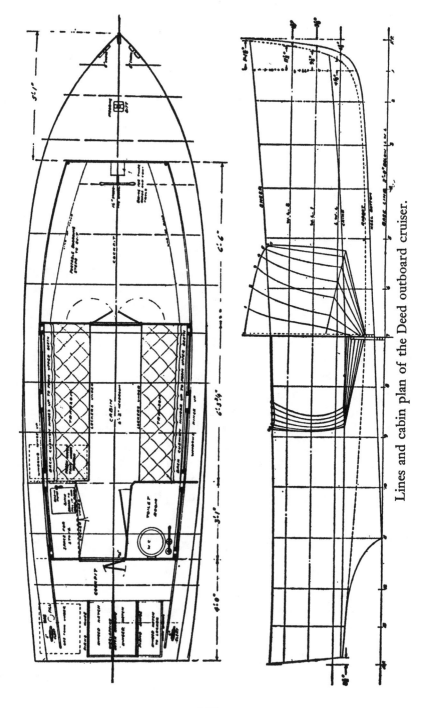

Lines and cabin plan of the Deed outboard cruiser.

HOLIDAY, 26 FT.,
SMART AND PRACTICAL
Designed by TOM GILLMER

NOVEMBER, 1944

WITHIN the dimensions of 26 ft., 4 in. L.O.A.; 20 ft. on the water line; 8 ft., 8 in. Beam and 3 ft., 11 in. Draft, Mr. Gillmer has embodied the following thoughts:

Herewith for size you will find a rather small (26 feet 4½ inches overall, 20 feet on the water) boat, but with a rather full bodied hull somewhat reminiscent of North Sea boats. The rising bow and deep sheer with well rounded sections should be of some influence in making her easy in a seaway. Her lines fair out clean below the water and in spite of her beam (which is not excessive, 8 feet 8 inches) she will not embarrass her owner either off the wind or on. She will go well in company with most any boat her size.

In the rig we have these features that make for utility and simplicity. First, the recommended rig is the simple jib or fore and mainsail with genoa. The spinnaker on a pure cruising craft was deemed unnecessary. The rig is entirely inboard with double jumper and running backstays. To attain a suitable area without spoiling the aspect ratio it is impossible to rig a standing backstay on any craft of this type and size. There should be no difficulty with the rugged slide arrangement on the runners.

In addition the designer is skeptical about standing backstays. Such construction requires a thorough job involving the proportionate cost of a long strap which through fastens outside the transom to the sternpost; otherwise it will eventually, as it has in many a similar design, pull off a transom plank.

The sails are the designer's fetish, loose footed throughout; while it involves working the jib, this is of little consequence in comparison to the advantages. The advantages are these: 1. Closely realizes the ideal airfoil section. 2. Section is adjustable by clew outhaul. 3. Load-

189

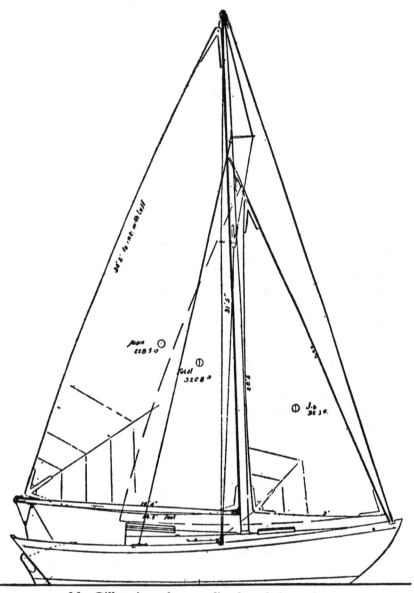

Mr. Gillmer's 20 ft. waterline knockabout sloop.

ing the foot at the clew alone, the upper twist is reduced to a minimum. 4. Easier and simpler to put on and take off than laced or slide foot. 5. Easier to reef. 6. Sets properly and beautifully without so much fitting and hauling. What more than this can a man ask from a suit of sails?

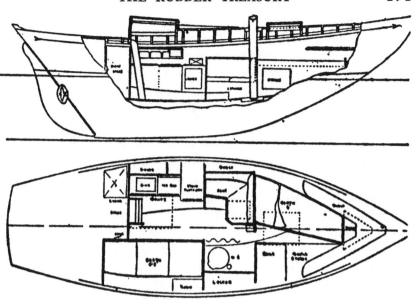

Holiday's cabin plan.

Now to the hull and some more contestable features. Why the outboard rudder? The question of appearance is a matter of taste. I like it better; it looks to me more seamanlike and less like the tail of a water bird, for which there is use only in flight. Practically speaking, the rudder can always be seen. For example, a friend of mine in his R boat last summer happened to drop a vital pin from his rudder post; he was without control for some hours, not knowing whether his rudder had dropped off or not. There is very little that can happen to a rudder hung on good gudgeons which comes up outside with a direct connecting tiller. An overhanging stern below decks is totally wasted space; it generally is the place where dry rot starts first, and soon. It is almost impossible to inspect or repair without tearing up the deck. Leaks are often prevalent where the rudder post comes through the hull. Finally, the outboard rudder design is simpler to build. (In all fairness, for racing hulls of less beam the overhanging stern increases the waterline length when sailing, consequently with greater possibilities for speed.)

The simple inboard sloop rig was chosen because it is undoubtedly the handiest. 228 square feet of sail in the main should not be too much work even for the kids to bend on or take off or hand under way. She will reef three bands deep, thus cutting her sail area to about half. An accumulating winch will keep the stainless halliard always in place with no halliard coils to fuss over.

Although the rig shown herewith is no doubt the simplest sort and handiest for most, there are some who prefer the divided rig.

It is obvious from the accompanying drawings that the most unconventional feature of this boat is the lack of any trunk or form of raised cabin. This form of construction has much to recommend it. First and foremost it makes for a stronger and more rigid hull shell. However further arguments for the convenience and livability of this type vs. the conventional trunk should be brought out. To obtain standing headroom in a boat of this size involves a trunk or doghouse so high that the profile of the boat becomes all out of proportion. Consequently good sitting headroom must be resorted to. There is sufficient freeboard here to allow good sitting headroom anywhere in the cabin. Then there is a definite lack of that trunk knuckle that always cracks the back of the head when sitting down.

The next most important feature of this flush deck arrangement is the unobstructed view ahead for the man at the tiller. The profile is kept in true form and the sheer line is dominant.

In this design the companionway is somewhat larger than usual. It is no attempt to substitute for a doghouse, but it is convenient above the one spot in the cabin where standing is better than sitting. The large hatch before the mast makes an airy, light and accessible forward end of the cabin.

The cabin ends at a break in the deck which forms a short bridge deck above the engine space. A large cockpit extends from there aft to the transom. The tiller extends into the cockpit through the transom, allowing the mainsheet to lead to a swivel fastened in the transom above the tiller.

Into the cabin plan itself—here the designer hesitates. If any part of a boat is personal it is below decks. There are infinite possibilities for infinite tastes; it is the owner's preference, or at least it should be. Yet there are so many boats, good boats, whose cabin layouts look strictly like a rubber stamp. After admiring the lines and rig of many boats it is often a disappointment to go below.

Herewith then is a cabin layout that I think best conforms to this type boat with due consideration given to the average demands and desires.

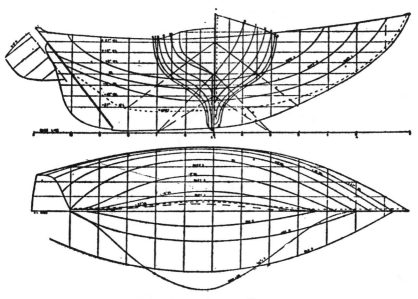

Holiday's pleasant lines.

First the galley is not large and perhaps those with greater appetites or culinary abilities would demand more room here. The galley is compact, with all the necessary articles. It is slightly more adequate than the one on my own boat and I have experienced some very adequate and often comically elaborate (for a 25 footer) meals served from it. However in the last analysis what article is in most demand from the galley? A coffee pot needs only a burner and a little water.

The important item, according to a friend of mine who has lived on boats (mostly small, with and without headroom) for fifteen years, is to have a handy place to sit near the stove. It is herewith presented as a corner seat. This also makes an adjacent spot to eat in weather not suitable for meals topside. A drop shelf or bracket attached to the side of this seat can make a handy table.

In a boat without headroom it is necessary to have convenient spots to sit. A transom berth on the starboard side, the corner seat on the port and a wooden bin top forward distribute the sitting room in an adequate manner.

To some there might be an objection to valuable room being occupied by such construction as this corner seat. This space could probably be adapted to hanging or stowage space. The matter however is a consideration to be decided primarily by the employment and locality of the boat. For sailing here on the Chesapeake during the regular season space for the stowage of hanging clothes would be a definite waste. There is adequate stowage in this plan exclusive of the space occupied by the corner seat except for those who demand a very complete wardrobe.

The cabin will accommodate a couple with considerable comfort and the absence of bulkheads or a trunk alley will give a justifiable impression of spaciousness to the interior.

The specifications on this design call for a rugged boat of moderately heavy construction. However the use of laminated strength members and flush deck assist in acquiring great strength without the addition of extra weight. The boat should be able to take it.

COMFORT IN 30 FT.

Designed by P. L. SMITH

NOVEMBER, 1934

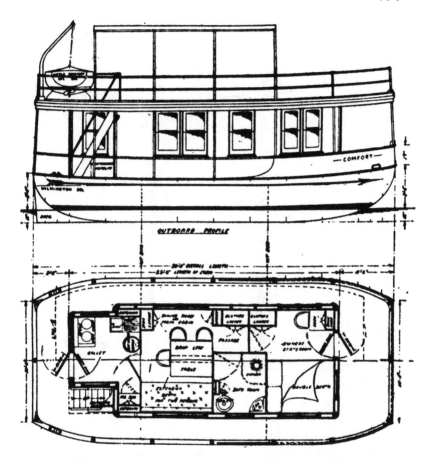

A WILMINGTON, DELAWARE, yachtsman wanted a welded steel houseboat that he could move to a different location each summer, towing it with its 10 ft. tender, *Little Comfort*, which is carried aboard.

Dimensions: L.O.A. 30 ft.; Beam, 13 ft. 6 in.; Draft, 12 in.; Depth of hull, 3 ft. 6 in. Except for flared bulwarks, all surfaces are flat for easy and economical construction.

A SLOOP, OR SCHOONER, WITH THREE CABIN PLANS, 30 FT.

Designed by s. s. CROCKER

JANUARY, 1932

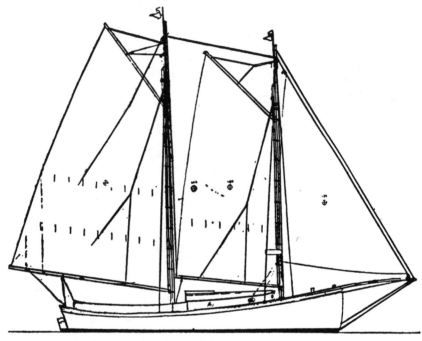

The Crocker hull as a bald headed schooner.

S. S. CROCKER has the following to say about this 30 foot 3 inch overall boat which can be rigged as sloop or schooner, and which can have any one of three interior layouts, as shown on the enclosed plans:

"The boat is of the following dimensions, length overall, 30 feet 3 inches; length waterline, 28 feet 7 inches; beam, 10 feet 8½ inches; draft, 4 feet 5½ inches.

"I have designed this small auxiliary, with large accommodations, in order to meet the present day desire for low first cost. I have en-

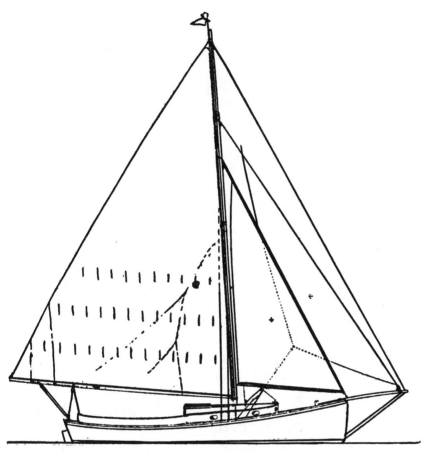

The Crocker hull as a sloop.

deavored to keep the construction costs down without in any way sacrificing strength or ability—for instance, the model is such that it does not require outside ballast for stability, which makes toward a double saving in first cost, i.e., there is no keel pattern to be made or metal to be cast, and the keel foundation is of one siding, eliminating costly hewing with broad axe and adz. Then, as this type of boat looks right only when plainly finished, the cost of expensive trim is eliminated and saved.

"A glance at the plans will show the remarkable amount of room both below and in the cockpit, making the boat most desirable for cruising or day sailing.

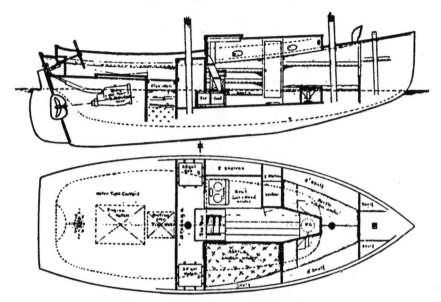

One style of schooner cabin plan.

"The fish well serves the double purpose of fish well and scupper for the large cockpit. It is an element of great safety, as in case the cockpit should ever be filled with a sea, the water would disappear instantly through the well.

"The Marconi sloop would cost somewhat less to build than the schooner as she would have fewer blocks, spars and less rigging.

"There are at present several small yards which are willing to build boats of this type at a surprisingly low figure. I actually know of two yards which build her now at a saving of $1,000 over last year's price. I figure this boat could be built complete this year for approximately $3,000."

Remember, that was 1932.

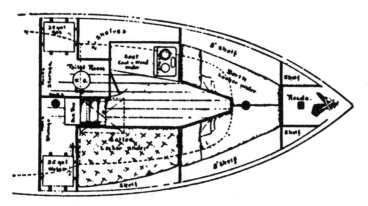

Same hull with alternate cabin plan No. 2.

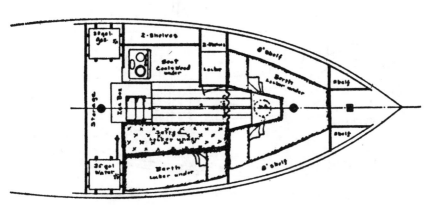

Yet another cabin plan for this flexibly styled craft.

199

SEA WITCH, A PACIFIC
OFFSHORE CRUISER, 35 FT.

Designed by HUGH ANGLEMAN

JUNE, 1945

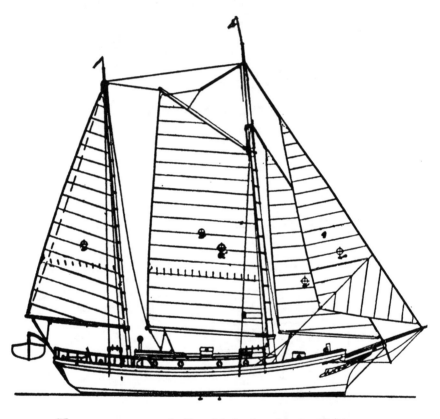

THIS coaster-type hull, with its handy rig, has become popular with Pacific Coast cruisers. In 1951, *Sea Witch* won the Honolulu Race on corrected time.

This 35 footer has the comfort and the accommodations of a much larger boat. She has a large main cabin, a separate owner's stateroom and an enclosed forecastle with bunk and head for a paid hand. The principal dimensions are as follows: 35 feet overall, 31 feet 6 inches

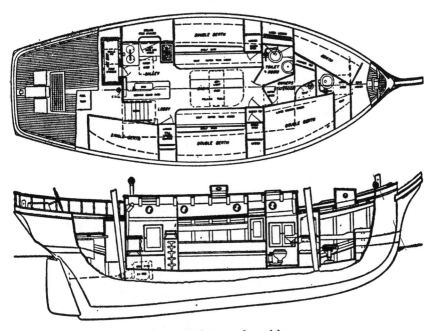

Sea Witch's ample cabin.

on the water, 13 feet 3 inches beam, 5 feet 6 inches draft. Total sail
area is 821 square feet and her displacement is 26,068 pounds.

The galley equipment and power plant are modern in every respect and she carries two 100 gallon water tanks and a ninety gallon
gasoline tank. No detail has been spared to lend her the charm of an
old time sailing ship. The traditional clipper bow and sprit, the dead-
eyes and lanyards, the monkey rail, the deck gear lockers and the
painstaking joiner work below, all reflect the craftsmanship of the
master shipwright. The *Sea Witch* sleeps eight, including the paid
hand. She is sturdy and easy to handle under any conditions. Power
suggested is a Gray Model 4-22 with 2 to 1 reduction gear.

CYNOSURE, 100% CRUISER, 36 FT.

Designed by WILLIAM HAND

Described by GIDGE GANDY

DECEMBER, 1927

ALTHOUGH much printer's ink has been spread in the discussion of the ideal small auxiliary cruiser, I cannot resist a desire to add a word in praise of a certain little vessel which, in the opinion of those who have sailed her, is the perfect craft of this kind.

I write of a boat that is now far beyond the stage of theory and experiment, having been in commission 14 years and proven her worth upon many cruises which have extended to Nova Scotia, to Cuba and into the Gulf of Mexico. She has encountered the changing moods of the Atlantic, the Straits and the Gulf and negotiated many harbors of the Eastern seaboard, yet time and distance have left no scars and she is as able and attractive as the day she was first launched.

I claim that the question of the ideal small cruiser is best answered in *Cynosure*, ex *C.D.B.*, ex *Fundulus*, a shippy little ketch built in 1913 by the Greenport Yacht Basin & Construction Co. from designs by that genius of the drawing board, Wm. H. Hand, Jr., through whose kindness her lines and sail plan are here reproduced.

Her principal dimensions are: 36 ft. o.a. by 31-ft. l.w.l. by 10-ft. 2-in. by 5-ft. 2-in. draught. Her sail area is approximately 650 sq. ft. and her construction is heavy and of exceptional workmanship.

In the Spring of 1926, I had the good fortune to purchase her from Ted Sibley at Cambridge, Maryland, and sailed her from the Virginia Capes to Vineyard Sound and from there southward to the Florida Keys and up the Gulf Coast to Tampa Bay, from where I made a cruise to Cuba and return.

Cynosure has proven to be just large enough for ocean cruising in safety and with a fair degree of comfort for three or four men, yet small enough to be handled conveniently by one man. Her draught is sufficient for deep water sailing and to allow full headroom in the

202

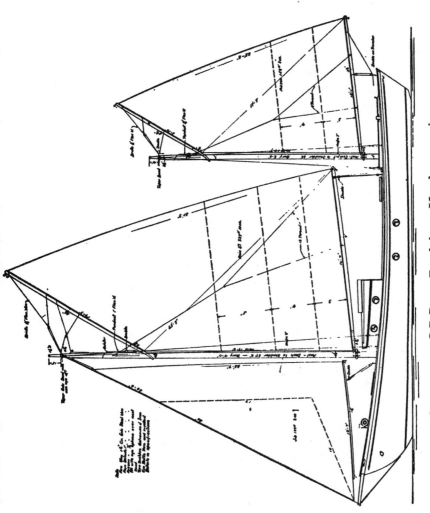

Cynosure, ex *C.D.B.*, ex *Fundulus*, a Hand masterpiece.

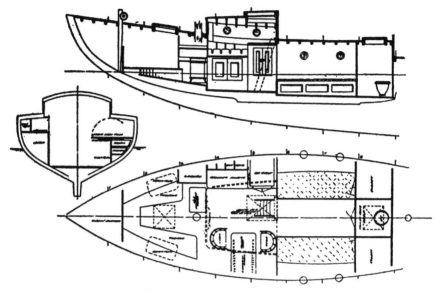

Cynosure's unusual, but practical cabin plan.

cabin, yet she can enter almost any harbor and her skipper can conveniently use the one-fathom curve on the charts as a guide.

With exception of rare occasions when curling seas have slopped over her rails, she has shipped green water on but one occasion, a memorable night when we thrashed to windward against a snortin' No'ther in the Gulf of Mexico under full sail, at a time when able fishing smacks ran under the beach and anchored. Our decks would have been virtually dry that night had we furled the mainsail.

When *Cynosure* is close hauled to a hard wind and heels over to the pressure on her canvas, her bows rise instead of falling as is the case with hard bilges and broad after waterlines. This tendency to lift her head, combined with her high freeboard, makes her unusually dry in a head sea. She "eases" over and through the crests of seas and, in some mysterious manner which I have been unable to fathom, avoids falling into the black troughs when the seas are short and steep.

She performs best when running before a quartering sea. Her sharp stern with its high, flaring freeboard is an excellent feature of her design and affords a dry cockpit in heavy weather. As she descends into a trough, her full bow sections come into play at the proper moment and I have yet to see water top her forward rail. Her

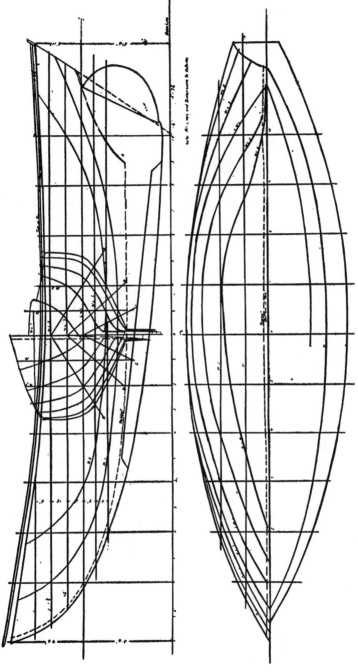

Cynosure's lines, which pleased all her owners.

moderate forefoot and the deep drag of her keel avoid any tendency to broach, even when running surf.

In fact, she is an excellent surf boat, despite her weight and draught. Last August we ran several of the New Jersey coast inlets and one day, when running Barnegat bar with an on-shore breeze and a heavy ground swell, she made the crossing in as fine style as any skiff could have done it.

Owing to the course of the narrow channel through the bar, it was impossible to hold her dead stern-to when a huge comber roared down upon us. Down the forward slope of that hill of water she raced at a pace which backed her sails against a fresh breeze! Yet she showed no tendency to broach nor disobey her helm and crossed the bar with only a little spray on her after deck.

Cynosure behaved equally as well with a Northeaster blowing against an ebb current in the Race; during a run before a quartering sea off the Delaware Capes; and when driving before a hard North wind against the Gulf Stream off the Florida coast.

Even with wind and sea abeam, she is fairly dry and has an easy motion like that of a large ship. She seems to time her roll intentionally to the action of the sea.

She will carry sail until the canvas leaves the bolt ropes. Since I have known her, we have shortened sail for weather but four times and not a reef knot has been tied! Her lee rail has been buried but four or five times and a previous owner informs me that he has never seen her rail under.

Although we did once carry sail until she buried to her cabin top during the gusts, and have carried full canvas on other occasions when commercial windjammers had shortened, I have not yet repaired nor replaced a sail, spar nor foot of rigging and she still carries the same Burrows sails and the rigging that Ted Sibley gave her in the Spring of 1925 and apparently the same sticks and spars with which she was equipped in 1913. The hull has never strained and no water has come through her seams, so far as we can tell.

Unlike many cruisers, *Cynosure* is no workhouse for her crew. We sailed on and on, through the months, without a man aboard showing calluses or blisters on his hands.

Her snug little rig is a toy for a lazy man. No heavy work at the halyards nor the sheets. No back-stays to shift. No reefing. No crawling out on bowsprit nor boomkin. No reason to go aloft, for there is nothing up there to foul. To swing her about or to gybe, one merely rolls the wheel. One man on watch usually finds it convenient to attend to everything and the watch below sleeps on.

Her sailing qualities are a pleasure, for she possesses no temperamental traits. She invariably does what one expects of her and is altogether dependable in any situation. In fair weather or foul, she will luff, pay off, come about or gybe exactly *when* you want her to and *how*.

Under any and all conditions she steers with such ease that a child can handle her. She will steer herself when close hauled, excepting in unusually heavy weather. Under favorable conditions at sea or on smooth inland waters, she will steer without a helmsman with her sheets well off. By steering herself, I do not mean with locked steering gear nor a Manila Mike on her wheel, but with the rudder swinging free.

When the helmsman is sailing a course, he finds that the lubber line rarely swings far and that she will "average" the course with uncanny accuracy. Usually a halfspoke turn of the wheel or less will straighten her out when she swings.

With three or four men taking four hour tricks at the wheel, we have sailed courses upwards of a hundred miles and sighted the objectives over the bowsprit. A few weeks ago we sailed 177 miles from Tampa Bay entrance and picked up the Key West blinker buoy, dead ahead.

Although her ketch rig will not point very high, her full lateral plane causes her to hold on and I have learned that a half-point is about the limit of leeway under full sail.

Cynosure is a comfortable home for fellows who know how to be comfortable aboard ship. Below decks she has room for broad berths, galley, water and gas tanks of ample capacity and stowage space for spare equipment and supplies necessary for an extended cruise.

Three large deck openings, eleven hinged port lights and a ventilator over the galley admit light and air to the "downstairs" parts.

Her deck arrangement is the best I have ever seen. The short cabin affords a space of 100 square feet, forward of the cockpit. Here, a Penn Yan eight foot dink reposes on the port side. To starboard, there is plenty of room for the boys to stretch out and smoke or sleep during the long runs at sea, or to work at odd jobs when in harbor. This broad deck, over which we often stretch an awning, has proven the most comfortable feature of *Cynosure*'s design.

The little ship's easy motion in a seaway guarantees three square meals every day and plenty of sleep, a happy faculty not found with every 36-footer.

Now, if you believe my statements relative *Cynosure*'s seaworthiness and comfort, you will not expect me to claim that she is a hellbuster for speed. She is not. And yet, she is certainly not a tub. She seems to take care of herself surprisingly well against boats of her size and class. Throughout a 2500 mile cruise, we averaged about five and a half knots by judicial use of her motor during calms, which drives her a little better than six knots. However, I don't believe I have ever seen her do better than seven knots, either under sail or motor. I have seen her beat against a wicked sea and make better than two and three-quarters knots to windward, with the motor silent.

Cynosure's appearance? Well, no boat has ever been a good boat that did not look the part. She looks it. The stumpy, business-like rig seems to belong to the hull and her bow, stern and middle belong to one another and look like something which is a complete idea in itself.

When she enters a fishing port, you should see those leather skinned fellows look her over. She is truly the cynosure of all eyes which have been accustomed to gaze over salt water. More than one old-time deep water man has stepped aboard with a "Captain, she looks like a smart little vessel," or some such remark which makes my pride a difficult thing to live with.

To help prove my claim that *Cynosure* is the craft I claim her to be, I must quote the words of her original owner, Mr. E. H. Wardwell, who sailed her to Nova Scotia and who writes, "I have always regretted the sale of *Fundulus* more than anything I ever did. I have never had her equal since and certainly have missed her as I would an old friend or sweetheart."

Also the words of Mr. Ezra Bowen, her second owner, who, with his wife as shipmate, sailed her from Portland to Philadelphia, who writes: "If you ever want to sell her I should be glad to hear from you."

Her third owner, I do not know, but Ted Sibley, who sold her to me, writes, "You took away my dream ship."

David S. Bechtel, who acted as agent in the last and very likely the final sale of this craft, writes, "If I had a dozen more like *Cynosure* listed, I could sell them all, quickly."

It remains for Jack Hanna, sage of Dunedin, to mention *Cynosure* in classic terms: "I was glad to know that you had bought a regular ship. I know the reputation of this craft, under the name of *Fundulus*, very well. She is said to be one of the best jobs Hand ever turned out.

"To every creative worker comes a time when, for some unknown reason, his old bean is hitting on all six and, without knowing why, he does it. He turns out a masterpiece that proves better than he dreamed of.

"Probably Leonardo da Vinci didn't guess, when he painted Mona Lisa, that that picture was going to stand the world on its head for hundreds of years. And probably Bill Hand didn't think *Fundulus* was going to be more beloved of all owners than many of his big famous schooners."

THE IDEAL WORLD CRUISERS
by Various Designers

Periods of impending social disturbance inspire cruising men to plan for world wide voyages, or at least for trips to quieter places. In 1941, THE RUDDER asked several outstanding designers to outline their "perfect ship" for a world cruise. To their contributions the editor has added a couple that appeared outside this series. These ingeniously planned yachts may offer a suitable ending to this section on Dream Ships.

A 36 FT. WORLD CRUISER

Designed by RALPH WINSLOW

JUNE, 1941

My GENERAL experience in designing boats for men contemplating a world cruise is that most of them could afford an investment of not more than $6,000 or $7,000. They did not want a paid hand and were planning to cruise with one or two companions, making a total crew of three. Also they generally wished accommodations for week-end cruising for two couples and an occasional larger party. I doubt the wisdom of building a boat suited solely for a "world cruise." She should be usable for general cruising when the voyage is completed, and I feel that a craft can be designed that is suited for both.

My selection of a "World Cruiser," taking into consideration these thoughts, would be a modern marconi knockabout yawl. She is 36 feet 6 inches overall, 27 feet on the water, 9 feet 9 inches beam, 5 feet 9 inches draft, freeboard at the bow 4 feet 4½ inches, least freeboard 2 feet 8 inches and at the stern 3 feet. The overhang forward is 4 feet 4½ inches, aft 5 feet 4½ inches. Sail area is 610 square feet. Ballast outside is 7,500 pounds, inside about 1,000 for trimming. Displacement is about 20,000 pounds.

I have selected this rig because I believe the knockabout yawl, with no bowsprit, has the best combination of safety, ease of handling and speed possible for this size of craft. The mainsail is only 365 square feet in area. It is the largest sail and it should not be beyond the ability of one man to handle it.

Most long voyages are made in the season to take advantage of broad reaching winds, and I suggest a large genoa or reaching jib. While a design should be produced that will reach or run well, I would not overlook windward ability as it might be necessary sometime to claw off a lee shore. It is also essential for ordinary cruising, after the voyage is over.

The design should have a great deal of stability so she can carry

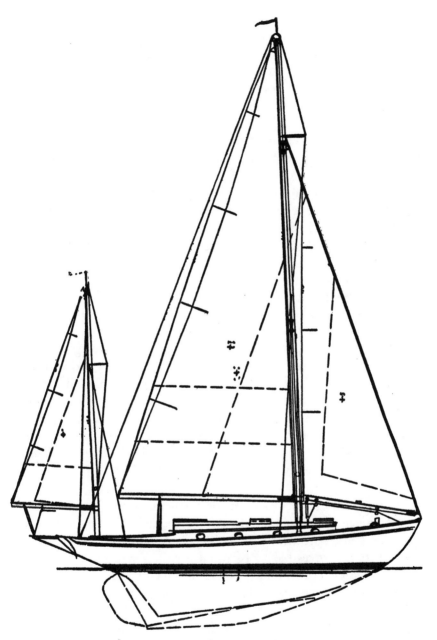

The Winslow 36 ft. knockabout yawl.

sail in a breeze but I still would want a fast craft, to get from port to port as quickly as possible.

I would have two complete sets of sails, one of about 8 ounce material for sailing in any wind in which whole sail could be carried, and also a complete set of heavy sails of areas equal to about close reefs for the lighter suit. These are to be cut up and down and strongly made.

For the rig I would suggest modern fittings, winches and other labor saving devices, but they would be about 20 per cent over-size for a strength factor of safety. The mainmast would be hollow, others solid. I believe the new improvements in rig and fittings will greatly outlast the older type and if over strong would never give any trouble. Some spares could be carried, such as extra wire and a few fittings.

For outside ballast I would prefer iron, straight on the bottom for easy beaching or hauling out, and extending the entire length of the keel for protection in case of grounding. Iron is much stronger than lead, is not damaged easily from grounding on rocks or coral and is less expensive than lead.

The hull construction should be strong but not cumbersomely heavy. I believe in proper engineering and close spacing of frames, floor timbers and deck beams which, combined with good workmanship and proper fastening, is to be preferred to the massive construction of seagoing vessels. The example of construction sizes would be about as follows: keel, 4 inches by 21 inches, stem sided 4¾ inches, frames steam bent 1 13/16 inches, on 9 inch centers, planking 1 3/16 inches thick, deck beams 2¾ inches deep, sided about 2½ inches, 1¾ inches, 1¼ inches, decks ⅞-inch 5-ply Weldwood canvas covered.

For the interior I can think of no better arrangement than the conventional one with forward stateroom, toilet and clothes closets, and galley aft, particularly if the details of this layout are carefully thought out. It gives plenty of room for three persons, a spare berth for an occasional guest and if wisely arranged sufficient storage space for all necessary boat gear, spare food storage, etc. The top of the ice box can be used for a chart table handy to the cockpit, and arrangements could be made for charts, books and navigating instruments. The ice box would be handy when in port but at sea, of course, would be used only for storage as no ice carried would last long enough to be worth while.

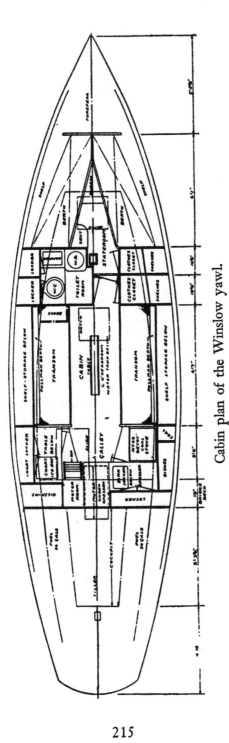

Cabin plan of the Winslow yawl.

215

In the cabin I would have two pipe berths upholstered so that they could be used for back rests or lowered and hung at any angle for sleeping purposes at any angle of heel, and also a liberal supply of book shelves.

There should be a good-sized oilskin space and the motor should be accessible for overhauling, with a good storage space for spare parts, oil, grease, etc.

For a motor I believe a 4-cylinder gasoline engine of about 20 hp. with 2 to 1 reduction gear would be excellent. There are two or three makes of small diesel engines of about 15 to 20 hp. that could be used with good fuel economy, although gasoline is probably more available than diesel fuel in most places.

All hatches, etc., would be given special construction for water-tightness, and all openings into the cabin would be screened. High double wire life rails would, of course, be installed (not shown) for safety and there would be chocks and lashings for carrying the small boat, bottom up, on top of the cabin trunk, the main boom being kept high for this purpose. Water would be in a tank below the cabin with two compartments piped so that it would not all be lost in the bilge if there was a leak.

I believe a yacht of this size and type would make a most desirable craft for extended voyages, a fine sea boat, stiff, able, fast and as comfortable at sea as one could expect for the investment.

There should be a proper sea anchor with the necessary gear, with containers for sea smoothing oil. For anchors I would use the new Danforth type which can be light but are most efficient, the heavy one need be not more than about 40 pounds or possibly less.

She is a craft that could be handled by one person to the watch without unnecessary physical strain. With a crew of three one to the watch is about all that could be expected what with the necessary work of navigating, cooking and vessel upkeep.   R.W.

TRUE COURSE, A 40 FT.
WORLD CRUISER

Designed by J. MURRAY WATTS

JULY, 1941

TRUE COURSE was designed by J. Murray Watts of Philadelphia for an owner who plans to take a trip around the world—as soon as conditions allow it.

She carries an unusual rig that is not often seen nowadays, at least on craft of her size. *True Course's* dimensions are 40 feet on deck, 34 feet 3 inches waterline, 11 feet beam and 5 feet 8 inches draft. Other designs in this World Cruiser group have had overall dimensions of 61 feet (Schock), 46 feet 8 inches (Alden) and 36 feet 6 inches (Winslow). Total sail area is 1,090 square feet, broken into small sizes in the mainsail, main topmast staysail, main staysail, fore staysail, main topsail, fore topsail, foresail, jib and flying jib. She is equipped with an auxiliary engine and an electric lighting plant.

The steel construction is heavy, using 3/16 inch shell plating and 2½ inch by ¼ inch frames, spaced 17 inches. The deck and cabin trunk are each 3/16 inch plate and the cabin top is ⅛ inch. The stem bar is 3 inches by ½ inch, and she carries five tons of ballast composed of boiler punchings in tar cement.

Sails are "up-and-down" cut, best practice for a suit to be used on a long cruise, and the square sail rig has proved its value many times on other ships. The yard on the foremast is a familiar sight on *Yankee*, and Robinson got his money's worth out of his on *Svaap*. In fact he says that when he arrived at Tahiti "For a month this sail had been off but once, and then only thirty hours. It was worn. The yard lacing was temporarily patched in many places. The sail itself was practically blown out of the boltropes half the way around. It would have to be almost remade before it could be used again. But if anybody should ask me I should say it was *some* sail."

The layout below decks is an example of the belief that cabin space should be cut up so that at sea you can't be thrown far in any one direction before fetching up against something solid. The motion of

217

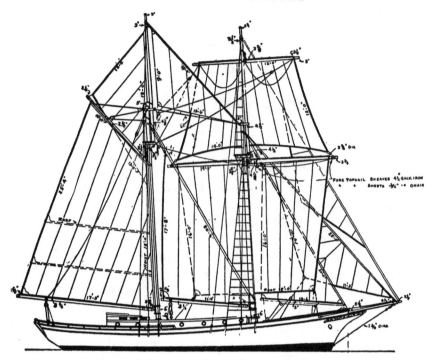

Sail plan of the 40 ft. topsail schooner.

a small boat in dusty weather *can* make the crew feel that they'd rather be tossed in a blanket. W. W. Nutting, after he had sailed his 46 foot *Typhoon* across the North Atlantic in November, said that when he started out he was in favor of leaving the cabin all open to make it more roomy, but afterwards he thought that a bulkhead here and there would be handy at times. He sometimes slid so far that the momentum when he hit was almost enough to break a leg.

From the deck the companionway leads down to the galley, which is thus handy to the cockpit, and is separated from the remainder of the cabin by a bulkhead and door. The toilet occupies the other side of this section. A navigator's desk three feet long is built in forward of the galley bulkhead, and lockers for oilskins and clothes are placed to starboard. An oilskin locker in this position is handy, because the cabin of a small boat almost inevitably becomes water-soaked in sloppy going. For one reason, the watch coming below cannot help but drip water around if it has been wet outside. With a locker here

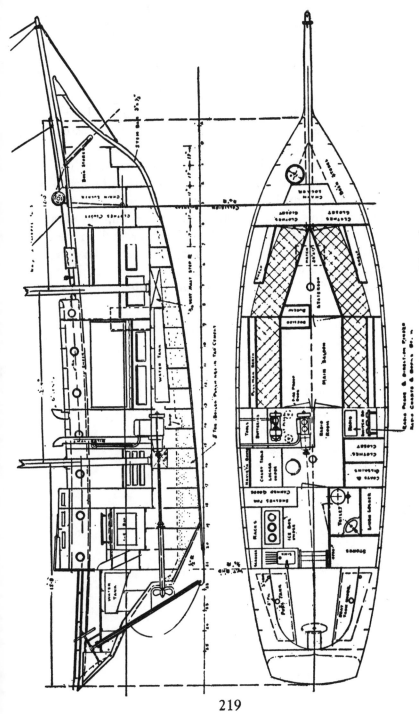

Cabin plan of J. Murray Watts' world cruiser.

they can house their oilskins and clothes and then go on into the cabin for something dry to put on (if they have it).

The motor and electric lighting plant are installed in a compartment of their own on the port side, with shelves for batteries. The engine is set off side to clear the mainmast, and the angle is also calculated to counteract the starboard drive of the screw. Its location makes it "get-at-able" which is a good point in case repairs are necessary. The radio equipment is opposite the engine room.

Forward of these "working quarters" comes the main cabin of the ship, 6 feet 4 inches in length. This has the usual bunks to port and starboard, and a small dresser. A stateroom with two berths is placed forward of this, with the trunk cabin extending for about 18 inches over the after end of it. A good sized hatch is built in the deck, and forward is closet space and room for stowage in the forepeak.

The ship is practically fireproof, because of her steel construction, and she is ceiled with Masonite which also provides good insulation.

A 42 FT. WORLD CRUISER

Designed by JOHN G. HANNA

FEBRUARY, 1942

JOHN G. HANNA designed this husky ketch for a New Jersey owner who intended to use her for family cruising in the Caribbean. Right now, of course, is not the time for a pleasure jaunt at any considerable distance from the home base, but although actual construction has been postponed until the sea ceases to be a battleground every detail of the design has been worked out with a conscientious care interesting to examine.

The owner wanted a comfortable ship on which he, his wife and two boys could spend the winter months cruising leisurely around Cuba and adjacent islands. Living accommodations more than merely adequate were a prime requisite under these conditions, and the sail plan was kept down so that she could be handled with a small crew. She has a 40 hp. diesel for an auxiliary, and a small gasoline generator to provide electricity for the refrigerator, radio and lighting system. The cabin plan has been kept simple, and the galley and chart table, both of which are frequently skimped in a small boat, have been given the space they should have.

The principal dimensions are 42 feet overall, 13 feet 4 inches beam and 4 feet 10 inches draft. Ballast is 13,000 pounds. Sail area is 900 square feet, divided 224 in the jib, 450 in the mainsail and 226 in the mizzen. In addition she has a storm trysail of 170 square feet and a "sea" spinnaker of 302 square feet. For fuel she can carry 210 gallons of diesel oil, 36 gallons of gasoline for the generator and 25 gallons of lubricating oil. She has a fresh water tank of 170 gallons.

The entire design, of course, has been planned for simplicity, ease of handling and comfort. The ketch rig is not meant for speed, and the hull is too chunky to keep up with a racing machine, but she could weather many a blow that might be disastrous for other craft of her size. She has a decided amount of initial stability, which means she can sail on an even keel when slimmer and deeper ones are forg-

221

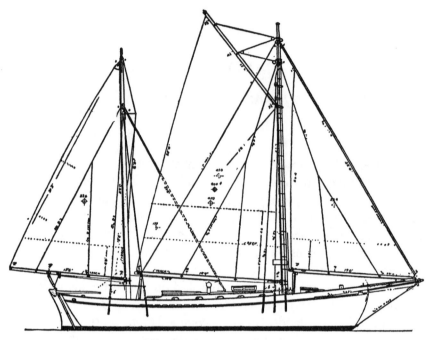

The Husky Hanna ketch.

ing along rail down with everything loose in the cabin piled up on the leeward side.

The cockpit has been kept small, with ample deck space around it for sitting, and a bridge deck that deserves its name and is not merely a door sill for the companionway. Under the bridge deck is the engine room, which is unusually deep because of the double-ended design. A hatchway with ladder leads to the starboard side of the motor while to port there is a seat with a space for tools under. The motor is placed as low as possible, which gives an advantageous shaft angle, and the exhaust line is led aft to a T and discharges athwartships. Gasoline, fuel oil and lubricating oil tanks have been placed in the engine room. The 500 watt generator is put aft of the main power plant to port while the batteries are to starboard. The entire compartment is separated from the rest of the ship by a bulkhead that is practically watertight and fumetight.

The steps to the main cabin lead down from the bridge deck to port of the centerline, and directly at their foot on the port side is the navigator's table, with drawers and shelves to take instruments and

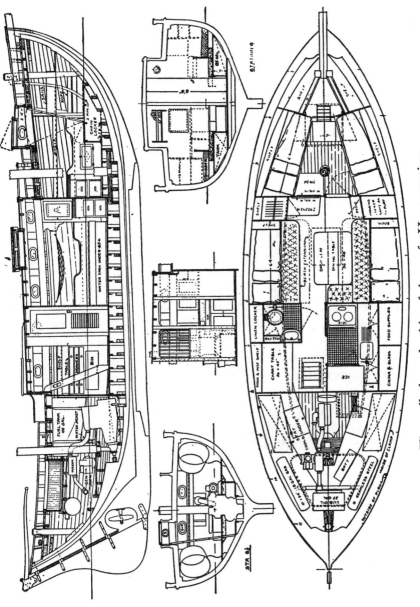

The well planned cabin of the 42 ft. Hanna cruiser.

charts. The owner evidently has had his fill of charting courses on a dining table with rolled or folded charts dug up from under the bunks. This "navigator's niche" is the real thing, and is handy to the companionway where the deck watch can duck below to check the course or verify a strange light.

The galley is placed to starboard, on the other side of the companionway ladder, and the plan view shows it so well that there is no need to comment. A Shipmate stove has been used, with a locker underneath it where an alcohol stove is stored and may be used at times when the weather is too hot for a coal fire. The toilet, across the alleyway, has its forward bulkhead even with the fore side of the galley.

Two permanent bunks have been provided, each a full 6 feet 4 inches long, and a settee has been built inboard from each to provide sitting accommodations during the day. The L shape of the starboard one makes a comfortable lounging spot, and also makes an additional seat for the table. Both settees have extensions for use as bunks. Shelves and hanging lockers have been placed on each side of the cabin forward of the bunks, and beyond the main living quarters is the stateroom, with two bunks 6 feet 3 inches long, shelves and a dresser. A hatchway with port lights in the side provides light and air, and a ladder which swings forward out of the way affords quick and easy access to the deck. The chain locker has been placed low, and the pipe through which it leads means that mud won't be flying all over the stateroom whenever cable is paid out.

PROSPECTOR, A 42 FT. KETCH

Designed by THE CONCORDIA COMPANY

JULY, 1942

THE ketch was designed by the Concordia Company, of Boston, and the designer states that she was named *Prospector* because her owner was one up in the gold fields of Canada. Her dimensions are as follows: 42 feet 7½ inches overall, 38 feet 6 inches on the water, 12 feet 6 inches beam, 6 feet draft and a displacement of 37,800 pounds.

In 1936 it was decided to build, and a ten volume correspondence ensued between Quebec and Boston. Everything was planned so that a man with two hands and some ability could make repairs or replacements far away from boat yards and machine shops. The cabin was to be really comfortable for two plus a hired hand. Also space for two occasional guests.

Prospector No. 1 was built at Scott's in Fairhaven. Her mast was a bit too far forward for proper headsails, but this did make a good sized gaff rig mizzen possible even if the latter had to be stepped on a tripod over the engine. While building, the boat was greatly admired; she was a lovely model with fine lines and still a lot of boat and carrying capacity. Everything was set, and the *Prospector* was about to be launched when yard, boat and all burned up. All that was found of the propeller was a drop of bronze. The engine was a Gray and was repaired, and is now used in another boat. The keel was saved and is now used in *Prospector No. 2*.

The second boat was to have the same hull but a dog house over the cockpit was added. Minor alterations were also made in the interior. A good work room aft with tool bench, chart table, engine and a bunk, big main cabin with galley aft. Toilet and lockers by the mast and then a big comfortable stateroom forward.

Work was begun in the summer of 1940 on the owner's back lawn a few yards from the river in Fort Lauderdale, Florida. A wood called acana was brought from the islands for a keel. Madeira was

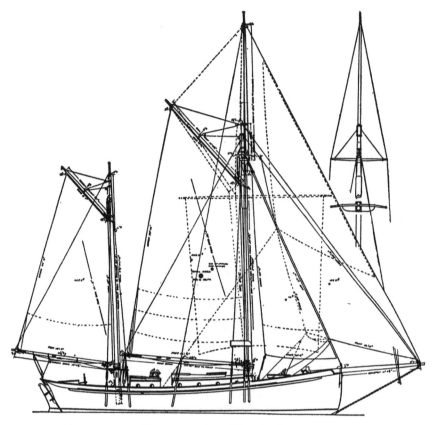

Prospector's tall ketch rig.

found for bent frames and deck beams. Teak was used for decks. Long leaf yellow pine for planking.

Special galvanized boat nails were ordered for fastenings. Iron bolts, iron keel, iron chain plates. No chance for electrolysis due to different metals.

Prospector's loose-footed sails worked out beautifully. They set well, worked well, looked well and furled well. A big loose-footed jibheaded mainsail may not work satisfactorily but a loose-footed gaff sail is all right. Her 56 horsepower Gray moved her along well and without any disturbance. The owner reported after a cruise to Nassau, and was enthusiastic. A Northerly had been blowing for some days, and the stream was really boisterous. The boat behaved well and averaged 6½ knots. Crossing the banks she did 7½ and 8 knots. She

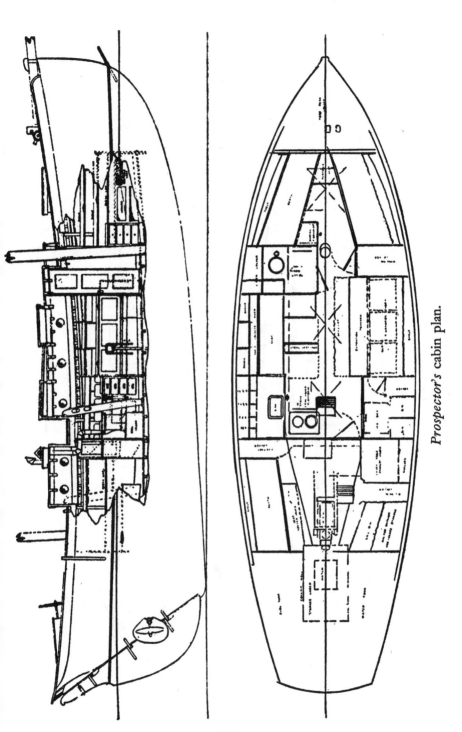

Prospector's cabin plan.

227.

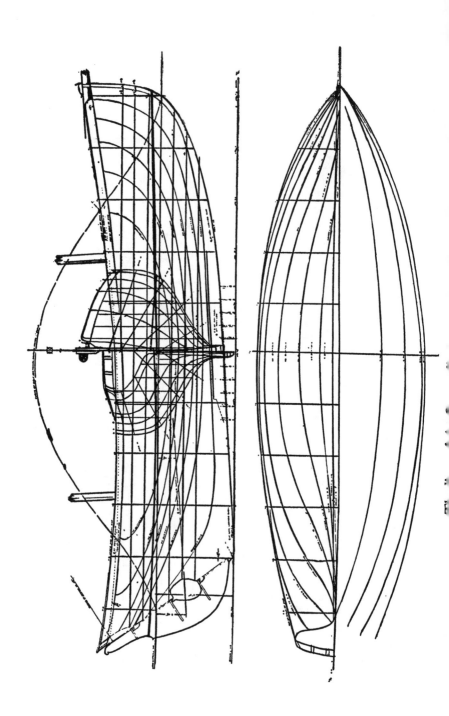

228

sails beautifully on the wind. Under power alone from Northwest light to Nassau she averaged 7½ knots at 1,400 r.p.m. All in all a highly successful little ship, which will give many years of faithful service.

MALABAR XII, A 46 FT.
WORLD CRUISER

Designed by JOHN ALDEN

MAY, 1941

THE RUDDER asked John Alden, noted Boston naval architect, what design he would recommend for the long ocean passages that are part of a world cruise. He replied that his *Malabar XII*, launched in August, 1939, embodied his ideas of the ideal ship provided a few changes were incorporated.

Malabar XII is 46 feet 8 inches overall, 34 feet 3 inches on the water, 12 feet beam and 6 feet 9 inches draft. She carries 12,000 pounds of iron ballast in the keel and approximately 3,000 pounds of ballast inside. Her sail area is 1,043 square feet in jib, staysail, main and mizzen. For auxiliary power she has a Gray 4:52, with reduction gear. The designer's requirements were that she should be capable of cruising in comfort in such waters as the West Indies and Caribbean, give a good account of herself in the Bermuda run and be adaptable for early spring and late fall cruising in New England waters. She has turned out to be an able boat for such use.

The low deckhouse with its two berths has proved itself extremely comfortable in service, and its use allows room for water tanks with 150 gallons capacity. The high freeboard made the decks dry and did not interfere with speed, for she has been fast in both light and heavy weather. *Malabar XII* is perfectly balanced under staysail, main and mizzen, and also when a large jib-topsail or genoa jib is set.

The changes Mr. Alden would make if he planned to set out on a world cruise are as follows:

Increase the beam from 12 feet to 13 feet. This will interfere only slightly with speed, and gives better accommodations below, more deck room and, above all, more initial stability. She will be a more livable boat at sea, and she'll sail at much less angle of heel.

Increase the water capacity by another 100 gallons, making a total of 250 gallons, and provide ample baffle plates.

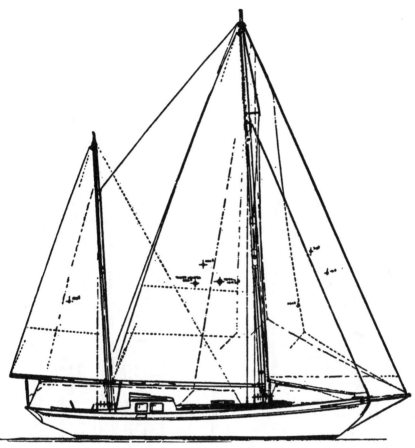

One of the famous Malabars.

Remove the large glass windows from the deckhouse and substitute smaller ports to provide against the eventuality of breakage.

Lengthen the bridge deck at the forward end of the cockpit by about 2 feet. This will make the well smaller, so that if filled by a sea it would not offer the danger of a bigger volume of water, and at the same time gives room for additional stowage space below.

Move the galley to the present location of the stateroom, amidships on the starboard side, and turn the present galley into a stateroom. For cooking in rough weather at sea the aft galley is much better from the standpoint of motion. It could be left open and made part of the cabin, so that on long voyages the space below would not seem cramped.

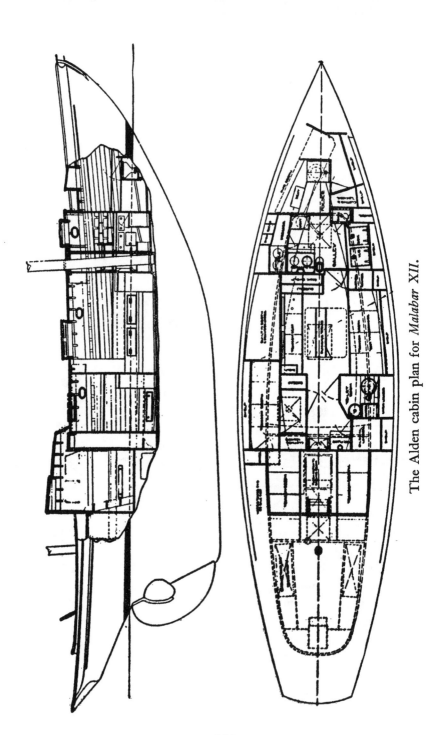

The Alden cabin plan for *Malabar XII.*

It is worth noting that Mr. Alden would not alter the sail plan or the rig. He feels, as do many others, that the ketch offers many advantages for ocean cruising. He would also hold to the marconi rig. The only suggestion that we would offer, and we do so in the full knowledge that it comes from the warm security of an office chair, is that more freeing ports be provided. The ship has a moderately high rail, and it's a good idea to get rid of a deck load of water as soon as possible.

MARCO POLO, 55 FT. WHALE BOAT

Designed by L. FRANCIS HERRESHOFF

JANUARY, 1945

MARCO POLO, a Venetian of about the year 1300, was one of the first great travelers who wrote up his adventures and told marvelous stories of foreign lands. Apparently one of the great secrets of his success was that he could travel light and could adapt himself to all conditions. Comfort and show were not the main objects of his life, but to get onward and visit strange places was more to be desired. So, like its namesake, this *Marco Polo* is planned to travel efficiently. It would have been easier perhaps to draw some wallowing tub with easy motion to lay at sea like a painted ship upon a painted ocean, with fuel gone and food and water rationed, a thousand miles ahead before next station.

The *Marco Polo* is designed mostly for driving under power and is shaped to accommodate a great variety of power plants, either single, twin or triple screw. Her length, fifty-five feet, may scare some people, but the cost of a boat or vessel is nearly in proportion to her weight. Length is only one of the four factors which influence weight, or displacement; the other three are width, depth and shape. The fact is, a long lean boat is easier to build than a short one of the same weight with full lines.

The principal objects tried for in the design are:

1. A very long cruising radius under power.
2. A sail plan that can be handled by one man on watch.
3. Extreme seaworthiness (the whale boat model).
4. Shallow draft which not only will allow her to visit out of the ordinary places but often will avert serious disasters.
5. She is cut away aft so that she will lay-to a sea anchor with her head well into the wind, and a balanced rudder designed to swing all the way around.
6. Her wind resistance is cut to the minimum for laying at anchor in strong winds and to drive economically under power.

234

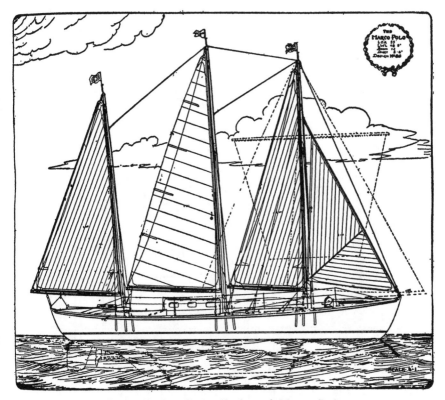

The easily handled sail plan of *Marco Polo*.

7. Her construction is simplified for economy in building as much as is compatible with strength.

8. She is arranged to sleep either four or five people, and planned to be run with one man on watch so that the watches can be four hours on and eight off. This allows a cruise to be a pleasure, but when one is not sure of eight hours' unbroken sleep the cruise is only hard work and drudgery. Few yachts have large enough hulls and small enough sails to allow this combination.

Three masts are adopted so great shifts in center of sail plan can be made. In running in heavy weather the sail can be way forward and prevent broaching-to; in laying-to the storm mizzen can be well aft (where it should be). The foremast and mizzen are very strong for heavy weather and set up-and-down-cut sails, while the mainsail is a crosscut sail on a lighter spar and easily and quickly taken in,

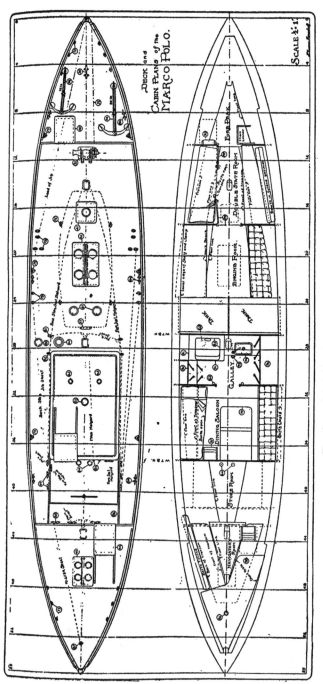

Deck and cabin plan of *Marco Polo.*

236

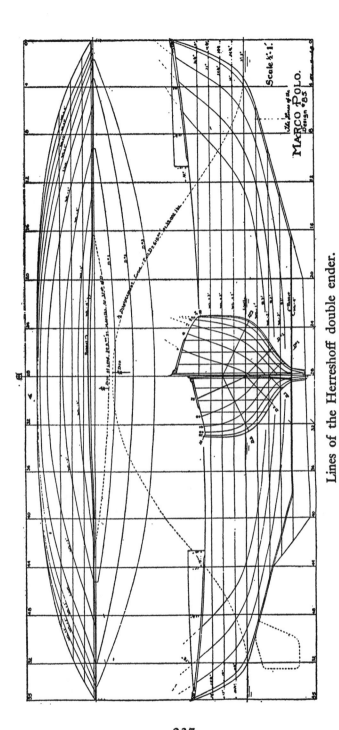

Lines of the Herreshoff double ender.

237

Her spars and rigging are according to the latest scientific racing practice, but much heavier and stronger. All unnecessary top hamper is done away with to reduce chafe and wind resistance. The booms are rigged with strong forward guys to prevent them from slatting around or gybing.

On this long narrow hull three masts are almost necessary if each sail is to be a high narrow airfoil. Three masts also almost entirely do away with the necessity of reefing, for one or more of her several sails can be taken in to accomplish the desired reduction of area, so that, although reefs are shown on the sail plan, they seldom would be used, thus there will be no necessity of considering roller reefing gear—that contrivance which is never entirely satisfactory and adds to expense.

In light weather with a beam wind she sets a large balloon jib forward on a removable boom or nose pole, which is shown in dotted lines together with a light weather overlapping foresail which goes on the fore boom and has a club sheet.

The small sail plans show various combinations of sails, but in running in heavy weather there is a bifurcated trisail hoisted on a track on the fore side of the foremast and set like small heavy twin spinnakers, and it is believed she will be partly self steering with this rig in heavy weather.

All of the working sails are hoisted or lowered from the cockpit and have downhauls so that in a squall at night the man at the helm need not leave the cockpit. However she is rigged with good life rails should he venture out for some other reason. She has no gunwales or bulwarks, for these only hold seas on board while the waist high life rails will hold a person on board and let the seas pass from under.

One of the features of the design is to have a place to carry a really serviceable tender, which few vessels of this displacement can do, but my experience is that an easily rowed, light tender adds to the pleasure of a cruise very greatly.   L.F.H.

AN 80 FT. WORLD CRUISER

Designed by EDSON B. SCHOCK

MARCH, 1941

COMPLYING with the request for the design of a yacht suitable for a cruise around the world I would suggest for your consideration the advisability of an auxiliary ketch of the approximate dimensions of 80 feet overall by 61 feet on the waterline, 19½ feet beam and 11 feet draft, either gaff or jib-headed rig as you would prefer. I would suggest a gaff rig as most of the trip, from New York, through the Canal and south and west across the Pacific would be largely off the wind. A square sail might be of some advantage under certain conditions while a balloon jib would prove to be of very great benefit.

The accommodations for your party of three should require two staterooms, one double and one single, and in addition it would be advisable to have an extra stateroom for your captain and also radio operator should you consider it necessary to carry one.

The crew's quarters should have accommodations for three.

The sail area would be about 2,800 square feet in the working sails, and the auxiliary power a 100 hp. diesel engine with 650 gallons of fuel oil and 1,200 gallons of water.

The lighting would be by D.C. current from a diesel generator and batteries which would also supply current for electric refrigerator and anchor windlass.

The general arrangement would consist of a separate engine room aft which would contain the fire fighting equipment in addition to the propelling machinery and auxiliaries.

Forward of the engine room would be a double stateroom having two berths, lockers, bureau and stowage space.

At the foot of the companionway would be located the chart table and oil skin locker, while opposite same a toilet room with shower for both salt and fresh water furnished by electrically driven pumps, together with discharge pump for discharging waste water overboard.

239

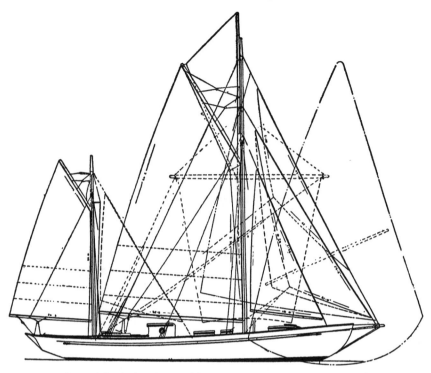

The 8o ft. Schock world cruiser has plenty of sail area.

Forward of the saloon would be located the two staterooms, one of which would be for the captain. The galley would occupy the full width of the yacht and be equipped with large refrigerator, food storage and store space of all kinds. The stove could be either a coal and wood stove or one using bottled gas, in which case it could be so installed as to remain level when the yacht was heeled. This would make it much easier to prepare meals when under way which would be the case practically all the time.

In the design of the hull it would be advantageous to keep the displacement rather light in order that she would ride easily and lift to the seas thereby keeping her out of the class of heavy displacement yachts which are frequently referred to as half tide rocks when they are so heavy that they do not rise readily in a head sea.

The construction, if of wood, would consist of double sawn frames with either yellow pine or Douglas fir planking below water and teak above with teak decks and all upper works of teak.

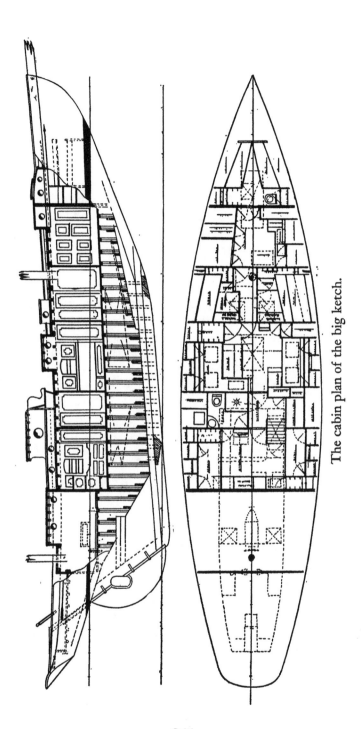

The cabin plan of the big ketch.

Standing rigging to be of stainless steel with bronze turnbuckles and bronze fittings. Life lines would run from bow to stern and boat davits would be of sufficient reach to place boats in their cradles on deck.

Ballast would consist of approximately 30,000 pounds on the keel and about 20,000 pounds inside placed about on a level with the cabin floor so as to ease the rolling thereby making for comfort and less strain on the rigging.

My idea in suggesting a ketch rig is largely due to the fact that the short booms, together with their height above the water eliminate to a great extent the liability of tripping and consequent danger of having a broken boom to contend with when many miles from a repair yard. It also reduces the size of any one sail thereby making for easier handling.

A yacht of this type and size, measuring about fifty tons gross, would make ample room for all and not be too cramped for such an extended cruise. She would prove very seaworthy under all conditions.   E.B.S.

THE CARE AND FEEDING
OF YACHTSMEN

There are books and articles galore on the maintenance and repair of boats. Yet, most of this work is done by fitters and mechanics, despite the much advertised pleasures of doing one's own boatkeeping.

Only the largest yachts, however, boast a full-time cook or doctor, for the feeding and medical care of the ship's company. From THE RUDDER'S *wisdom come these effective articles covering two fields wherein the small boatman must fend for himself.*

Frd. S. Cozzens

COOKING FOR FUN AFLOAT

by CHARLES H. BAKER, JR.

FEBRUARY AND MARCH, 1938

Mr. Baker's gustatory gilhickies really taste as good as they sound. What M. Escoffier's directions are to the landbound kitchen, Bake's Cordon Bleu Pierre recipes are to the galley afloat.

BEFORE any salt-encrusted readers bound on deck and say that this subject has already been done in books and that cooking at sea is never any fun anyway, let me hasten to explain.

Now we've sailed some quarter million miles in ships, larger and smaller, and have seen our share of stove-side police. No one knows better than ourselves that thankless lot of any Galley Slave. He rates every aid and comfort. His life is just one round of damns, dishes, and duckings. He scarcely gets the evening meal cleared up and snugs himself down for a snooze when the midnight watch barges off to drip slickers in his slumbering face and command hot coffee—or else. Hardly is this cross borne, and once more parallel with the keel, when the four o'clock watch stamps below like a brace of fiends to drip more icy slickers down his pants and growl things about hot soup. Barely can the poor Slave doze again before it is full day and the whole condemned ship's company arises to a man and screams for ham, eggs, hot cakes, coffee—and the entire vicious parade marches on again. Combined with such minor addenda as scalds, burns, broken shins and toes, the whole business is a sort of marine mayhem without benefit either of clergy or court.

But we somehow feel that all yacht cookery isn't done crossing tide rips in a fifty-mile dusting. We don't tabulate figures showing hardtack pemmican, dried prune, or thyroid tablet consumption for three men, a girl, and goat, on a two-year jaunt through the South Seas. We do, however, list a few kinks proven in practice.

244

So here's a hot grog to all fellow Galley Slaves, at least they know there's one friend out on that great big bunch of salt water who sympathizes with their wretched lot. So good chance!

TOMATO JUICE MORNING STIFFENER, *à la Marmion*

A brain child of our own while stormbound back of Old Point Comfort for four days with a seventy-mile gale outside. . . . One-half clam juice and one-half tomato juice is better still, and is guaranteed to make the cabin boy slap an admiral's face. *Serve really cold or not at all.* Enough for three.

3 cups canned tomato juice	Quarter clove garlic, crushed
2 teaspoons scraped onion pulp	1 teaspoon celery salt
2 teaspoons Worcestershire	2 dashes Angostura bitters
1 tablespoon lime or lemon	2 teaspoons grated horse-radish
1 teaspoon sugar	1 good dash Tabasco

Rub through fine sieve and discard by-products, of course. Put in shaker with plenty ice and shake plenty hard. Serve pronto.

HARLEM BISCUITS, OR MUFFINS

Christened not from geographical hail port but due to delicate mulatto color. They may have laughed when we went to the Shipmate, but here's one prescription for seagoing popularity. . . . Just add enough sifted cocoa to biscuit or muffin dough to tinge lusciously. Brown.

DEVILED VIRGINIA HAM BISCUITS

We've always preferred Underwood's right from our first boyhood sail in a Kirk Munroe canoe out to Alligator Reef Light of Upper Matecumbe Key, aged twelve. . . . Roll out biscuit dough ¼-inch thick, cut to size, spread one round with deviled Virginia—or other—ham; clap on other round. Brown in hot oven around 400°. Grand with salads and lunches generally.

WAFFLE THOUGHTS AND FANCYINGS

Once the average cook pours batter in iron the mind has left the body. Let's try and be a little original with this grand dish. Serve jams or orange marmalade instead of the eternal near-maple syrup. Much neater in a seaway. Grate a little orange or lemon peel in the batter; donate a couple of extra eggs for quality; a little grated nutmeg in batter is also good. Really crisp them.

JIFFY COFFEE

This is an old camping trick we learned in British Columbia, and especially helpful to Galley Slaves. . . . Allow *heaping* tablespoon fresh coffee to each cup water. Drip through twice. Never let the made coffee boil. Strain through two thicknesses of cloth, seal in mason jar with airtight ring. Put by ice. Presto—in four hours clear as crystal, keeps fresh a long time with flavor and aroma undissipated. Just heat as needed, but don't ever boil. Worth its weight in platinum when feeding the offwatch.

THE MARITIME MATTERING OF FRIED PIES

Ever since our first boyhood reading of Kipling's *Captains Courageous* we've envied Harvey and Danny the fried pies they swiped cookie on *We're Here.* Later in practice we found a happy yachting fact: Dried fruits work better for this job than fresh, for the water in the latter literally tries to explode under the intense heat of boiling fat. As a weather-bound cheerer for a grousing crew fried pies can't be beaten. . . . Make a simple piecrust; ready mixed is okeh. Stew up dried apricots, apples, prunes, peaches, or mixed fruits, in a very little water. Cut crust into 6-inch circles. Heap fruit on half this, fold over and pinch tightly with dampened fingers. Prick center with fork tines for vent. Brown in deep fat kettle with wire basket at 370°. Fry only two at a time to keep from overcooling fat. Lift out with pancake turner. Use Crisco or lard, for butter won't stand heat. . . . Marmalade or any jam is grand also. Temperature right when 1-inch cube of white bread browns in precisely one minute.

DRESSING UP THE LOWLY SCRAMBLED EGG

Scrambled eggs show often at sea, for obvious reasons. And without being overly economical here's a way to use up left-overs and change this bruised and battered barnyard fruit into a voluptuous thing out of proportion to origin and effort involved. . . . To pan of lightly beaten eggs add any of the following in amount suitable to larder, pocketbook, or taste:

A little chili sauce. . . . Bits of chopped cooked ham, bacon, kidneys, sweetbreads, cold meat, fowl. . . . A tomato, well-chopped and tossed in frying butter for few moments. . . . A trifle of finely chopped mild onion and green pepper ditto weds well with the thought. . . . Season exotically with: A little Worcestershire and dash Angostura; a pinch or two of marjoram or basil; a dash or two of tabasco. . . . Canned or cooked flakes of *firm* fish—like tuna, salmon, and the like; canned or fresh-chopped shrimp meat, crab, lobster, mushrooms; chopped cooked okra, a canned artichoke bottom, chopped, stuffed, or ripe olives; chopped parsley with a trifle of chopped onion tops. . . . Season with imagination and we have something here!

Words to the Wise on the Preparation of Those Typically Limey Products—Kippers or Bloaters

All too many females, both sound in wind and limb and otherwise serviceable aboard ship, turn up the nose at these grand delicacies—just as they do to sound Holland gin and certain cheeses. One feminine whiff in a seaway can cause a Galley Slave Trunk-Cabin Murder Case worthy of our friend Dashiell (Thin Man) Hammett. . . . To mollify and deceive such tender cases, first squeeze on the juice of a lemon or two limes, then poach—freshen is the word—kippers in a pan half boiling water, half milk of sorts. Ten minutes, drain, and butter-fry lightly as usual. Much of strong taste and odor is thereby voided.

Poor-Boy Meat Sandwich

This is no copy of a Reuben's three-decker, but invented through necessity. The only thing poor about it is the name. . . . Split a 10-inch loaf of crusty French bread down center, slightly scooping out each half. Rub first with a cut garlic clove, paint richly with butter, then load one-half with all the sliced cold or hot cooked tongue, beef, pork, lamb, veal, chicken, or what not it will tote. Paint this succulent mountain with mild mustard, bestrew it with thin lengthwise slices of dill pickle or India relish, crown with four paper thin slices of mild onion. Dust with a slight gift of hand-rubbed dried basil or marjoram, a trace of celery salt, or some walnut pickle is not amiss. Skewer this monumental erection with toothpicks—being careful not to forget the latter in eating enthusiasm as they can puncture the toughest mouth-top—take both hands, brace elbows firmly on cabin table or deck, open wide and munch. Without seeming to be crudely mercenary this is a smart way to note the liability of possible future dental bills in any fiancée, and furthermore indicates a companion piece of cold Bass—or other valid brew. Also strong jaw muscles, and time.

JIFFY BARBECUE SAUCE FOR ALL SORTS OF ROASTED MEATS

This is mighty close to the deep-south Barbecue Sauce we've known from childhood. To a small bottle of decent ketchup add a quarter cup vinegar, two tablespoons mild mustard, one of brown sugar and plenty of black pepper. Simmer up once; ready. The best possible basting for roasts during the last half hour, and marries any proper gravy with compatibility and loving kindness.

WORDS TO THE WISE ON THE IMPERATIVE NECESSITY FOR A HAND PEPPER MILL FOR BLACK PEPPER

No chef worth his weight in celery tops ever uses canned ground pepper. Let's get a dollar wooden hand pepper mill, buy enough for a year in whole peppercorns for fifteen cents, and grind into pots on food as needed. Pepper, like coffee, has a real aroma when fresh. Even has a taste all its own entirely aside from the mere fact of being hot to taste. Indispensable to salads especially.

SMOKED OR SUGAR-CURED HAM STEAK AND APRICOTS

This originated on a Bimini cruise to fish with Ernest Hemingway on his good ship *Pilar* in 1936.

Slice ham at least 1 inch thick, stand for a while in water, or poach ten minutes to freshen. Brush with any good cooking fat. Make a paste of the following: ⅛ teaspoon each ground allspice and clove, one teaspoon hot dry mustard, 2/3 cup brown sugar, enough vinegar to moisten well. Put in greased pan, surround with two cups of soaked apricots and brown in medium oven around 350° for an hour. Baste frequently. Apricot likes ham very well.

WORDS TO THE WISE: ESCHEW RICH CREAM SAUCES, MAYONNAISE, AND SUCH ON ROUGH DAYS

One word of advice from one who has wrestled Ole Davil Gulf Stream too often to be amused: After seeing all sorts and conditions of men and women stricken with *mal de mer*, regardless of race, creed, morals, fortitude, age, or political party—don't start them out with rich pily salads like chicken or potato; greasy or over rich foods.

Jiffy Cocktail Sauce for Shrimps, Oysters, Clams, Crabs, or Lobsters

Here's one just as good as Oscar ever thought up at the old Waldorf. Whip up half a cup evaporated milk, same of ketchup, same chili sauce, juice of large lemon, dash of cayenne or tabasco, salt to taste, and a level tablespoon of scraped mild onion pulp. Some admire a teaspoon or so of walnut pickle—although this mars color, it adds taste. Season hot as can stand. A little grated horse-radish is optional. Chill this really cold; chill glasses, chill food.

An Exotic Cocktail of Lobsters and Gin, or Shrimps Will Do as Well

Don't develop antisaloonleague complexes or accuse us of joking, for it's delicious. We stumbled onto this one in Barranquilla, Colombia, out of Puerto Columbia where Americans voyage in search of emeralds, oil, jaguars, and senoritas—during a jaunt from Guatemala's west coast to Havana. Personally we prefer Holland gin, due to its odd taste, in this sauce. To one cup mayonnaise add a third cup chili sauce, a tablespoon or two of lime or lemon juice, a dash Angostura, two tablespoons thick cream, Worcestershire, tabasco, and salt to taste. Donate one teaspoon of gin per serving. Mix again. Must be chilled well along with cooked lobster or shrimp meat.

Ten-Minute Canned Corn Chowder de Luxe

Too often canned food cookery skips all originality after wrestling with the opener. I defy any Paris chef to complain of this one we worked up while put-putting up the Dismal Swamp Canal recently.

1 can Del Maiz or other canned corn	3 tablespoons butter
3 rasher salt pork, chopped fine	3 potatoes, average, sliced thin
1 medium sized onion, sliced thin	1 pint evaporated milk
2 tablespoons sugar	Salt and cayenne, to taste
Enough flour to thicken	2 cups water

Brown pork gently, and simmer potatoes fairly tender. Drain, mix everything well, reserving a tablespoon of butter. Simmer up once, meanwhile melting reserved butter and flour gently together in small pan. Work smooth with some juice, stir in well. Simmer a minute more, and serve with pilot biscuit.

A Regal Nantucket Chowder of Hardshell Clams—
Quahogs to Us

Everyone knows the watery insult which passes for Boston Clam Chowder from coast to coast. A Rhode Island man will stare down any Cape Cod addict, advocating tomatoes and not cream, and mutter things about his barnacle covered ancestry. We hereby give you our Ace Clam Chowder—the Chowder to End All Chowders. We found it under roof of an outfit who cared about chowders. All we need is a decent spice shelf, the four herbs which no cook can be without, celery seed or celery salt, all the rest is easy. It serves eight.

4 dozen medium sized clams; steamers will do if no hardshells
1 big mild onion, chopped fine
1 teaspoon anchovy paste
1 pint really thick cream
2 tablespoons flour
3 egg yolks
1 dozen whole allspice
Salt and pepper, to taste

Celery seed, 3 teaspoons
½ teaspoon bicarbonate soda
1 quart milk
⅛ pound butter, or more
3 tablespoons fine chopped parsley
½ teaspoon mace
Thick bottomed kettle; or double boiler

2 good pinches each of following herbs rubbed fine between palms: Thyme, marjoram, summer savory; two bay leaves

Don't risk lacerated hands; open by steaming *briefly* to loosen shells. Put clams through coarse blade of food chopper, save all juices. Put in double boiler with herbs, spices, celery seed, onion. Cover with quart and half of water. Cook an hour, timing from time lower pot boils. Put through sieve. Let settle once, discarding final gritty residue. Turn back into clean double boiler top again, add soda. Heat milk and cream separately, and stir in clams well. Melt out butter and work flour smooth, *but never brown*. Add some broth and stir into pot. A jigger of sherry or white wine is optional and commendable right here. Beat egg yolk lightly and stir in at last minute. Serve and sprinkle parsley on each plate . . . Send for us!

Night Watch Hurry-Up Chowder

Here is our one concession to haste and need—and why is it that everything bad has to happen in freezing rain squalls at 2:10 a.m.? . . . Once, when we needed something good and hot and quick Eric Devine

—the best Galley Slave we've ever shipped with—whipped up this accidental masterpiece.

1 can vegetable soup	Cayenne and Worcestershire, plenty
1 soup can boiling water	heated pilot biscuit for all hands
Handful stale bread	
1 can clams in their juice	

Haggle off can tops, mix, heat hot, eat. Work bread in soup. Dunk with pilot biscuit first heated on top of stove. A bay leaf and two or three pinches of the usual herbs would make this still better—bay leaf discarded when serving.

A Superb Stuffing for Baking Fish Such as: Bluefish, Cods, Haddocks, Bass, or Snappers

Besides the two imperative rules of having butter sizzling in baking pan before fish goes in oven, and basting frequently—it is the stuffing which can make or break the chef's reputation. This is well-tested, sure.

2 cups bread crumbs, or more to suit fish	Enough milk to moisten *slightly*
	½ teaspoon sage
2 crushed bay leaves	1 teaspoon summer savory
1 medium onion, chopped fine	1 tablespoon vermouth
Salt and lots of hand-ground black pepper	4 tablespoons melted butter

Stuffing must be fairly dry and of character, not soggy-wet. Mix stuffing in bowl, testing by taste to check force of pepper. Stuff fish previously wiped off with damp cloth; sew up. Brown in hot oven around 400°, baste often. Allow about twelve minutes per pound. A covered roaster is best, uncover for last few minutes to brown. A dry baked fish is like a tweaky spinster—friends seldom return for further acquaintance . . . Lemon or lime juice brushed over fish is always excellent. Use at least half tablespoon butter per pound of fish for basting in pan.

Words to the Wise on the Tradition of Serving Pilot Biscuit with Soups, Stews, and Similar Fodder, Afloat

The landlubber who serves regular soup crackers on a yacht would probably tie a granny knot in his dinghy painter, and frostbite his bride to a portside ladder, or throw his garbage to windward across a commodore's epaulets . . . One of our biggest biscuit outfits at last makes them up in handy packages. They keep well in damp weather, but unless just opened, benefit from a moment in an oven or in a pan on top of stove burner.

Oyster Pan Roast, à la Marmion

One November it was blowing great guns off the Virginia Capes and we lay in Norfolk for a couple of days—and Norfolk to us always means Smithfield peanut-fed, smoked hams, and oysters. Eric Devine got the proceeds of a bushel, donated the overflow to all the assembled yachts in harbor, and we ate oysters in divers ways—of which this was one of the best. First comes the sauce:

For each serving of one dozen oysters allow the following: Juice of a lemon, two rashers of smoked pork—browned crisp beforehand—a teaspoon of scraped onion pulp, two dashes of tabasco, a teaspoon chopped parsley, half teaspoon Worcestershire, three tablespoons butter, and salt and pepper to taste . . . Pork should be minced very fine, mix everything and bring to simmer . . . Meantime simmer oysters in own liquor until *barely starting* to curl on edges. Pour on sauce and simmer up until you count twenty—slowly—dashes of paprika top it off, and have we a bottle of chilled Chablis, Rhine, or Moselle handy? . . . Personally we've later found that a tablespoon of sherry in with the sauce adds a touch not to be ignored.

Down in Florida where the coral reef water is that haunting blue green which no man can describe, fish—big and small—really do strike baits. Shellfish and crustacea haunt shallows and rocky holes. All sorts of important and rare food bits are constantly being tossed into the yachtsman's ice box, consumption of which back north not only would amputate sizable chunks out of his bank balance but put him in that rarified class affording forty foot starboard launches and the fifteen dollar check-for-two. Yet all through the Florida Keys, Bahamas, and West Indian waters generally, such things as pompano, guava paste, avocadoes, red snapper, seedless Persian limes, coconuts, green turtles, and stone—or Morro crabs—are matters of daily occurrence.

The Vital Matter of Those Armor-Plated Reptila—Turtles to Us—Clear Green Turtle Soup, Royal Bahama Style

This was added to our list cruising to Bimini and Cat Cay, and whipped up by Jim Aranha, the best chef in all Alice-Town. Six cups:

Green turtle, meat and bones, 3 lbs.
Salt pork, 2 tbsp., diced fine
Butter, 2 tbsp.
Calipee, yellow fat of turtle from
    lower shell, 1 piece for garnish
Fine sieve

Water, 2½ qts.
Onion, 1 small, chopped
Lime, juice 1, average size
Tart white wine, or sherry, ¼ cup
Salt and hand-ground black pepper,
    to taste

Thyme, basil, 2 pinches each; 4 bay leaves tied with string

Cut up meat and simmer in slightly salted water for three hours, or long enough to make a really strong, tasty broth. Add all seasonings, butter, pork. Simmer slowly two hours longer and put through fine sieve. Add lime juice, wine. Add tablespoon diced calipee for each serving, and simmer fifteen minutes in clear soup. A thin slice of lime goes into each cup . . . Now uncork your finest dry white wine!

Words to the Wise on the Menace of Too-Early Salting of Stews and Soups Which Are to Be Reduced by Boiling

Let's not be hoist by our own spinnaker booms through believing that salt, like water, vanishes in steam. No, all salt stays in the dish, so save the salting until soup is nearly done. Same for stews.

Turtle Stew-Soup, Key West Style

We picked this up cruising the Marquesas west of Key West last July, fly-fishing for, *and catching*, tarpon.

Scald meat to remove skin, using knife. Put enough cut up meat in kettle to suit, add half pound diced salt pork lightly fried out with a couple of big diced onions, three quartered tomatoes, a couple of sprigs each of basil and thyme; four bay leaves. Smother until lightly browned, cover with cold water and simmer until meat is good and tender. Usual practice requires another big onion and two sliced tomatoes be fried out with another rasher of pork, and when tender add. Season highly with salt, hand-ground black pepper, half a teaspoon powdered mace . . . Cut up some of the *calipash*—green fat from upper shell—into ½ inch cubes. Add to stew, turn in a quarter cup sherry. Simmer gently for fifteen minutes longer; discard bay leaves and serve.

Bahama Island Whelk—or "Wilk"—Stew-Soup

Ernest Hemingway once said "Whelks are strong fodder, but they can save life," which is one reason we list this recipe—should some yachtsman find himself marooned with the larder low. Whelks—called "wilks" by the natives—are huge salt water snails found clinging to tide rocks on many of the Bahama Islands. They are not strong if prepared correctly. This is a tested recipe.

Whelks, 2 doz., per size   Onion, 1 big one
Salt pork, ¼ lb.   Black pepper, and salt, to taste
Thyme, 1 teaspoon   Worcestershire, ditto
Bay leaves, 3 or 4   Tomatoes, optional; canned okeh

Put into boiling water, shell and all. After a few minutes drain; tap shell until Mr. Whelk falls out. *Cut out sand bag;* cut body from tail. Body is white meat—tails are green or yellow. Pound separately in canvas bag or with maul, until tender. Parboil separately for ten minutes and discard water . . . Now cover white meat with three or four quarts water —*cold* please—add herbs; simmer until tender. Fry out pork and tails; when tender turn into stew and simmer ten minutes longer. Discard bay leaf; add a little sherry if in the medicine chest.

Words to the Wise on Building a Real Shore-Side Cooking Fire with Wet Wood or Non-Existent

Simply take a tomato or other empty can; half fill with water and pour half an inch of gasoline on top. Draw the schnozzle out of range and toss in a match—and there we are. Being unenclosed it is as safe as one of Old Aunt Sephronia Fittich's bayberry candles. Add another dose of gas when burns out; relight. A right hot fire right now, and won't easily blow out. Try it when driftwood is coy.

West Indian Conch Chowder—the Very Finest Soup of Them All

This, gentlemen, is the Number 1 Chowder of the world—and our brief experience covers that seafood catchall—Bouillabaisse at Pascal's in Marseilles, odd and chancey brews with fish cooked and apparently raw along the China Coast from Saigon to Chingwangtao at the gateway to Peking; Swan's Island, Maine, Newport, Cape Cod, and Gloucester clam chowders; shrimp and crab gumbos in Charleston, Sea Island, and New Orleans . . . Conch chowder has what the others lack. It delights the taste buds, stiffens spines, renews the outlook of faltering manhood, enables the weary chance-ridden skipper to face life and its varying challenges with outlook refreshed, battery charged and undismayed.

Europe grants America few food superiorities: Stone or Morro crabs, our oysters, Virginia ham, canvasback duck, dried beef, sweet potatoes, and New Orleans gumbos; red snapper, pompano, and wild rice. Ten dollars tells a plugged centime that if any Paris chef met a Florida Keys or Bahama conch eye to eye, cooked, and tasted it, he'd have them flown Pan-American Airways to Paris in dry ice. Conches lead clean lives in clear water, have dazzling white, sweet meat in abundance; their shells are heavenly pink affairs. . . . To get one out of shell with no native to help: Take the boat's hatchet, don gloves and with near corner chop out the groove at very back end of shell spiral where it meets the point. There the tail crook-end hangs on. Once detached, out drops your conch. Trim off all yellow portions and claw—which is the animal's foot. Use the tough yellow part for reef fishing bait—than which there is none better as it is tough as rubber and hangs on the hook regardless. For eight:

Conch white meat, 1 doz.	Tomatoes, 3 or 4 average
Salt pork, 1/3 cup, minced	Onions, 2 large, minced
Lime, juice 2; or lemon, juice 1	Thyme, 1 tsp.; 4 bay leaves
Potato, 4 cups diced small	Sherry, ¼ cup; *added at last*
Garlic, 1 clove, crushed well	Salt and black pepper, to taste

Pound conches with potato masher, mallet, or back of heavy knife; mince into 1 inch square. Fry out pork until light brown. Take heavy iron chowder kettle and build as follows: Pork grease, conch, onion, tomatoes, seasoning; then repeat, and repeat again; cover with water. Tie bay leaves with string and toss in. String enables to catch and discard later. Cover with hot water. Simmer slowly until conch meat is tender— about two hours, then add potato. Be sure to stir frequently to keep from sticking to kettle bottom; and simmer *slowly*. Potatoes will be done in twenty minutes or so; stir in sherry, discard bay leaves. Pilot biscuit "floaters" are Captain's orders. Key West style: omit tomatoes entirely, add three cups of rich milk—evaporated or fresh.

Words to the Wise: Conch Bouillon Is Not to Be Ignored

Ten minutes parboiling of chowder conch meat in slightly salted water makes a broth which is to the stoutest quahog brew as a composite of Madame du Barry, Mae West, and Gypsy Rose Lee, would be to Elsie Dinsmore . . . Mix half and half with tomato juice, season with 1 tsp. onion pulp (scraped) per serving, celery salt, lime juice, and Worcestershire—to taste; shake with ice or chill well. It'll make the Swiss navy tackle the whole British fleet!

CHARLEY FROW'S BISCAYNE BAY YACHT CLUB CHOWDER
PARTY FISH CHOWDER

The formula originated in great secrecy years ago. Several claim to be
the parent; however, we take authority from Charley who has cooked it
for 400 guests for the last several years.

Ingredients	For Six	For One Hundred
Firm white fish, boned	2 lbs.	35 lbs.
Potatoes, diced small	2 lbs.	35 lbs.
Onions, diced small	¼ lb.	5 lbs.
Green sweet pepper	1 pepper, diced	16 peppers, diced
Tomato soup or juice	4 tbsp.	3 10 oz. cans
Butter	2 tbsp.	1¼ to 1½ lbs.
Evaporated milk	1 tall can	16 tall cans
Seasoning	To taste	To taste
Tabasco	3 dashes	About 1¼ tsp., to taste

Dice salt pork to ¼ inch cubes, and fry brown. Add 1 pint *boiling*
water for six; 2 gallons for hundred. Simmer for an hour. Add peppers
and onions; simmer 10 minutes . . . Add ¼ inch diced potatoes; simmer
5 minutes then add fish and everything else—fish cut into pieces 1x1½x½
inches thick. When all is tender draw off fire, and only then add butter
and milk. Stir gently always so as not to break up fish. And keep adding
just enough water to cover, as it boils away. Last year Charley added
chili powder—about ½ tsp. per six people, with good results. Herbs could
be bay leaves—allowing 2 per six portions. Sherry also, 1 tbsp. per six . . .
Fish used: grouper. Personally we rate fish as follows: 1st Jewfish of 50
lbs. or less, grouper, rock hind, gray or mangrove snapper, Lane snapper
—any white, firm fleshed fish, and there's a tongue twister. All are easily
caught in these waters.

HOW TO PREPARE STEAKS OF TUNAS, KINGFISHES, WAHOOS, AND
OTHER LARGE AND LUSTY PISCATORIAL ENEMIES OF
MAN, BOAT, AND TACKLE

Down in Gulf Stream and reef waters all former ideas of fish cookery
need revision. Sometimes, with fresh grub low, the little ones just don't
bite or we don't bother to fish for them. A chicken tuna steak, wahoo, or
any of the big mackerels is prime food—yet the very sight of the culinary
problem in one of these monsters has caused suicidal tendencies among
many sea cooks! We finally adapted a famous century-old Basque dish

snapped in Spain in 1931, which is also very similar to the Marseilles Frenchman's version. Garlic makes the dish. Olive oil is essential. Big fish should be braised.

Cut into 1½ inch thick steaks. Put in deep dish and marinate in lots of the following: 1 part lime juice (or lemon) to 1 part olive oil; or same using tarragon vinegar. Into this toss a garlic clove crushed in a bit of the fluid, a pair of bay leaves crushed between palms, a handful of parsley, chopped (if there is parsley); 2 teaspoons thyme, also crushed. Toss together, and stand for an hour—letting the comparatively tough meats acquire discretion and merit. Next heat a cup of olive oil in our biggest iron skillet, and while getting hot slice a huge mild onion (red best) thinly on bias, another crushed small garlic clove, and three average tomatoes with skins scalded off, quartered . . . Now turn in a can of beef bouillon, ½ cup common white wine, season highly with salt and hand-ground black pepper. Discard lime juice. Cover and simmer slowly for an hour. Remove fish steak with pancake turner and put on hot dish. Rub sauce through sieve, discard debris and pour sauce over fish. A few chopped capers add final touch. *Voilà!*

SIMPLE BROILING SPREAD FOR FISH STEAKS OF ALL KINDS— INCLUDING OUR NORTHERN SWORDFISH

Let's depart from the usual and create something really tasty—with not one bit more effort than ordinarily required. In the first place every fish that swims—especially all the mackerel tribe—benefit from an hour or more marinating in a little mildly salted lime juice. The one great enemy of all broiled fish is dryness—butter won't stand the intense heat, so *always use olive oil when first searing, nothing else,* if possible. A little garlic rubbed on the fish steak—both sides—then dicarded—does not add breath trouble, and tunes up the ensemble as nothing else does. If garlic objectors are aboard—and God help us—use scraped onion pulp instead.

Score all *large* filets or steaks—3 inches apart—to let heat penetrate. Broil all mackerel filets flesh side only. Sear first both sides, then spread with any of the following and cook more slowly:

Devling butter: Cream two tbsp. butter with one tsp. dry hot mustard, and a few drops Worcestershire. Spread thin after first searing—later using lime juice marinade and then brushing with olive oil. Try the same using anchovy paste instead of mustard. Season with tabasco. Try a dash Angostura. A touch of onion and garlic is really essential. Spread with: one tsp. dry mustard, one tsp. Worcestershire, two tbsp. ketchup or chili sauce, one tbsp. melted butter, one tsp. onion pulp.

The Same Goes for Broiled Crawfish—Spiny or Rock Lobster to the Northener

Big crawfish—like all big lobster—should be parboiled five minutes or so—starting in *COLD* sea (or salted fresh) water. Split, brush with lime or lemon juice, then olive oil; sear, then spread with above sauce and finish broil. Herbs, walnut ketchup, all add nice touches.

Two Fish Sauces of Proven Quality

One from Fort de France, Martinique: Rub six sardines through sieve —small sardines—cream with four tablespoons butter, juice three limes, a teaspoon of fine chopped parsley, a teaspoon scraped onion pulp. Brush over fish when it comes sizzling from broiler or bake pan.

A *Piquante* sauce for baked fish. Add a little water to basting in pan, which last should contain plenty of butter from start. Add a little finely minced spring onion top, a big pinch basil rubbed between palms. Reduce this in small pan, add two teaspoons mild French mustard, two cups cream sauce, a dozen chopped capers. Simmer all up together once, and pour over fish.

Cream Sauce: The universal Foundation White Sauce of the World— two tbsp. butter, two tbsp. flour; one cup cream for fancies, milk for usuals. Salt and cayenne to taste—about ¼ tsp. salt does it . . . Melt butter in *clean* enameled pan or saucepan, work in flour. *Do not brown.* Add warmed milk or cream a little at a time, working out all lumps. Season, simmer once, then rub through fine sieve. That's it.

Words to the Wise on the Utter Fallacy of Plunging Lobsters, Crawfish, Langoustes, Langostas, Prawns, Ecrevisses, or Any Crustacea into Boiling Water

If you believe that a snake's tail doesn't stop wiggling until sundown and toads give warts, skip this advice. Boiling water makes any flesh tough —from sea or land. Start the process with *cold* sea water—or *cold* salted fresh water. Put in the varmint, fetch to a boil. He goes bye-bye just as though he'd been put under an ether cone—and can't feel anyway. Result: tender flesh. We've seen many a big lobster made tougher than rubber by the boiling plunge. It takes no longer and the brute is done almost when boiling starts.

Baked Trunk Fish, à la Ernest Hemingway

Ernest rates this among the best four of all sea fishes. There are two species: Called generically "Box Fish" or "Trunk" Fish; the other sometimes called "Cow" Fish have tiny horns over eyes. They frequent rocky holes in flats or reefs, and when tide is low may be taken with small drag seines, cast nets now and then, or with the tiniest possible hook. Have no scales, the body being armor plated with sections of thin bone . . . Dish may be varied through imagination and daring—with the whole herb and seasoning shelf like stops on a Wurlitzer organ: The tiniest touch of garlic pulp, a moistening of white wine or sherry, a pinch of herbs, what not . . . Open fish from vent to chest, draw, wash out. Fill with fairly dry bread stuffing seasoned to taste, mood, and larder. Bake in moderate oven until shell opens at joints and starts to peel. Peel shell and slice. The sauce is up to the chef. This gourmet's delight rates the finest chilled white wine we can find—and Montrachet is best, with a Rhine like—well, buy the best the region affords. Or Moselle; or Chablis. We give you a toast: "Here's to the girl who eats rye bread!"

Chicken Tropical or Tahiti Chicken Baked in Ripe Coconuts

Two winters back we wound up a jaunt into the back-country of Colombia with a gourmet's tour of Barranquilla—an incredible town born of oil and emeralds, where ancient buildings rub shoulders with smart American villas.

Cracking the coconuts is the tough part. Proceed as follows:

Husk mature, but not dry, coconuts. Drill out two "eyes" with sharp knife point, and aim the first one toward enemies or you'll take your own picture with a vicious squirt. Put on stone or hard board and tap hard with hammer near eye end. A crack, once started, will run almost symmetrically around diameter—making a lid. Never try to saw off, as we read once in a famous magazine. *That's* a chore, for who's going to hold the coconut from spinning, we found? Cut out some of the kernel, trim off brown part, and reserve with lids. Now get:

Fowl of tender years, masculine, feminine, or neuter, 1 plump one	Sweet green pepper, 1 small
Onion, 1 medium, diced fine	Canned chicken broth, 1 can
Evaporated milk, 1 can	Enriched coconut milk, 1 cup
Butter, 2½ to 3 tbsp.	Del Maiz canned corn, 1 cup
	Bay leaf, 1 broken
	Seasoning, to taste

Fresh broth may also be made by simmering chicken rack and bones in enough lightly salted water to cover. Cut up meat into small pieces, cover with broth, and enriched coconut milk made as follows: Grate kernel into small pan, add cup coconut water, simmer gently five minutes. Pour through cloth, and wring out coconut cream from grated kernel with vigorous twist. Put in all ingredients except cooked corn and simmer gently until chicken is nearly tender. Ladle into large half of shells, tie cap on with string or circle of copper wire, bake in hot oven, standing shells in ½ inch water. Half an hour does the job. Personally we prefer to omit the corn, and donate a teaspoon of sherry to each shell—stirred in when served.

I'A OTA—TAHITI'S OWN FISH SALAD ADAPTED TO THE GULF STREAM; FROM CHARLES (MUTINY ON THE BOUNTY AND THE HURRICANE) NORDHOFF, TO US, TO YOU

Nordhoff from his Lafayette Escadrille days—down to his fine work with James Hall, needs scant introduction. The dish is universal throughout Polynesia. We quote Nordhoff:

You take a fish of not less than five pounds weight and in the pink of condition, remove the two fillets, and cut them into pieces about one inch square and half an inch thick . . . You then put these in a fairly deep dish to "cook" in citric acid for not less than one hour and a half—enough lime or lemon juice to cover . . . At the end of this time throw all the liquid away and serve fish in one of two manners:

(1) With raw thinly sliced mild onions and French dressing made of salt, hand-ground black pepper, lime juice and olive oil. (Vinegar will also do, but not as well.)

(2) Better still, in a sauce made by grating fresh coconut kernel into part of the coconut milk, and squeezing in a cloth after simmering for five minutes. Skim cream on top before straining the rest. Add to this cream: Salt, white pepper or cayenne, thinly sliced raw onion, and a bit of garlic if you like.

The fish is anything but raw for it is *completely cooked* in the citric acid. I think you and your friends would pronounce this dish a most delicious variety of hors d'oeuvre, and it is widely known and appreciated in the South Seas as a specific for the man who has looked too long upon the flowing bowl the night before.

KEY WEST "OLD LIME SOUR"

This is a universal condiment used throughout the Keys for flavoring salads, dressing various kinds of cooked fish, crawfish, and so on. A little adds a very strange and convincing touch to any salad dressing, and it is absolutely necessary to any proper Conch Salad—or as the natives call it, "Conch Souse." Making is simple: Put two cups of freshly strained lime juice in a bottle. Add three level teaspoons of salt. Stand in a moderately warm corner of the kitchen and when it has stopped "working," cork and keep in cool place. Use any time. Try on cold crab, crawfish, lobster, added to *lime juice* French dressing.

Conch Salad, More Properly Called "Conch Souse"

Here is a sun-rise spine-stiffener par excellence; for morning-after blues it stands second to none. As we have already inferred, conches are to the lowly clam what the *Normandie* would be to the first Robert Fulton steam packet! This proportion serves six, and is a modified recipe of souse we have eaten several times on *Pilar* when off for Stream fishing.

Wash six conches, trim out white meat, pound tougher portions lightly, and mince very fine. Mince the following vegetables as fine as is practical: Three large mild onions, three tomatoes, two green peppers, vinegar (tarragon best) ¼ cup, lime or lemon juice (lime best) ¾ cup, six tablespoons olive oil, dash or two tabasco, two teaspoons Old Lime Sour—see above—and season to taste with salt, hand-ground black pepper, and two tablespoons Worcestershire . . . Mix well and set to chill at least an hour before serving; two or three hours is better, as that marinates flavor in. We add two pinches thyme to our Souse, and rub two bay leaves between palms also, just for luck.

A POT TO COOK IN

by ROBERT NEILSON

SEPTEMBER, 1944

For those who are not inspired to wrestle with the compli-
cated tit bits of Mr. Baker, this basic cruising cookery of Mr.
Neilson offers an efficient and satisfying solution, contribut-
ing to mental composure and physical ease.

AFTER a lifetime at sea with and without indigestion, my own
opinion on the matter is that the best solution is found in a com-
promise between two extremes. While no man should starve and
languish at sea, neither should he set sail with the idea of indulging in
one long continual gastronomical debauch. Unfortunately there will
inevitably and always be some element of doubt in the understanding
of just what is or is not over and under eating.

Thus, to illustrate the point more clearly and to get out of this
haze of theory and conjecture, let us take up a few practical tried
and proven menus with a discussion of their merits from any and
all angles.

First, a good and not unusual breakfast in warm climates and one
that would be hard to beat is as follows:

1. Oranges, grapefruit, papaya, bananas, apples or any fruit available, fresh or canned or dried, eaten from the half-shell or more
   or less *au naturel.*
2. Choice of several cold breakfast cereals with canned milk and
   white or brown sugar.
3. Coffee, toast and marmalade.

On Sundays, or possibly twice a week, the above can be varied
by adding or substituting bacon and eggs, pancakes or cornbread
with bacon, and so forth. All the possible and rather minor variations
of the above menu cannot be gone into here, since conditions and
combinations of supplies on hand, prevailing weather, locale, indi-

262

vidual tastes, etc., all go to form the deciding factors. The important point is that such a breakfast is extremely easy and quick to prepare and, fully as important (at least to the cook and/or dishwasher), it is just as easy and quick to clean and wash up after. And, in spite of the protests of past abnormally distended stomachs, it is more than nourishing enough to maintain a high standard of health and cruising vigor.

In cold weather the only change necessary to the above menu is to substitute a hot cooked cereal or porridge for the cold. Oatmeal, cream of wheat and many others have long been available with the three minute cooking time feature. It is well to make sure you are getting this variety when purchasing supplies, as the long and short cooking varieties of the same brand often come in almost identical looking packages. By using a double boiler the preparation of the quick cooking cereal requires but little time and practically no attention; simply stir the mixture for a minute or so until it comes to a boil and then place over the boiler, where it can be forgotten, within reasonable limits, without danger of scorching. Again double boiler technique makes the pots far easier to wash, since it does not form a hard baked on residue as do pots when put directly over a fire, and it also conveniently provides its own hot washing water from the bottom receptacle. Sea water of course is always used in the lower boiler.

For lunch a husky buxom sandwich is hard to beat as an ideal solution to the main course. In nearly every case it can be so manufactured as to suit individual tastes as well as the state of supplies on hand. Shore bought bread should be available for the first three weeks or more out, and thereafter perfectly satisfactory sandwiches can be made with the large rectangular soda crackers or water biscuits. French bread and hard rolls keep the longest, while whole wheat and raisin bread last but poorly. As a staple and durable filler peanut butter or Kraft's processed cheese in jars are hard to beat, especially when supplemented by canned butter or mayonnaise or both. And there are a few hundred other items that can always be used as a palate tickling variation—numerous varieties of canned meat spreads; tongue, ham and the like; canned tuna, salmon or sardines; a fried egg every now and again; fresh cheese from the last port with mustard; and the list goes on and on.

When long at sea there usually arises within most people a distinct craving for pickles, both sour and sweet; and the sandwich lunch should be fortified accordingly. Olives (stuffed, ripe and natural) also make a pleasant variation and addition. Smoked herring and raw onions are usually appreciated by most crews, either as a main filler or simply as a palate teaser.

As a dessert in warm climates, and also as a sort of substitute for much missed fresh salads, canned fruit (or fresh) is always appetizing. For some reason, probably the tangy tartness, apricots and applesauce usually rank most popular in this field, as do baked apples, packed whole with two or three in a can. The large sweet peaches, although appetizing enough at times ashore, somehow lose their appeal after a long stretch at sea. Fresh fruit can obviously be substituted for the canned variety, in fact it *should* be if there is any danger of its spoiling; the great temptation to use the canned fruit, especially in hot weather, is due as much to the richness and tastiness of the abundant juices as to the fruit proper. With this in mind it is a good idea, when opening a can of fruit at noon, to pour off some of the juice into a glass and set aside until midafternoon or evening, when it will be greatly appreciated in the form of a fruit ade or as an ingredient in some stronger and more fortifying beverage.

For a lunchtime drink coffee, tea, cocoa, soup, vegetable or regular fruit juice or fresh lemonade all fill the bill perfectly, according to the dictates of climate, tastes and prevailing conditions. Even fresh water tastes good a month out.

On Sundays or biweekly a rice pudding or one of the convenient arrowroot base puddings in many flavors can be whipped up as a special morale booster, served hot or cold to suit the temperature. (And incidentally arrowroot in any form is very beneficial to harassed digestions.) Dried fruits, even prunes, all taste good at sea when properly cooked up with spices. Their greatest disadvantage is the relatively large amount of fresh water required in their preparation. This disadvantage however can be reduced to a minimum by the use of a previously recommended Flex Seal cooker which not only conserves fresh water, but fuel, time and energy as well. Also, when cooking dried foods of any kind which require much fuel and water, it is a conserving practice to cook up enough to last for a week or so; such articles keep splendidly and a wide mouthed glass jar should be at hand for just that purpose.

Now for dinner, and taking up three meals all at once like this already makes a cruise appear to be just one long culinary grind, simple as the menus have been. When cruising in the tropics it often happens that the temperature below decks at this time of day flickers well above the 100 degree Fahrenheit mark. In such circumstances the unhappy cook, with sweat rolling into his eyes and streaming off his steaming torso, is very apt to view the prospects of a relatively ornate, piping hot supermeal with a definitely jaundiced eye. Nevertheless shortly after sundown in such climates it often turns distinctly chilly and the crew, especially the watch on deck, appreciate the warm glow of a hot meal under their belts.

The miracle chef at work on a five course dinner.

In such circumstances I eventually hit upon a dinner technique which reduced time, heat and labor to a welcome minimum, yet which at the same time produced a completely satisfactory hot meal. By actual test such a meal on a pressure stove will raise the temperature of the cabin a bare eight degrees and take thirty minutes from start to finish, though for twenty minutes out of the thirty you can follow the example of the heavy cook in the sketch, or if you are the outdoors type you can go on deck and gab for twenty minutes. In other words, there is only about ten minutes of actual labor involved. One burner of the stove and a two gallon pot are all that are required in the way of equipment. And here is a typical pot-dinner menu:

1. Hot soup, with choice of twenty-one flavors.
2. Chicken and noodles, or meat balls with spaghetti and tomato sauce, corned beef hash with boiled egg atop, spaghetti and cheese, or any of a number of similar items which come in cans or sealed jars.
3. Any canned vegetable as desired.
4. Any fresh vegetable that can be cooked in salt water. For example, potatoes, onions, hard shelled squash, carrots, corn on the cob, turnips and green peppers, to mention the most common. (And these will keep in just about the order mentioned.) In the tropics small green papayas can also be boiled and served as a vegetable, tasting like very tender squash.
5. For dessert a couple of bananas (or regular cooking plantains) can be thrown in and eaten as a vegetable if desired, or with brown sugar and milk.

To bring about this miracle dinner simply fill the two gallon pot about half full of sea water and place on a wide open burner; place therein, on their sides if possible, all the cans and jars selected for the meal with their labels removed. If placed on end the boiling will make them rattle like a dozen castanets. On top and in between place the vegetables, and later on the bananas, all with their jackets on. This latter precaution prevents them from absorbing too much salt, and besides they are far easier to peel after boiling. Bring to a boil, cook for twenty minutes, and dinner is ready.

In cases where the fresh vegetables are rather antique, they may have to be cooked a bit longer. They can be left in while the cans and jars are being removed, opened and served, by which time they should be well done. It takes twenty minutes of boiling to thoroughly heat through the contents of a medium sized can. In opening a heated can jab an air hole through the top, the while holding a piece of paper or cloth over the top, then open in the regular manner; this lets the expanded air from the inside come out harmlessly, but do it in the sink to avoid any muss. As is evident the entire meal is ready to serve all at the same time (a not too easy trick even in a well appointed shore kitchen).

Besides requiring only one burner and practically no attention except for the serving, this process literally does away with any dirty pots altogether. Never neglect that side of the picture when mulling over articles on the various phases and techniques of sea cookery.

Here again there are many optional variations that can be worked in to suit the cook's spirit, the larder, the weather, and so on. For example it is a good idea to have a deep frying pan that will snugly fit into the opening of the two gallon pot. Then, when you have a special yen for a cheese or cream sauce, or a pudding for dessert, you can start it off for a minute or so on the other burner and then allow it to finish cooking by simply placing the pan over the top of the pot, merely double boiler technique on the grand scale. Fried fish, ham, eggs and the like can also be similarly treated and thus kept good and hot for the final "Come and get it." You will come across many other uses for the combination as you go along.

Hot biscuits or cornbread, with honey or syrup, can be served as special treats when weather, temperatures and state of sea and minds indicate. However baking with me is always associated with two usually unpleasant conditions, a relatively large amount of pre-messing about and measuring and mixing, and an excess of heat. (The latter condition of course can also be a blessing in cold damp weather.) The former condition can be reduced to a minimum by the use of one of the many brands of prepared flours now on the market; the latter in hot weather must simply be endured and sweated out. But unless you are a superskilled galley mechanic calmish seas should be the order of the day for a baking program.

A splendid item to relieve the baker in seasons of stress and at the same time to quiver the palates of a languishing crew is canned cake and gingerbread. The cake comes in several flavors, chocolate, devil's food, cinnamon and fruit, and is quite a treat a month or more out. In fact it is so excellent that, after once using, it would be hard indeed to go back to the old fashioned messy bake-your-own routine that would tax the patience of even a true martyr. Furthermore it allows you to "let them eat cake" even in the midst of a howling gale, and the novelty of that fact alone should boost any smothered morale.

Many sea cooks consciously or unconsciously make things un-necessarily hard for themselves and indirectly for all aboard. For instance fresh fish, and most other meats for that matter, are ninety-nine times out of a hundred fated for the frying pan. This has two bad results: a greasy frying pan is one of the most difficult and messy utensils to wash, and fried food is always the most difficult to digest. A simpler and better way is to boil (or stew) fish; boiled fish, especially where large coarse fish are concerned, can be delicious. Cooked in chunks in the bottom of the double boiler, a cream sauce can be brewing the while above; and this double operation is far easier, both in the actual cooking and in the cleaning up, than the single act of frying.

Again if you are lucky enough to have knocked over a wild pig, goat, rabbit, fowl or what-is-there, stewing them is from any angle the most satisfactory technique. For one thing all such meats are only too often definitely on the tough side, and stewing softens them up considerably and makes them more palatable. In fact, where shaky teeth, bridgework or the portable type are concerned, stewing might even be said to be a necessary procedure. This writer still whistles through a gap in his lower front jaw where a tooth collapsed under the strain of an encounter with a hunk of roasted wild goat. Here of all times a Flex Seal cooker is worth its weight in shoe coupons, since the cooking under pressure not only shortens the cooking time but also tenderizes the meat in the process, with of course the usual conservation of water.

The previously mentioned two gallon pot is also practically a necessity where lobsters or large crabs are to be on the menu. The ability to drop them alive and whole into a pot of cold water is a blessing, and their best flavor is thus preserved. The necessity of having to hack them up into small pieces for a small pot is both messy and laborious to do as well as disastrous to the resulting flavor. In case of emergency it is well to remember that a five gallon gasoline can (the type that gas is shipped in, two cans to a wooden case) makes an excellent boiler, either aboard or especially on shore parties. Simply cut out the top and nail a wooden crosspiece in the opening for a handle. They are ideal for packing personal gear, cameras, food, etc., when going ashore, keeping them dry and protected against hard knocks; and later they can be used in cooking up the day's bag on the campfire. Truthfully, they come in so handy that it is almost worth while carrying extra case gas aboard just to get the empty cans. And in spite of their seeming vulnerability, they will last for an amazing time and stand a lot of abuse.

A labor saving detail about the galley is to save all the empty tin cans from one meal to the next. They can often be used as mixing cups for cream sauces, for melting butter or shortening, or as receptacles for waste fat, coffee grounds and other messy garbage; when finished they can be heaved overboard as is, thus saving a lot of unnecessary small pot washing. In wild battened down weather the system is especially appreciated, making a regular garbage pail unnecessary and greatly facilitating the small irksome chores about the galley.

Somewhat along the same labor saving line, although not exactly within the sphere of cooking itself, is the abolishment of dishwashing by the simple expedient of using paper plates. Paper plates may be more associated in most minds with Sunday picnics, but on any cruise they are just as convenient and far more welcome. On a thirty foot ketch I have stowed a supply sufficient for two men for six months without the slightest difficulty or overcrowding, and the drudgery they saved I love to think of even to this day. Whether you are going around the world or just halfway around and back, paper plates will go a long way to make your passages pleasanter. And considering initial expense and breakage of regular plates, the paper variety in the long run is probably no more costly; in any case they are worth a few cents of any cruiser's money. I have found the ordinary five and ten variety perfectly satisfactory. Two sizes only are really necessary, the regular dinner sized plate and the small scalloped rectangular saucers. Paper cups, at least to my mind, are not practical since ordinary glasses or cups are too easy to rinse out over the side, and also because the paper ones are near impossible for hot liquids. No small advantage of paper plates over any other kind is the fact that, when laden with hot moist food, they are practically nonskid, no matter on what sort of a surface they are placed. They do not leak, but the moisture comes through just enough to make them stay put most anywhere. To anyone resigned to the dismal task of scraping greasy plates and attempting to wash them in sea water it will indeed be an exhilarating gesture to gather up all the plates in one fell swoop and simply give them the "deep six."

A similar supply of paper towels in rolls, while not indispensable, is a godsend to any cruising cook and/or cleaner-upper. Their uses are so many and varied that it would be impossible to take them up here; suffice it to say that once you have cruised with a rack of them as shipmates you will not want to do without them unless you have to. To mention just one point alone, they can make a dish cloth unnecessary, and anyone who has ever drifted into the lee of the average craft's dish rags will understand what I mean immediately. It too often is like getting into the warm breeze off a dead whale. (Note: Cooks or dishwashers are not to be blamed for this state of affairs, as the odor is caused from having to rinse out said cloths in salt water. Hand towels and even clothes will also suffer accordingly.) The towels like the plates are light and can be stowed here and there in all sorts of odd out of the way corners; and the quantity thus stowable will surprise you (at least it does me).

In conjunction with the towels it is a good plan to have a bag of small rags hanging convenient to the galley. They are ever useful in scouring the dirtier pots and pans. Again like the plates and towels, they too are throwaways.

And there is no need to worry about messing up the oceans with a streaming wake of paper utensils. Those seas have been messed up for centuries in more ways than one, yet they are still the cleanest part of the globe. Besides you will make better friends with the albatrosses and the gooneys by serving them their dinners on floating plates, and that is not meant so jokingly as it may sound, for you get pretty attached to the birds on a long passage.

It is to be understood that most of the foregoing applies to small craft, twenty-five to forty feet overall, on long cruises with short crews, one to three men (or women). Where larger craft or crews are concerned there is no good reason (excepting occasional spells of bad weather) why the ordinary shoregoing technique of cooking should not be carried out perfectly satisfactorily without any change whatsoever. It is only on the smaller scantily manned craft that ingenious wrinkles and time- and labor-saving practices really reveal their true values. Under such circumstances, as nowhere else, is the full meaning of that ancient wisecrack, "Necessity is the mother of invention," so appreciated and understood.

SINGLE HANDED EATING

by JOHN P. RILEY, JR.

JUNE, 1952

Mr. Riley solved the eating problem quite simply in his 34 day voyage from San Francisco to Hawaii in a 30 ft. Hanna Tahiti type ketch.

A TYPICAL dinner under way was prepared with a minimum of effort and practically no time out from sailing. A half bucket of sea water went on the stove to boil. A can of meat such as enchilada was tossed in as well as a can of spinach, peas or corn. I also put two eggs in the same bucket to boil hard for breakfast and lunch the next day. From time to time I added a can of soup to the dinner menu. These cans were opened one at a time by an opener that took the top completely out of them. Dinner always was eaten off the top step of the companionway ladder (directly out of the can). When I had one foot planted on each side of the ladder I was darned hard to throw. The hot can was held in one padded gloved hand, leaving the other hand free for eating or grabbing, whichever seemed most necessary and desirable at the moment. As each can was emptied it was an easy matter to decide what to do with it. Next the spoon was swished in the same bucket of hot sea water and the dishes were done. I always finished off with delicious canned brown bread such as is served with Boston baked beans. It will always be the first thing on my stores inventory. Dessert consisted of a small can of fruit such as apricots or pears and a small can of fruit juice, usually tomato or grapefruit. Breakfast started with a one-a-day type vitamin pill and a can of fresh fruit juice. When sail was hoisted, and I settled down for my sixteen to eighteen hour watch I broke out last night's hard boiled egg and ate it with an apple, an orange and some cookies. Again no dishwashing was necessary. Lunch was the same as breakfast with a Spam sandwich or peanut butter sandwich sometimes added. I al-

271

ways looked forward to a Hershey bar at four o'clock. Not one of my five dozen eggs spoiled or broke. Each egg had been dipped for five seconds in boiling water before my departure. If I do not spell out my fresh water consumption the reader will think it a misprint. During the entire thirty-four day trip I consumed only three and one-half gallons of water. I measured it out, a half gallon at a time, and kept account in my log. I had taken a lot of canned fruit juice for daily consumption and to guarantee liquid ration if my water tank sprang a leak. This system worked so well that I sometimes went several days without being thirsty. Fresh fruit and the moisture in canned fruits and vegetables also contributed liquid.

THE PHILOSOPHY OF FIRST AID

by LOUIS H. MERKER, M.D.

OCTOBER AND NOVEMBER, 1950

Behold, a doctor who talks like a man—and a yachtsman, at that! This is the best first-aid-afloat digest that has appeared on the horizon,—full of sense, sound advice, and wit.

YOU DON'T NEED two college diplomas. You don't have to be a doctor, to give good first aid.

First aid, like philosophy, is an art, not a science. Therefore this will not be a scientific discourse. There will be no high sounding words. In fact, extremely simple terms will be used. When you are on the water, you must think and act quickly. The less you have to remember, the more likely you are to remember it well.

On the one hand, first aid means more than a few bandages and a bottle of iodine. On the other extreme, it does not mean any "Dr. Kildare" stuff. It does not mean any major operations on the cockpit floor. There is a middle of the road. If you follow a few simple rules and a few simple remedies, you will save many a cruising day and sail with "peace of mind."

Now what does first aid really mean? First aid means: You are the first one there. Simple quick remedies at first may be better than a blood transfusion later. Also, remember you are only a substitute. You are merely doing a part of a job until help arrives. So do not do too much, and don't do it too long. Give yourself a time limit (four to six hours). It is true, many emergencies respond quickly to simple treatment. That's how we doctors get our reputations. However, beyond a definite time do not prolong treatment. Get help.

Just a word about the first aid kit itself. It should be a strong sturdy box, preferably homemade, and best when made of wood and brass. The usual metal first aid kits you buy ready made become rusty almost overnight. Never lock your first aid kit. If it comes with a built-in lock and key, open it up and throw the key overboard. Invariably when you want to open the kit in a hurry the key will be in your pants pocket, in the new suit at the club locker, thirty miles away. Let us begin with artificial respiration.

If you do not know how to swim, don't worry about it too much. The average non-swimmer is a cautious fellow. He wears a life preserver when he goes on the forward deck. He is usually ten times more careful than the good swimmer. Only good swimmers get into trouble. They are careless about their steps on deck. They rarely wear life preservers. They forget one thing: When they accidentally fall overboard they usually bump their heads, and swimming ability does them little good.

So let us dive into artificial respiration. Artificial respiration, no matter how crudely or inexpertly applied, is still better than no breathing at all. I am not going to burden you with the extreme niceties of the technique. You can get all that from any Boy Scout or Red Cross manual. You will probably forget three-fourths of the maneuvers during the first accident. If, however, you learn a few basic principles you will never forget them.

Artificial respiration has many uses. I will tell you a secret. Many doctors in New York City have never given artificial respiration in a drowning case. I, like many other medical men, have given artificial respiration many times for other conditions. For example, electric shock cases need it. On a boat a sensitive guest may touch a few spark plugs while the motor is running, and suddenly stop breathing. Accident cases, head injuries, often need it. Your guest may fall down the companionway and stop breathing.

In the operating room cases often stop breathing, due either to too much ether or to a plug of mucus in the windpipe. A guest of yours may swallow a chicken bone the wrong way, and need help. Or else your guests may start drinking highballs as soon as the motor starts. (Alcohol and ether are first cousins.) Six or eight hours later they may be so high that one of them may try to imitate an angel, and stop breathing. So you see why you should know a bit about artificial respiration.

As soon as you get your man aboard, act fast. Also act sensibly. Do not delay. Drop him on his belly on the cockpit floor and get busy immediately. Don't drag him into the cabin. You'll have less room to work in. Your assistant can cover him with a blanket, loosen his clothes, remove anything in his mouth (chewing gum, false teeth). Never try to pour liquor down his throat. Remember, he is unconscious. It will not go down. Besides, it's a waste of good liquor. Take a few stiff drinks yourself, because if you are going to give artificial respiration, brother, you'll need it.

The latest, most approved method of artificial respiration is the back-pressure arm-lift system. It can be used in all cases, except where the victim has an arm injury. Here's how the U.S. Army training circular describes it:

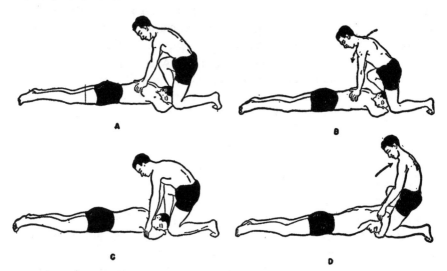

The new, back pressure, arm lift method of artificial respiration.

BACK-PRESSURE ARM-LIFT METHOD.—*a. Position of the victim.*—Place the victim in the face-down (prone) position. Bend his elbows and place his hands one upon the other. Turn his face to one side, placing his cheek upon his hands.

b. Position of the operator.—Kneel on either the right or left knee at the head of the victim and facing him. Place the knee at the side of the victim's head close to the forearm. Place the opposite foot near the elbow. If it is more comfortable, kneel on both knees, one to either side of the victim's head. Place your hands upon the flat of his back in such a way that the heels of your hands lie just below the lower tip of the shoulder blades. With the tip of the thumbs just touching, spread the fingers downward and outward. See "A" in the illustration.

c. Compression phase.—Rock forward until the arms are approximately vertical, and allow the weight of the upper part of your body to exert slow, steady, even pressure downward upon the hands. This forces air out of the lungs. Keep your elbows straight and exert pressure almost directly downward on the back. See "B."

d. Expansion phase.—Release the pressure, avoiding a final thrust, and commence to rock slowly backward. Place your hands upon the victim's arms just above his elbows, and draw his arms upward and toward you. Apply just enough lift to feel resistance and tension at the victim's shoulders. Do not bend your elbows, and as you rock backward, the victim's arms will be drawn toward you. The arm lift expands the chest by pulling on the chest muscles, arching the back, and relieving the weight on the chest. Then drop the arms gently to the ground or floor. This completes the full cycle. You are now ready to repeat the cycle. See "C" and "D."

e. Cycle timing and rhythm.—This cycle should be repeated about 10 to 12 times per minute at a steady uniform rate to the rhythm of Press, Release, Lift, Release. Longer counts of about equal length should be given to the "Press" and "Lift" steps of the compression and expansion phases. The release periods should be of minimum duration.

f. Changing position or operator.

    (1) Remember that either or both of your knees may be used, or you may shift knees during the procedure with no break in the steady rhythm. Observe how you rock forward with the back-pressure and backward with the arm-lift. This rocking motion helps to sustain the rhythm and adds to the ease of operation.

    (2) If you get tired and another person is available, you can "take turns." Be sure, however, that you do not break the rhythm in changing. To change operators move off to one side while your replacement comes in from the other side. The replacement begins the *press-release* after one of the *lift-release* phases, while you move away.

Now let us consider what you are trying to do. Are you trying to get water out of his lungs? Forget it. There is very little water in his lungs if he is a ten to twenty-minute submersion case. Stoppage of breathing was due to a reflex spasm of the windpipe. It is only the cases that have been in the water several hours or more that become waterlogged, but then you cannot help them anyway.

Let me tell you another secret. There is plenty of air in his lungs, but it is not circulating. That air is doing him as much good as your money in the bank, on Sunday. You can't use it.

How long should you continue artificial respiration? The rule says, at least four hours. Even though he is not breathing and you cannot feel a pulse it may still be there, so feeble that you can't feel it. There are many reports on record where success finally came after eight hours of artificial respiration.

But all this does not concern you. You are only a part time doctor. While you are giving artificial respiration someone is at the wheel, heading for the nearest harbor. Try to notify the Coast Guard. If you have a ship to shore telephone, use that. If not, you may meet a boat with the tall thin antenna signifying a telephone aboard. Stop for a moment and tell them of your plight. They will notify the operator, and the Coast Guard and an ambulance will be waiting for you at the dock.

When the victim begins to take a few breaths of his own, by all means let him. Don't think you are through. Merely sit back on your haunches and watch him carefully. Very often he will stop breathing again, and you will have to begin the rhythm all over again. So don't lose time. However some of them snap out of it quickly and forcefully, actually become violent at times. They all open their eyes and ask the same question, "Where the heck am I?" and want to jump up.

Here the patient is in the biggest danger of all. Do not let him get up, even if you have to sit on him. All organs of the body need oxygen, but the heart actually lives on it. The heart took the biggest beating of all in this episode. If he gets up suddenly there is a great danger of a heart attack, regardless of his age. So keep him down. Keep him covered. Support his head on your elbow and feed him hot tea or coffee. If he is an old hardened boatman don't waste his time, but feed him whiskey immediately. He'll probably ask for it anyway. Give him diluted whiskey preferably. Straight liquor may make him gasp, choke or cough, and he may stop breathing all over again. Dilute his whiskey with Pepsi-Cola, Coke or Seven-Up. He needs the sugar for quick energy. For that matter give everybody a drink, and take some yourself. But the patient stays down on the floor. He does not move until the doctor arrives and takes over.

We will now get down to brass tacks. How much does it cost you to insure a thirty foot cruiser against all the usual hazards? You know. I don't have to tell you. Can you get your boat insured for about fifteen dollars a season? No, of course not. You will pay that much to a good mechanic for a couple of hours work on your motor. The total cost of the contents of your first aid kit will be about fifteen dollars. This will cover you all summer, for your guests and crew as well. And you may not use even one-fourth of it. What you and I are interested in is this: 1. All are simple proven remedies. 2. All are harmless, even if taken unnecessarily. All may be repeated at regular intervals. 3. They work beautifully.

Now let me tell you about my old dean at medical school. He was a typical success story. Poor farmer's son had come to the big city and made good. He became dean of the school, and treated all the millionaires in town. His favorite statement used to be: "If I were ever shipwrecked on a desert island and had to grab a few medicines in a hurry, I'd grab four. First and foremost would be whiskey. Second would be aspirin. Bicarbonate of soda would come third, and last but not least would be codein."

Some of the medicines I will mention will need a doctor's prescription. Write your family doctor and tell him your are preparing a medical kit, an emergency outfit for your boat. Send him a list of the medicines. The chances are that you will receive the prescriptions in the return mail. That is the advantage of having a private physician. The probabilities are that he owns a boat himself.

I am quite sure if the old dean were making the same lecture today he would add to his list the sulfa drugs, penicillin, and that new magic drug called anti-histaminic. It appears that each company makes it but gives it a different name, so I will mention the first one I ever used, benadryl.

Please believe me, you do not have to worry about habit formation from codein, or bad reactions from the sulfa drugs. The reason is simple. You do not develop drug addiction in six or eight hours. You are only a part-time doctor, remember? Neither do you get any reactions from the sulfa drugs in six or eight hours. The reactions we usually get from drugs occur in hospitals after three to five days of constant dosage.

Now, let me explain briefly the actions of a few drugs: First, benadryl (which is easier to say than "anti-histaminic"). Benadryl came out several years ago as a good remedy against hay fever, and also works very well against these: asthma, hives, eczema, and all illnesses allied to allergy. Allergy simply means being sensitive to something, whether it is strawberries, pickles, ragweed pollen or dust. Patients soon discovered that benadryl helped cure a cold equally well. After all, getting a cold might be called being sensitive (allergic) to germs. Many people noticed that benadryl made them drowsy and gave them a good night's sleep, which did no harm if taken at night. It is not a sleeping pill, and causes no habit formation. Also it calms the nerves while making the patient a little drowsy. Here you have a medicine which is good for hay fever, asthma, hives, skin rashes, and helps you to get a good night's sleep. Furthermore it will dry up a cold if taken early.

Along came big business and made a billion dollar proposition out of it. I can't blame them too much either. Big business took a substance like benadryl, combined it with aspirin and caffeine, and now you have the famous new cold killer that you see advertised in double page ads in all the newspapers. But when you are developing a cold while on a boat, why not do this: Take one benadryl, one aspirin, and one cup of coffee (which contains caffeine). You have here the almost identical mixture present in the famous cold killer pills. Incidentally it is much cheaper this way, and much safer to know exactly what you are taking.

Secondly, let us talk about whiskey. All pleasure aside, we shall consider it purely as a medicinal agent. Whiskey relaxes both body and mind, dilates blood vessels and improves the circulation, which is why it produces that warm glow all over. It comes in handy after a storm, cold weather, or while getting on or off that sand bar. Whiskey is good in attacks or spasms such as heart attacks, kidney stones, etc.

The third medicine on the dean's list was bicarbonate of soda, the wonder of all wonder drugs. Of course everybody knows bicarbonate of soda is good for indigestion, gas, acid, ulcers of the stomach. The ulcer case lives on bicarbonate or something similar. It can do no harm. It is good in food poisoning. It is good in all skin conditions you may get on a boat. Put a tablespoon of bicarbonate in one quart of cold water, apply compresses to the inflamed skin whether it's sunburn, hives or poison ivy. Use a teaspoon of bicarb in a glass of water as a chaser to other medicines. Bicarb can be used as a tooth paste, gargle, and mouthwash. What more do you want for ten cents?

Now we come to aspirin. Everybody knows aspirin, the pain killer, good for colds, etc. What most people do not know is that aspirin is a good sedative. Take two some night when you can't fall asleep, and you will find it gives you a good night's rest.

Codein is the last item on the venerable dean's list. Codein is for that special extra pain which aspirin alone cannot relieve, for the broken arm or severe sprain.

Remember, all these remedies are simple, harmless and efficient.

Now, let's get down to cases. We will begin, on top, with *headache*. You are beginning that weekend cruise with an unpleasant throbbing sick headache. Remember one thing, the cause of headache. The commonest cause is nerves. The strain of a possible storm coming up, that leak from the stuffing box which will bear watching, or maybe your mother-in-law is aboard. The next common cause for headache is indigestion, gas, etc. Then again you may be developing a cold or sinus attack.

Everybody runs to the aspirin bottle first, and that's perfectly all right. But let's make like a doctor now. Knowing that most causes of headache are nervous in origin, how about adding a benadryl to the aspirin? Then if you add bicarb as a chaser you are taking care of any indigestion as well.

You now have a nice mixture, benadryl for the nerves, aspirin for the ache, bicarb for indigestion. If you add a cup of coffee to this you are even improving on the fancy cold killer or headache pills.

You must get quick action in a headache. It should respond in about one hour. If the headache has not responded in two hours, repeat the mixture but add codein to it. In other words, one codein, one aspirin, one benadryl. This is not too much medicine either. I will tell you a little secret. Aspirin, codein and benadryl are a favorite combination written by doctors on many a prescription for various aches and pains. It can be taken without question, and repeated once or twice for that extra special ache or pain.

Remember your time limit. If the headache is not gone in four to six hours, or is still present in the morning, after the night before, go home. Headache may be the warning signal of many a more serious condition. Don't assume all the responsibility.

We come next to another subject, the small *infection* (or festering), for example a boil on the neck, or an abcess on the hand (from a splinter). That little pimple on your neck Saturday morning suddenly becomes a big boil Saturday night while you're moored at Lloyd's Harbor. Or that splinter in your hand Friday afternoon may suddenly puff up like a balloon Saturday evening, with a few red streaks going up your arm, and maybe a little fever besides. We used to call that blood poisoning.

Now we need the "miracle drugs," sulfa and penicillin. Use both. Don't worry about any reactions. You are using them for a short time only. Give plenty. A good dose would be: two penicillin tablets (100,000 units per tablet) and two sulfa tablets (standard dose). All sulfa medicine needs bicarbonate of soda as a chaser. One teaspoon in one glass of water. This type of medication (sulfa and penicillin) has to be repeated every three or four hours to saturate the body with it. This goes on during the night also. Chances are that the boil or abscess will be down to pimple size the next morning. It may not need any help at all, or will be a small matter entirely.

Another important subject to touch upon is *skin diseases* which occur on the boat or during the cruise. This is a simpler matter than you think. All rashes which occur aboard ship are recent ones. (We call them acute.) The man with a chronic rash knows all about it. He has been to his doctor or skin specialist and is treating for it. He is no problem to you at all. Any new rash on the boat is therefore very recent.

Treat them all as though they are allergic in character. (They probably are.) Whether it is sunburn, poison ivy, nervous eczema or a seafood rash, remember it is due to sensitivity, to what you came in contact with. First of all, give the medicine used in all allergic conditions, one benadryl, with bicarb as a chaser.

Now, concerning the rash itself, follow a well established medical method. I will quote the words of a skin specialist: "The worse the rash, the wetter the remedy." So at the beginning of a red hot rash (whatever the cause may be) apply cool compresses of bicarbonate of soda solution (a tablespoon of bicarb to every quart of cold water). Keep applying these compresses until the condition has cooled off. After several hours, when the rash is much better, you may start applying calamine lotion, known as the "pink lotion." Shake the bottle, pour some on a piece of gauze, and use the gauze like a powder puff to cover the area you want. When this lotion dries it leaves a pink powder on the skin. At night cover the entire area with plain yellow vaseline. The next morning the rash may be a whole lot better, and no problem. However keep giving bicarb and benadryl every four hours to fight the rash internally.

From now on, when I mention B and B, I mean benadryl and bicarb, not benedictine and brandy.

To repeat, remember that hay fever, asthma, hives, eczema, many skin rashes, are due to allergy, meaning sensitivity to something. For all of these use B and B.

Now we come to *eye accidents* aboard ship. As a rule it is not mud in your eye, but usually a cinder from the smoke of a passing tugboat, or a small particle of steel which apparently can be wafted on the breeze. Don't rub your eye, which is dangerous. You may actually rub the particle right into your eyeball. The procedure is as follows: First pull down the upper lid. This causes tears to form, and may wash out the foreign body. If this does not succeed, then you must locate where that foreign body (or cinder) has lodged. After all, there are only three places where it can be: 1. Lower lid. 2. Upper lid. 3. The eyeball. Look at the lower lid first. That's easy. Just pull down the lower lid and look. If you see the black cinder, take a corner of a clean handkerchief and wipe it out. If it is not there, tackle the upper lid. Here you have to evert the lid, which is simple. Pull the upper lid down, place a match stick or tooth pick against it, and bend (evert) the lid upward against the toothpick. Now you can see the inside of the lid. If the cinder is there, wipe it out.

However, if it is not on the lower or upper lid, then it must be on the eyeball itself. Now you're in trouble. Never fool around with the eyeball. Keep your hands off. Put a patch of gauze over the eye and go home. You can easily blind that eye by rough handling, and causing scratches and scars. Even the average medical doctor sends his patient to an eye specialist if there is a foreign body on the eyeball. You may not always see it. To spot a black cinder on a black background (the window of the eye) is looking for black on black, worse than the needle in the haystack.

There is another terrifying eye accident which may happen

aboard ship, *burns of the eye*. A man lights a match for a cigarette (close to his face). The match, for some reason or other, explodes or falls apart, and some of the flaming sulphur hits the eyeball. This happened on my boat. Secondly, a man may get acid in his eye when handling his batteries. In the galley some fat in the frying pan may spatter up into someone's eye. You now have an eye burn. Whether acid or alkali does not concern you a bit. You have a concentrated painful burn of the eye, and it may cause permanent damage. You must dilute and weaken the chemical burn with lots of water.

Here I quote from a medical journal, written for medical men, by an eye specialist: "Dunk his head in a pail of water, meanwhile keeping the eye open. This is usually very satisfactory. After this has been done, then you have time to send the patient to the specialist for further treatment."

Now we come to the *fish hook in the finger*. This may be trivial, but can become complicated. As you know the fish hook is pointed with a barb. In other words, it's a one way hook. To try to pull it out backwards would rip the finger apart. You should do as follows: If the hook is in the finger, all you see sticking out is the shank. The point is inside the flesh. Take some iodine and paint the shank (the remainder of the hook) thoroughly. Tell the victim what you are going to do. Then push the hook through completely until the point comes out on the other side. Now it is a comparatively simple matter to cut the tip off with a pair of cutting pliers, and pull the rest of the hook back out the way it came in. However, if the hook is buried in the palm of the hand, then you're in trouble. You cannot pull the hook out. You'd rip the whole hand apart. Neither should you push it through two inches of flesh to the top of the hand. You may hit a nerve and paralyze a few fingers. You might go through a blood vessel and cause an internal hemorrhage. So, fold your tents like the Arabs, and as silently steal (or sail) away. Cover the hook with gauze and bandage, and go home. Your private doctor will have to inject novocain in the hand (like your dentist before an extraction), and cut down in the muscle to get the hook out.

The subject I'll take up now is probably the commonest and most abused of all, namely, *indigestion*. You and I know that the average boatman lives in the frying pan. I have read articles about galley cooking, where the frying pan was the main part of the article. The average boatman's menu can be listed as follows: Fried eggs and bacon, fried sausage, French fried potatoes, fried hash, fried everything.

As a doctor I have often wondered why more boatmen do not get ulcers. Of course everyone knows that ulcers of the stomach are a psychosomatic affliction, meaning that the brain has a lot to do with the ulcer formation. If a man has a lot of turmoil, nervous tension, frustrations, etc., more acid is formed in the stomach, and more ulcers develop. Maybe yachting gives the boatman so much real pleasure that it counteracts the frying pan. Of course this is merely the writer's personal opinion.

What do we mean by indigestion? We mean the sour, acid, bloated, nervous, "butterfly feeling" in the stomach. This usually comes after something you ate (or drank). Nervous indigestion may be the cause of eighty per cent of the cases. Please do not underestimate the nerves. They can make a monkey out of you. A cold may start with indigestion. A seafood dinner (allergy to shell fish) may cause it. The first and safest thing to do is to take a teaspoon of bicarbonate of soda in one glass of water.

Remember, ulcer cases live on bicarbonate a lifetime, and do quite well on it. Remembering also the possible nervous or allergic factors, give him a benadryl with the bicarb. He should get immediate temporary relief. So we are back to B and B. It is always a safe combination, even if used unnecessarily. It will never do any harm.

If there is a problem of constipation associated with it, consider milk of magnesia. It is the only laxative I keep aboard. (There are many other good ones, but why complicate matters?) Milk of magnesia is a physic and also acts like bicarb at the same time. It neutralizes acid, helps gas, sweetens the stomach, and helps the bowels, all in one. Usually two tablespoons of the liquid are enough for an adult.

Diarrhea is another frequent visitor on board ship. Paregoric is a soothing syrup given to babies when they're teething. It surely will not harm an adult. So give your guest or crew two teaspoons of paregoric and a cup of hot tea. Stop all food for a while. This alone may slow down everything. If the diarrhea still persists after a few hours, treat it like any infection. An intestinal cold, food poisoning, etc., are caused by germs, just like the boil on the neck. So start with two tablets of penicillin, two tablets of sulfa (diazine), and use bicarb as a chaser. After this go home, because something else may be brewing.

The last cause of indigestion I mention will cause a lot of argument. So, let's argue. I am referring to *seasickness*. Here, I'm going to stick my neck out. Let me mention something which boatmen seem to forget. Boating is a hobby, and should be a pleasure. If your guest or crew gets seasick, drop him off at the first chance you get. Take him home immediately if you can. Why? Seasickness is contagious, mentally. It is very suggestive. Your remaining crew and guests will begin to look green around the gills and imitate him. It spoils the whole trip for everybody. Yes, I know you are going to mention dramamine and hyoscin, that the Navy uses it, etc., etc.

Here is where we depart from the Navy. When the farmer boy from Kansas enlists for a three year hitch in the Navy, and gets seasick a week later, the Navy cannot discharge him just because he is seasick. The Navy is stuck with him and must treat him. You are not stuck with your guests.

Some of the remedies have kickbacks or reactions. Some may give irregular heart beats. Some may make a person delirious (I'm referring to hyoscin). You don't have to bother with them. The best cure is to put the victim ashore, preferably under the shade of an old apple tree.

There is another good reason why you should put the victim ashore. This happened in Florida a few winters ago. A middle aged man and three others had chartered one of those fishing boats with four chairs in the cockpit. When they hit the Gulf Stream the man began to get seasick. He begged to be put ashore. They all laughed at him, and made comments as to his sporting blood. He even offered to refund them double their money. This time the others got really angry and called him much more than a bum sport. However when the man collapsed they rushed the boat back to Miami, and got him to a hospital where he died two hours later. He had had a heart attack. Remember this: a heart attack can imitate seasickness very much.

If an old hardened sailor, who's been on the water all his life, suddenly gets seasick, think of a heart attack. Don't laugh it off. You may have a lifetime to regret it. You are a spry, able bodied boatman, true. Some of your guests, however, may not be spring chickens any more. So don't assume too much responsibility. Go home.

Now let us get down to the really "big-league" stuff, the emergencies. These happen much less often, thank God. The first thing on the list can be the *fainting spell*. Of course it may be more than a fainting spell, but you don't know it yet. The real fainting spell means nothing. When he or she faints and hits the deck, it is just what nature (and the doctor) wants, and the patient needs. As his head is lowered, blood rushes back to the brain, and all is well in a few minutes. He snaps out of it, and usually expects your best brandy as a consolation prize. Fool him. When he comes to, give him some aromatic spirits of ammonia to inhale. This comes in ampoules (sealed glass tubes). You break one in a handkerchief and let them inhale it. If you always give brandy, fainting can become chronic.

There are a few other causes of fainting or unconsciousness. These are heart attacks, or strokes (hemorrhages in the brain). What can you do here? The answer is, very little. Don't move him. Always put a pillow under his head. (This improves the general circulation.) Don't get fancy. No massaging, rubbing, etc. No artificial respiration is necessary as long as he is breathing. Get to shore and hand this case over to a doctor as soon as possible.

Following this closely is a related condition, the *attacks or spasms*. Here the patient remains conscious throughout. He may be coughing, wheezing. He complains of pain in the chest or back. He is doubled up and in severe pain or distress. The main thing is that he is in a spasm, but conscious. You don't know what is wrong with him, but you do know he is in a spastic painful state. It may be hysteria, asthma, heart attack or kidney stone. The important thing for you to remember is that his nerves and muscles and blood vessels are all tightened up. You must relax him quickly and safely. Twenty-five years ago the internes on the ambulances used to give an old remedy which is still good and just as fast sometimes as an injection of morphine. It is surely much safer. The old reliable used to be as follows: 1. Two aspirin tablets. 2. A double dose of whiskey. The aspirin is a pain killer, sedative, and relieves spasm a bit. Whiskey relaxes muscles, blood vessels and nerves, as well as the mind. The combination acts like knockout drops, and that is exactly what you want. You want to knock out the spasm. Nowadays we add a benadryl to the other two. Benadryl helps asthma and the nerves as well.

To repeat, give two aspirin tablets, one benadryl capsule, a good dose of whiskey. This will relieve any spasm. Best of all, it will do no harm.

The next few emergencies are dreaded by everybody on board. First among them is *fractures*, or broken bones. Of course you don't always know whether it is a broken bone or a sprain. Therefore to play safe consider every injury or sprain as a fracture.

When we consider injuries like fractures, bleeding wounds, or severe burns, we come to another condition, known as *shock*. What is shock? Not to be too technical, shock is an "all gone" feeling. The victim feels knocked out without actually being unconscious. The man in shock feels low and acts low. His blood pressure and temperature have dropped. His heart action is low, weak and fast. He is in a cold sweat and very pale. He actually does not know and doesn't care whether he is coming or going. There are three things you should do quickly in shock. You are here first. Immediate treatment now may be better than two pints of plasma four hours later.

1. Position. Keep him flat. This takes the strain off the circulation. 2. Heat. Blankets, hot water bottle, hot drinks. 3. Stimulants. Coffee, tea, whiskey, or aromatic spirits to inhale. He will react from shock if you act quickly.

Now, let us consider the original condition which caused the condition. Here it is, a fracture. He is now going to have a lot of pain. Forget about the broken limb for the time being. He is not going anywhere. Don't fool around with small doses of aspirin here. You have to relieve pain and spasm quickly. Otherwise there may be so much spasm when help arrives that it may take days in the hospital (with weights and pulleys) to relieve or break the spasm before setting the bone. Give him double doses of everything you have: two codein tablets, two aspirin tablets, two benadryl capsules, and a good slug of whiskey in Coke or Pepsi. He needs the sugar energy for quick response. In a hospital he would probably get sugar (glucose) into the veins. It is just as efficient by mouth.

When he feels as though he owned Long Island Sound, then consider treating the fracture. Don't entertain any fancy ideas. You are not going to set any bones on board ship. What would a doctor do on board ship, without an X-ray? The answer is, nothing. The doctor has learned that from sad experience. All you want to do is to splint the bone, to prevent further damage and further pain. Where are you going to get splints on your little ship? That's easy. Every boat carries floorboards. Little boats have long ones, and fifty foot cruisers carry small ones, depending on what part of the boat you look for them.

The splint must always be longer than the bone you are supporting. For a broken forearm, about eighteen inches long, use a two foot floorboard. In a broken thigh use a board from his heel up to his armpit. Don't worry how clumsy it looks as long as the limb is held rigid. Use blankets or bedding to pad the boards. Use a few lengths of rope to tie the leg to the splint. Don't use up all your fancy bandages just to attach a splint. Let the doctor get fancy when he takes over.

Now we come to the *bleeding wound*. Suppose, while falling down the companionway, he struck his head against the edge of the bunk and opened up a big gash. Do not start pouring iodine all over him. You may burn him severely, and you may blind him if the iodine gets into his eye. This is one of the cases where a simple quick remedy at the beginning may be better than a blood transfusion later on. You must stop the bleeding. Apply pressure. Grab some gauze and apply pressure right over the bleeding area. Do not start looking in your manual for scientific pressure areas. Just apply pressure where you see the bleeding. Forget anatomy. Use gauze, a towel, or your shirt tail if necessary. Pressure does what clamping the blood vessel with an artery clamp would do. In about five or ten minutes, when the real bleeding has stopped and only a slight ooze remains, proceed to the next step.

After all, you have no sutures (stitches) aboard. So what? Neither have I. What do sutures really do? Do they heal the wound for you? No, they merely hold the wound edges together, so that it can heal by itself. You can use strips of adhesive for the same purpose.

Have one of the crew (the one with clean hands) push the edges of the wound together. Now you have a narrow red line instead of a wide gaping wound. Then take several strips of half inch or one inch adhesive plaster, and stick them over the wound, crossing it at right angles. If the adhesive does not stick well, hold each strip over a flaming match for a moment (an old hospital trick). This will rejuvenate it immediately. By the way, Scotch tape works very well instead of adhesive, and it always sticks. Now, with the strips of adhesive in place, put some gauze over them, wrap a bandage around the whole, and decide whether to go home or continue with the cruise. Do not worry too much about infection at this stage of the game. Give him two sulfa tablets, two penicillin tablets, and a bicarb chaser. If he is having much pain, you know what to do. Give him codein, aspirin and benadryl.

The other big emergency dreaded by all boatmen is the *severe burn* case. You have two quarts of steaming hot water on the alcohol stove, ready to boil those frankfurters for lunch. As the galley slave is getting ready to use it a speed boat dashes past and dumps two quarts of steaming hot water over her hands and chest.

The war has taught us many new concepts of burns. Burns often result in shock. When the skin is damaged the tiny vessels underneath become fragile and ooze into the tissues. If necessary treat the shock first, as previously mentioned, with position, heat and stimulants. Remember, a burn case needs a lot of fluids. The next thing to help is the pain. Severe burns give about the worst pain known. The skin is the source of all our sensations, and when that is burned you get plenty of sensation. Here again, do not spare the horses. To relieve the pain as well as the shock give plenty of liquor, diluted in sweet drinks. Give two codein tablets, two aspirins, two benadryls, and lots of fluids. Then after shock and pain are under control start treating the burn itself.

Do not remove the clothing roughly. Cut away the clothes from the burned area, but please do not pull off any clothing which is stuck to the wound. Why not? Because you will do just what you want to avoid. You may cause oozing, internal bleeding, and shock. Leave the adhering clothes stuck to the wound, wherever it is. Now take a lot of sterile gauze pads and soak them in bicarb solution. Use one tablespoon of bicarbonate of soda to every quart of cold water. Gently lay these wet pads all over the burned areas. Then take bandages and apply them very tightly over the gauze pads. The purpose of the tight bandages is to support the weakened tissues to prevent oozing.

The next thing to do is to give penicillin and sulfa tablets. Burns are notorious for getting infected. Force a lot of drinks into him and you will have surprisingly little trouble. Actually a hospital does not do much more. A hospital gives the burn case fluids, keeps him warm, relieves his pain and applies tight bandages. Then it lets the victim rest several days without changing the bandages at all. If your victim feels better several hours later (or the next morning) and demands a big breakfast, let him stay aboard if you wish. If he is convalescing what better place is there to do it than on board ship? If you want peace of mind check up with a doctor at the nearest port.

Another emergency which is dreaded aboard ship is the old fashioned "*bellyache*," accompanied by nausea, vomiting and a little fever. Think of one point immediately. If there is diarrhea with the pain and vomiting you can practically forget about appendicitis. Appendicitis is not an emergency operation. There is lots of time. The ruptured appendix that you hear or read about is usually a twenty-four to forty-eight hour neglected appendix. On a boat you know exactly when the pain began. If the guest had had pain that Saturday morning, accompanied by vomiting and fever, he would not have come aboard your boat. So you know almost to the minute when that pain began and you have time to make your plans.

Of course every schoolboy knows that no laxative is to be given. Also give no food at all. Food makes the intestines active and the appendix might be ruptured more rapidly. I see no reason why he cannot be given some benadryl and bicarb. It still may not be appendicitis. It could be a "frying-pan bellyache" food poisoning.

Even if the patient improves go home anyway. Once you have thought of appendicitis, take no chances. The responsibility is too great and the appendix is too tricky. Sometimes a hospital must observe a case several hours before it can make sure of appendicitis, even with all the scientific tests.

An unusual emergency, but one you will always remember, is the fish bone or chicken bone that gets caught in the throat. They usually lodge in a definite area—where the throat turns the corner into the gullet (oesophagus). This area can still be seen by the examiner with a bright light flashed into the mouth. Have the victim say "Ah—ah" while you press his tongue down with the handle of a spoon. When he says "ah—ah" it makes the tongue drop down and you can see the back wall of the throat and the beginning of the lower part as well. As this is going on, take a long pair of long nosed pliers, grab the fish bone and gently withdraw it. If you do not see it, give him two teaspoons of syrup of ipecac to cause vomiting. The act of vomiting may loosen up the bone.

Accidental poisoning is another condition which can happen on small boats where all supplies are crowded together in a small space. You have been to the rendezvous of the Bronx Power Squadron at Price's Bend. You had a meal at Jake's Sea Food place, and all the drinks fore and aft. At 3:30 A.M. you wake up on your boat with a terrific heartburn and indigestion. In order not to awaken the rest of the snorers you feel your way to the galley, grab the box of bicarb, dump a generous amount in a glass of water and gulp it down fast. Instead of the usual relief all the fires of hell seem to light up in your stomach. Something is wrong. Now you put on the lights and look at the box. Lo and behold, you took the wrong box. Maybe borax or silver polish. You are in trouble. Thank God, many poisons are slow in action so you have a little time. The thing to do now is to dilute and neutralize the poison immediately, so that it will become harmless while in the stomach. Secondly, after doing this, you want to bring it all up again.

So (1) break three or four raw eggs in a deep dish, mix them, and drink them down fast. Since every boatman likes fried eggs for breakfast, most boats carry them aboard. Eggs contain albumen, and this forms a chemical combination with many poisons. It also forms a protective lining on the stomach and renders the poison inert and harmless. (2) If you have milk aboard take three, four or five glasses of milk, one right after the other. If milk is not available drink about three, four or five glasses of bicarb in water. The purpose is to neutralize and dilute the poison and also to fill up the stomach, so that you feel you will burst. Now, when your teeth are about ready to float, bend over a pail, put your fingers in your mouth and try to force vomiting. If you succeed all is well. A stomach pump could not have done better.

If you cannot vomit take two teaspoons of syrup of ipecac and you will probably bring up what you ate last week. After all this, lie down and rest. You will need it.

I have left the subject of *fevers* for the very end. Fevers are most neglected and can be most dangerous. Saturday night, let us say, you have moored near Croton-on-the-Hudson or maybe in Huntington Harbor and one of your guests complains of not feeling well. He is hot, has aches and pains, maybe a slight cough, stiff neck, nausea, etc. His temperature may be 101 degrees. What have we now? I do not know, and neither do you, so let us do a little thinking. July, August and September are the best cruising months of the year. Pneumonia and pleurisy can also occur then. July, August and September, the best cruising months, are also the best months for polio or infantile paralysis. It is not "infantile" any more. Adults get it as often as infants. Ask the Navy how many cases have occurred among its sailors. It does not necessarily have to be polio. It may be an ordinary infection. Start with penicillin and sulfa right away, two tablets of each and a bicarb chaser. Repeat every three hours if you are stuck there during the night. Penicillin and sulfa may cure a pneumonia or pleurisy. The patient may feel better in the morning. This will not cure polio, but may make him more comfortable. In the morning go home.

You will notice that all through this discourse I have kept saying, "Go home." Why go home instead of taking the victim ashore, wherever you are? Suppose you are moored at Podunk on the sound. Usually it is a holiday and the local doctor there may be away on a cruise himself. He may even be a member of the Power Squadron and on a rendezvous on the Shrewsbury. Finally you locate some doctor who promises to come over as soon as he can. In about two hours he arrives and you row him out to the boat. He examines the patient and agrees with you that it is a hospital case. If you get an ambulance within one hour you are doing well. So within three and a half or four hours your patient is heading for some small hospital in a strange town, and with a strange doctor. In that same time, you could probably get home where your family doctor, who knows you well, would take charge. If hospital is necessary the patient will be near home where family and friends can visit without traveling forty miles.

And now, it looks like this is where I came in. First aid means quick aid, and short time aid. It means more than bandages and iodine, but not a major operation on the cockpit floor. It means knowing a few simple harmless remedies, like aspirin, whiskey, bicarb, codein. It means giving yourself a time limit, then if necessary getting help. The victim will be in better shape when you reach the doctor. Most of the time you will not need a doctor, and you will save yourself many a lost weekend.

EMERGENCY PROCEDURES

PAIN—Codein. Aspirin. Whiskey. Benadryl.

NERVES—Benadryl. Aspirin. Whiskey. Hot drink.

COLD, COUGH, SNEEZE, HAY FEVER, ASTHMA—Benadryl. Aspirin. Whiskey, Coffee.

SKIN—*Hives, Eczema, Sunburn, Poison Ivy*—Apply compresses of bicarbonate solution, vaseline at night, calamine lotion by day. Take benadryl and bicarbonate by mouth.

SHOCK—Position, flat. Heat, blankets. Stimulants, tea, coffee, whiskey, aromatic spirits.

INDIGESTION—Bicarbonate. Benadryl. Milk of magnesia for constipation. Paregoric for diarrhea.

TO FORCE VOMITING—Syrup of ipecac. Drink bicarbonate water, 3, 4 or 5 glasses, then put finger in mouth to induce vomiting.

ATTACKS—Whiskey. Aspirin. Benadryl.

INFECTION, ABSCESS, BOIL, FEVER—Sulfadiazine. Penicillin. Bicarbonate.

REMEMBER—Always bicarbonate as a chaser.

Emergency Kit

Sunburn cream. Eye wash (with eye cup). Rubbing alcohol. Thermometer (mouth). Eye cup, eye dropper. Q tips (cotton on toothpick). Bandage scissor, thumb forceps. Long nose pliers (to remove fish and chicken bones in throat). Bandages, 6 rolls of 3 inch and 6 rolls of 2 inch. Sterile gauze pads, one box. BandAids, one box. Adhesive tape roll, 3 inches wide. Mercurochrome. Cotton. Scotch tape (for use as adhesive on face and hairy parts).

Suggested dosage is noted after certain items

Whiskey. Aspirin, 1-2 tablets. Codein, 1-2 tablets. Bicarbonate of soda, 1 teaspoon, in water. Penicillin, 2 tablets—repeat every four hours (50,000 u size). Sulfa (diazine), 2 tablets—repeat every four hours. Benadryl, 1-2 tablets—repeat every four hours (25 mgm size). Aromatic spirits (ampoule), break and inhale. Milk of magnesia (liquid or tablets). Paregoric, 2 teaspoons. Ipecac (syrup), 2 teaspoons. Calamine lotion. Vaseline.

Put a bookmark in this page. Leave the end sticking out so that you can find it in a hurry.

THE HURRAH'S NEST

For many years, Tom Day conducted a department of this name in THE RUDDER *wherein oddments of information were collected. Quite often a paragraph containing an opinion or a single fact is remembered longer than the contents of a carefully composed essay. So may it be with these fragments.*

CHEBEC: SPANISH) OFF TARIFA
Warren Sheppard

Warren Sheppard

ON OBSERVATION

CONSIDERED from the practical point of the detective business the Sherlock Holmes stories are ridiculous; no man ever has or ever will ferret out crime and detect criminals by such methods. The only successful detectives are men who, having spent their lives with criminals, come to live, think and act like criminals. It is through becoming thoroughly saturated with criminality, detectives are able to trace and fix crime, not as many suppose from the act to the perpetrator, but from the perpetrator to the act. But outside of this, the Sherlock Holmes stories have done a marvelous amount of good in drawing men's attention to the worth of observation. Until they read these stories men did not appreciate that right under their noses not only for days, but years, were things they had never seen, and which unseen have played a part in making or unmaking their lives. It may be laid down as an axiom "He who observes the little things sees the great."

Just to show how few people closely observe, in fact observe at all, let me give a few cases that have fallen under my notice. I was sitting in a house the owner of which was disputing with a neighbor as to the age of the building. The owner insisted the house was over one hundred years old; the neighbor made the age seventy years. On being asked for his authority, the neighbor asserted that he had seen the date 1836 carved on a stone over the doorway. The owner, who had lived in the house nearly twenty years, denied that there was such a stone or inscription. To settle the matter we went outside and there was the stone and the figures plainly to be read. The owner admitted that although he had passed in and out that door thousands of times, he had never seen that inscription.

Another time in entering a strange harbor I asked a resident working on a small boat what the rise and fall of the tide was. After a pause he answered hesitatingly, he guessed it was about four feet. On consulting the tide books I found the mean rise and fall was over six feet. On calling the man's attention to this, he said, "He had never taken much notice of the rise and fall." In this I heartily agreed with him.

I have had men sailing with me, who for years have passed certain lights, and yet if you ask they cannot tell the duration of the flash, and sometimes not even the character of the light. Men own and handle boats for years and yet don't know the true dimensions. I have met men who did not know the over-all length, often by several feet, the width; few know the true draught, and how many men can tell the height of the mast, the diameter of the wheel, and not one in a hundred can tell anywhere near the consumption of fuel. An engineer, who admitted he had been running a certain type of engine for three years, could not tell the exact consumption, making several guesses all of which were wrong when we came to make the test.

One night a man in my watch said, "Do you know that the stars move?" "When did you find that out?" I asked. "The other night I happened to be sitting at the back of the house looking along its side, and I saw the stars come out and pass the corner. I never knew before they moved." Yet this man had lived on the rolling world for over thirty years.

A sure sign of a good seaman or skilful navigator is the roving eye. The man whose eyes rove is always a good observer. The first thing to look for in a seaman or navigator is the eye, then the hand.

The good seaman sees everything alow and aloft; his eyes are roving all over the vessel, across the sea to starboard and port, and ahead and astern. He notes every vary of the cloud, every change of the swell, every shift of the wind. He catches and interprets the phases of ocean life. Not a bird moves over the wave, not a fish breaks the surface but his quick glance catches the glimmer of the wing or the glint of the fin. To him the sunrise and sunset speak, foretelling the weather; he reads the clouds and questions the drift and color of the horizon. His eye and hand play together in this fascinating game of voyaging, and the ship laughs her way onward, contented under the watchfulness of an observing master.

The unobserving man is always stupid; it is the want of observation that dampens and deadens his faculties. The fellow who shuffles the deck with his eyes on the cracks, never holds his luff in the voyage of life, or runs the stretches of fortune, rolling and leaping before a flowing sea and a brisking wind.

If you who are aiming to be a good yachtsman or boatman want to succeed, observe. Let nothing be too small to interest you. Keep your eyes continually on the rove, make a point of trying to see everything, and from what you garner winnow out the grain, measure, weigh it, store it up, and in the future make use of it.

To start with, get a diary. Every day when on the water observe the sky, especially at sunrise and sunset; write down its appearance, especially the colors; then next day note what change in the weather. Do this for two or three seasons and you will be weatherwise. Note in your diary how the wind shifts, how the tide affects the coming and going of the breeze.

Make a habit of observing and it will repay you in the interest and pleasure it brings a thousandfold, and furthermore it will give you that skill and understanding which is essential to the making of a real seaman.　　　　　　　　　　　　　　　　　　　　　　　UNSIGNED.

MAKING PORT ON A SHOESTRING

by ROBERT NEILSON

FEBRUARY, 1943

Have you ever had to enter a harbor for which you had no chart? Here's one way to do it in safety.

HERE is a wrinkle that is worth while passing along. Although probably not original, in our particular case the idea was born of necessity. You may never have to use it but, like a lifeboat on a ship, when and if the need arises it may prove to be the only or best way out of a serious situation.

We were bound for Punta Arenas in Costa Rica through the Gulfs of Tehuantepec and Papagayo, when we banged head on into an apparently perpetual, stiff, steady, southeasterly Papagayo. With a badly fouled bottom, our progress for days was almost nil against the nasty steep seas and whistling wind. Too often we could have paced off our distance made good from the previous noon. With supplies running low and distance to go remaining unchanged from day to day, we were in one of those too numerous navigators' dilemmas.

Our best bet, aside from the disgusting alternative of turning back (and even that would have been risky with the calms and northerlies behind us), was to head on up into the corner of the bight, close hauled to the last fraction, and make a try for either Corinto in Nicaragua or La Union in El Salvador. As they both lay a couple of hundred miles to the east of our route, our charts did not cover them at all. Furthermore both harbors, according to the Sailing Directions, were involved and tedious. Necessity being the mother of invention, we made up our own chart. To have attempted to follow four or five

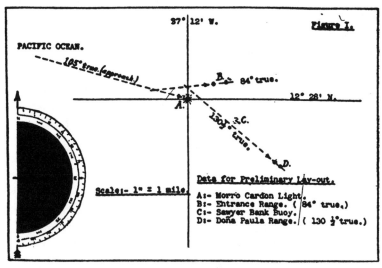

Figure 1. The preliminary placement of landmarks.

pages of closely written explanations and keep all the important points in mind while crashing about in heavy tide rips, taking bearings, and being preoccupied with a thousand and one other odd chores and duties, would have required the mind of a memory marvel. Somebody else can try it, not me. As to pilots, I would rely neither on their appearance when needed nor their methods of procedure if they should happen to appear. Generally, it can be said, they attempt to handle a thirty foot underpowered cruising ketch either like a 5,000 ton ship or like their own pilot boats. Under certain circumstances, the results can be mighty nerve racking and messy, if not actually disastrous.

Our only sources of information aboard on the harbors were the

Sailing Directions for the West Coasts of Central America and Mexico, and the H. O. Light List. The former gives directions, landmarks, depths and local conditions and information, while the latter gives data on the lights, beacons, buoys and ranges, with the exact positions of the more important ones. With these two books, a surprisingly complete and accurate chart can be plotted and both works should be, and generally are, found aboard any cruising craft.

As Corinto was the port we finally made, I have used it in the diagrams showing the progressive steps in plotting. As a starter, pick out some prominent outer landmark whose exact position is given in the Light List, and build the chart up around it. Thus, in Figure I, Morro Cardon Light (A), Lat. 12° 28' N.—Long. 87° 12' W., was taken as the central point. Use any scale suitable, depending mostly on the extent of the harbor and its approaches. At Corinto, considering the ranges, I used a scale of one inch equals one mile as being sufficient, although a larger scale could just as well have been used if felt necessary. In Bowditch, Table II, one mile is found to equal 1' of longitude at 12½° N. Lat., and, as one mile always equals 1' of latitude, our chart is in proportion. Other positions can be plotted using the ratio of one mile equals 1' of both latitude and longitude. For greater accuracy in the higher latitudes, you can convert the Difference of Longitudes of other positions into Departures and plot to scale, although a simpler method would be to get the proportion from a small scale chart, taking in the same latitude and using, say, 1' equals 1° of latitude and longitude respectively.

Now put in the 105° approach (from the Directions), which clears all outlying dangers. From such phrases as "about 300 yards north of Morro Cardon Light," and the range position from the Light List, run in lightly the 84° true bearing of the entrance range. Do likewise with the 130½° true bearing of the Dona Paula Range, and dot in the Sawyer Bank buoy.

Now check back over the Sailing Directions again. With "1,500 yards long in a NW to SE direction," Isla Cardon can be sketched in, similarly the various shoals and the white beacon southeast of the light. After locating Isla Encantada, run in the 65° true bearing of that range. Then sketch in roughly the end of Isla Punta Icaco and Castanones Peninsula. Locate the municipal wharf and light and run in the true north bearing to the anchorage off its outer end. Double check courses and distances and make certain they all jibe. Undefined points and comparatively unimportant shorelines can now be sketched in from the shaped up chart and the general context of the Sailing Directions. Right here is a good place to say that such helpful gems of advice as the following may be taken lightly, ". . . This house constitutes a conspicuous mark in the daytime when entering the harbor off Morro Cardon. This house has been reported to be practically obscured by trees." The Sailing Directions are full of such frustrating pleasantries. Try counting up to at least five before giving way to vexation (to borrow one of the S.D.'s favorite words).

Too much faith should not be put in using mountain peaks as guides or ranges. According to the book, the "conspicuous" peaks of Momotombo, Coseguina or Viejo are practically infallible as entrance guides. However, on approaching the coast about a half a hundred other conspicuous peaks loom up and cause confusion. Unless you are personally acquainted with Momotombo and his relatives, it would be just as well to skip the mountain stuff; you might easily pick the wrong peak. Put your faith in the unmistakable objects such as distinguishing lighthouses, beacons and such, and use the "conspicuous" peaks, trees and houses as a check (just in case you should happen to see them).

Figure 2 shows the finished product with all necessary and help-

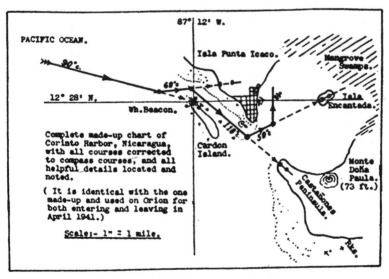

Figure 2. The reconstructed chart.

ful aids in place and all the courses changed to compass courses for safety and convenience. A mental note should be made of such remarks as "These range marks have been reported to be confusing in view of the fact that when a vessel is on the range line only the front beacon is visible," just so you won't worry if you see only one instead of two. (At least it makes a change from the all too common affliction of seeing double.) Notes on the colors, peculiarities and makeup of the various bluffs, islands and peninsulas should be put on the chart. (These were left off Figure 2 due to lack of space and to avoid confusion.)

Check over tidal data carefully, considering the circumstances before attempting to enter. Corinto has a rather formidable range with resulting rips, eddies and cross currents. In such a case, especially if you are a bit underpowered, should you find the going too hectic and wild in the outer reaches it would be wiser to stand by until the tide eases up before going on in to the narrows where conditions are sure to be worse. A short delay may prevent an indefinite stay.

Before closing, I'd like to say that I never have seen an official chart of Corinto. Thus, as in any chart so made up, there may possibly be some minor discrepancies in contours and such, but the channels and main points I'll swear to. It's as near correct as "damn" is to swearing. We entered and departed with the chart as shown, and we had no hair raising surprises or setbacks. Furthermore, everything was where it should have been. In fact, to be truthful, after all the plotting and figuring, the place even seemed familiar. What with some nasty tide rips and eddies, close-to rocks, an outcoming steamer and some frantic identification hailings with the local coast guard, I was more than glad we had not attempted to read ourselves into the anchorage. The chart repaid us a hundred times over for the little time and effort it consumed in making. So stow the idea away in your "wrinkle bag" and, if the need ever arises, you'll find it, like quinine in a fever, a real life (and craft) saver.

HOW TO KEEP A LOG

NOVEMBER, 1937

KEEPING a log is considered a dull, dry chore by the majority of yachtsmen who bother with it at all. And yet it can be made a very interesting and even instructive part of cruising if one will but go at it in the proper way.

The failure of most yachtsmen to keep logs is due in part to the nature of the very log sheets themselves. They are, for the most part, either too blank or too cluttered up with a lot of columns for meteorological data which will never be used and present such an imposing appearance that they scare the amateur skipper off. Many are too small for proper handwriting space; many are too big for convenient handling. Some are too frivolous and have no room for proper navigational data, being disfigured with drawings of anchors, mermaids, and blocked off squares for photographs and the vaporings of idle guests.

A proper log should be a combination of space for navigational notes and room for more informal stuff. The most satisfactory form is one with a page for entries on one hand and a blank page opposite for additional notes, comments, sketches of landmarks, or, interesting shore scenes, notes on the doings of the party, and photographs of ships, men, and ports encountered at the time. There should be only one log sheet for every twenty-four hours and one opposite blank "sketch page" to correspond. In the form suggested the sheets should be printed as shown, with blank backs so that the back of the form for one day will be the blank "chatter page" for the preceding one.

A log book should be printed on paper reasonably water resistant and should not include much over fifty pages. The hourly data sheet should be at the left as you open it up, and the blank page on the right.

The form suggested is one based on considerable cruising in all types of boats and is a "boil-down" of many types of logs. The columns shown represent the average number and character that are actually *used*. Oh yes, there are many more columns in the average

301

LOG OF THE _____

AT OR EN ROUTE FROM _____ TO _____ · DATE _____ 19 ___

THE RUDDER
The Magazine for Yachtsmen

TIME	NAUTICAL MILES	PATENT LOG	COURSE MADE GOOD	WIND DIRECTION & FORCE	BARO- METER	REMARKS
1 A.M.						
2						
3						
4						
5						
6						
7						
8						
9						
10						
11						
12 M.						
1 P.M.						
2						
3						
4						
5						
6						
7						
8						
9						
10						
11						
12						

A.M. { LATITUDE _____ LONGITUDE _____

M. { LATITUDE _____ LONGITUDE _____

P.M. { LATITUDE _____ LONGITUDE _____

DAYS RUN _____ NAUTICAL MILES

CRUISE RUN _____ NAUTICAL MILES

MOTOR RUN _____ HRS. _____ MIN.

FUEL CONSUMPTION _____ GALLONS

FUEL RECEIVED _____ GALLONS

FUEL ON HAND _____ GALLONS

A typical log page.

302

log—but nobody ever bothers to fill them out. So why have them at all?

The columns shown are sufficient to detail the course, speed, position, and handling of the boat—all the information that might be valuable for accurate navigation or for future reference when in the same waters. When used in conjunction with a blank page opposite, and properly filled out, one will have an interesting, human, but still not sloppy record of one's cruise.

The reasons for the form of the various columns are as follows: The first line "Log of the . . . ." should be finished off in handwriting thus—either "Motor Yacht Sea Breeze," "Schooner Yacht Endymion," or some similar expression including the name of the vessel. The date should always be entered in the proper space, and the "At or En Route From . . . . To . . . ." space should be filled out each day.

The time column is shown with every hour marked. This is conducive to regularity in making entries. If the hour spaces are left blank the log-keeper will likely skip several hours at a time and the log will have no value as a connected record of the movements of the boat.

The "Nautical Mile" column should be entered with the miles progressed up to the time of entry. The mileage used here is the mileage estimated, or spotted off the chart when working alongshore, and fixed by bearings or other observations. This is used when the log is not towed. If a log is used, then the Patent Log readings should be entered in their proper column. Patent Log readings should be taken every hour—or at most every four hours—when cruising offshore.

The column for "Course Made Good" means just that. You should not put in the course to be steered. That should be marked on a paper or card in front of the helmsman, or told him. The course made good—the course actually steered during the hour noted, is the only one that is of any use for future reference when working up a dead reckoning. Don't put down where you *should* be steering. Enter the course you *have* steered.

Wind Direction and Force will be of little moment to power boat men unless they know something about predicting weather conditions or wish to see what effect it may have on their boat's performance or fuel consumption, or want to figure leeway. Yet the information should be entered, if one wishes to do the thing properly, and the force figures should be Beaufort Scale (found in *Bowditch, American Practical Navigator* and many other navigation books).

Barometer readings should by all means be entered and they should be entered hourly. The record of variation of the barometer and *how fast* the variation is taking place is the only thing that means much when consulting a barometer. A single reading at any one hour is meaningless.

You will note that the space for "Remarks" is left big. Here is where most logs fall down. They leave far too little space for remarks, and remarks are important. They are, also, the most interesting entries in a log sheet.

The items that should be entered in the Remarks column are innumerable. They should include anything that affects the operation, handling, position, and performance of the boat. They should not include the "remarks" of wiseacres in the crew or similar rot. The place for that stuff is on the blank opposite "diary, photo, and what-not page." Don't defile your regular log sheets with silly or useless matter.

Some of the things that should always be entered in the Remarks column are the following:

1. Any change in the course of the boat (and how much).
2. Time of getting under way or anchoring.
3. Handling or shifting of sails (if a sailing vessel).
4. Vessels sighted, headlands passed, buoys "made," notes on character of bottom when anchoring, how much scope, time lights are lit, any unusual or important information regarding performance and handling of vessel.
5. Any navigational data, such as time of taking azimuth, checking compass, making soundings, etc.
6. Anything regarding waters traversed that would be of benefit in handling boat if visiting again in the future.
7. Any changes in number of persons on board and any accident, sickness, etc., of anyone on board.

It is usual to initial the entries, if several people keep the log.

The spaces at the bottom of the suggested log sheet are more or less self explanatory. The spaces at A.M., M. and P.M. Latitude and Longitude should be filled in with the actual hour of the sight.

Now, of course, you can have as many more spaces as you wish but it is silly to have more than will be used.

Keeping a log is like everything else. You have to get into the swing of it before you find much fun in it. But there is fun to be had, and the more you learn about handling a boat, the more value you will place on a well-kept, accurate log.

There are many reasons why a good log *should* be kept, even if you don't find any amusement in it. It eliminates guesswork in piloting and navigation. It affords a record of the boat's course and distance that is necessary for correct estimating of position if out of sight of landmarks, or caught in fog. It forces one to observe wind, weather, and the state of the sea and gradually learn to predict conditions. It makes one more conscious of the need for careful steering. Over a season it constitutes an invaluable record of the boat's performance. It provides fascinating winter reading after the boat is laid up and you are storm bound far from the water. A well-kept log is a character witness and proof of the boat's position and maneuvers if you are ever involved in a collision or other accident which may come to the attention of a court. Who knows—it may be worth its weight in gold some day for some such use?   UNSIGNED.

ON READING CODE

JANUARY, 1939

THOSE little dots and dashes that you sometimes hear on your radio, believe it or not, represent human intelligence being flashed through space to the very ends of the earth. Those blinking signal lights that you see the Coast Guard and Navy use are the same thing but they don't carry quite so far. The point of the situation is, though, that they are both in the same code and if you can understand one, you can understand the other. You, as a yachtsman, should know this code for you never can tell when it will be sorely needed. Rod Stephens tells a story of a small yacht evidently in some distress heading for some rocks. Those on shore tried to signal them with an ordinary flash lamp but no reply came from the yacht. Had anyone on the yacht been able to read those flashes, they would have discovered that a safe harbor was within easy reach but they thought the flashing light was simply a shore light and paid no attention with the result that the yacht hit the rocks and was badly damaged. During any offshore passage, even coastwise, you may wish to speak to a ship. Signal flags cannot be read at night and many times are not visible in full daylight. The flashlight will do the trick for you.

Most people refer to it as the Morse code, which it decidedly is not. Instead it is the Continental code adopted universally a number of years ago in place of the Morse code because it was simpler to read. The Morse code has several spaced letters that make it difficult to understand whether used for radio or for visual signaling where the Continental code has every letter and numeral different. The Morse code is used only in land telegraph lines with which we are not interested.

The Continental code, as used at sea.

The code diagram, printed herewith, is simple and fast. One can get to understand the characters in one or two evenings of practice— that is for sending, but for receiving the practice may take somewhat longer. Almost anyone can learn to send after a fashion without much difficulty but it will do you no good if you can't read what is sent back to you. You don't have to be any speed hound either for most visual light signaling is done at a relatively slow speed because of the

lag in the incandescent lamps used for the purpose. If you can receive
ten ten-letter words a minute, you can get by anywhere. If you can
take only five, you are still better off than not being able to understand anything at all. Under that you had best practice a bit.

In learning the code fix yourself up some kind of a key, a battery
and a buzzer or light. The key may be only a piece of spring brass
screwed to a board with a couple of brass-headed tacks for contacts.
You work this until you are thoroughly familiar with what the different characters are. Then you get someone else who knows the characters to send simple words to you. Two people, both learning, can
pick it up amazingly soon but one person by himself has a more difficult problem. You can buy what is known as an Omnigraph which
consists of brass discs with notches cut in their edges. You place these
on a clockwork driven machine and they will send you messages at
any rate of speed you wish. At one time the Victor people made
phonograph records of dot and dash messages that could be regulated

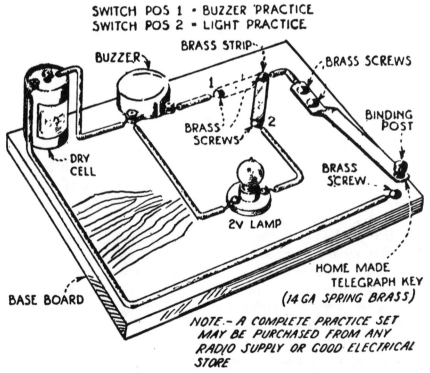

SWITCH POS 1 • BUZZER PRACTICE
SWITCH POS 2 • LIGHT PRACTICE
BRASS STRIP
BUZZER
BRASS SCREWS
BRASS SCREWS
BINDING POST
DRY CELL
BRASS SCREW
2V LAMP
HOME MADE TELEGRAPH KEY (14 GA SPRING BRASS)
BASE BOARD
NOTE.- A COMPLETE PRACTICE SET MAY BE PURCHASED FROM ANY RADIO SUPPLY OR GOOD ELECTRICAL STORE

A simple rig on which to practice code.

in speed on any ordinary phonograph. We believe these are still available. At any rate, it takes practice to learn to send and plenty of practice to learn to receive. Like anything else, the more you practice the more proficient you become and you may in time even get up to the speed used by commercial radio operators. Ship messages by radio frequently are sent at speeds of about twenty-five to thirty words a minute and some crack "ops" even knock 'em off at nearly twice this speed. After you once reach a speed of fifteen words a minute you can get all the practice you need right on your radio set.

The whole trick in learning the code is to do the entire thing by ear, not by sight. Forget what a dot and dash look like but instead say "dit-dah" to yourself and make the dit-dah automatically stand for the letter A. If you think "dot-dash" and visualize that in your mind, you delay your thinking by translating the dot-dash to the letter A and by the time you have done all that whoever is sending to you is three or four letters ahead of you and you'll never catch up. Do it entirely by ear; not by sight. Some people have tried to write down the dots and dashes as received then translate them later into letters but you can't do this and ever get any speed. Dit-dah must automatically mean A to you just the same as you look at the words in this article and automatically translate them into some semblance of a meaning. Once you get this it does not make any difference whether you receive the message by looking at a blinker light or listening to a radio. A fast operator can read code just as easily as you can read this page—automatically without a single thought of making . — into A. He never sees the . — but to him it is dit-dah which *is* A. The thing is instantaneous and as soon as you find yourself hearing dit-dah, then transferring it to . — in your mind and then, still in your mind into A, you are on the wrong track. Dit-dah *is* A without any further mental processes.

There are hundreds of abbreviations in use both by blinker and radio but most yachtsmen might better stick to plain spelled-out words and request the operator on the other end to do the same. The "Q" signals used in radio are not the same as the abbreviations used in visual signaling which includes the use of blinker lights.

The book entitled *International Code of Signals*, Vol. I, Visual Signals, and the other book called *International Code of Signals*, Vol. II, Radio Signals, are both available from the Hydrographic Office, Washington, D. C. Stamps are not accepted in payment. The first volume contains full instructions for sending and receiving abbreviated messages by visual signals while the second one covers the same thing in the radio field. The abbreviations are not the same by any manner of means although the code used is the same and since it would be a lifetime job to know both, it is better to stick to plain, spelled-out words.

The secret of really knowing the code is practice and plenty of it. Once you really learn the code you'll probably never forget it although without practice you may get a little rusty in your receiving speed. Receiving is the real trick as anyone can learn to send in a relatively short time. British yachtsmen nearly all know and use the blinker code but in America not one in 500 knows what it is all about. A knowledge of the code will add pleasure to your cruise and may be the means of saving your boat or even your life.

A mast head light may be very easily rigged with a telegraph key near the steering position. Watertight boxes for open bridges are also available. In these boxes a key is arranged in such a way that you can use it no matter what the weather. Some boats could be easily equipped with a white light on either spreader connected with the key. Regular navigation or riding lights should not be used.

UNSIGNED

HORSEPOWER—WHAT IS IT?

by C. F. LOEW

APRIL, 1933

If you are curious, this article can answer your questions. It will also show you a simple way to find out whether your own engine's horses are little or big.

A STORAGE battery salesman, in a burst of enthusiasm, and for the purpose of impressing his prospect with the diversity of his company's line, had laid before him a photograph showing the two extremes of battery sizes that were at that time being produced. One was a small motorcycle battery that could be held in the palm of the hand, the other one was a large power house battery, standing several feet in height, and weighing hundreds of pounds.

"You say," said the prospect, "that this little battery delivers six volts?"

"Yes."

"And this large one also delivers six volts?"

Again the reply was in the affirmative.

"I don't understand," continued the prospective purchaser, "why, if this little battery delivers six volts, this monster affair can do no better."

"Well," was the answer, "they're d——n big volts."

To many, it is a mystery why, as in the case of our battery illustration, there should be such a wide discrepancy in horsepower ratings of marine engines; why a small compact engine, such as used in light, fast runabouts, may be rated at the same, or even higher power than the much larger and heavier motor used in cruisers and work boats. The answer is: in the heavy duty engine they're d——n big horses.

The Kentucky thoroughbred has lots of speed, but cannot draw a load, and its life is usually short. On the other hand, the heavy draught horse can only plod along very slowly, but can pull a load many times its own weight, and lives a long life. He's a d——n big horse.

In choosing a marine engine, one must not be misled by horse-power rating, but must select one especially suited for the work to be done. We would not think of harnessing a trotting horse to a truck, nor is it conceivable that a draught horse would make a desirable mount for the bridle path. By the same token, we cannot expect satisfactory results from a heavy duty engine if we install it in a runabout or light express cruiser, nor conversely, from a runabout engine in a work boat or heavy cruiser. Just because a marine engine has a high rating, it does not necessarily follow that it will drive a given boat faster than some other engine of equivalent, or even less power. Neither does it always follow that the maximum power is obtainable. This maximum, or peak horsepower, is developed at some specific speed, and unless operated at exactly that speed, the full usable horse-power is not developed.

There is a very definite relationship between horsepower and engine revolutions per minute. After the engine is installed in the

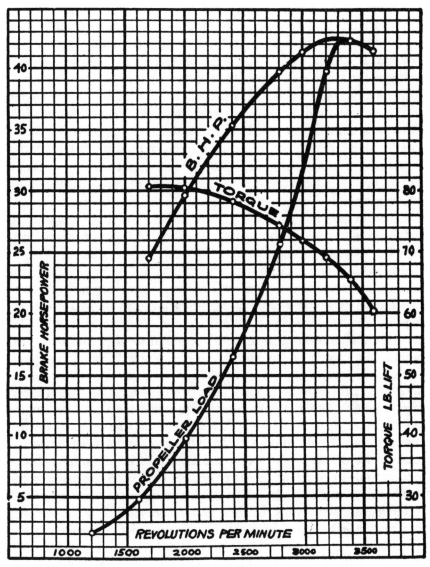

The relationship between RPM, brake horsepower and torque.

boat, the speed or r.p.m. will be governed solely by the size of the propeller. Therefore, if the propeller has too much blade area, excessive pitch, or is too great in diameter, the load on the engine becomes so great that it cannot turn at a speed that permits peak power output.

Now there is considerable difference between usable horsepower and useful horsepower. If an engine of given maximum horsepower rating is used, and it is found by experiment that the best boat performance can be secured with a propeller that holds down the engine revolutions below those recommended for highest power output, then the power at the lower speed represents useful horsepower, while the maximum, as rated by the manufacturer, represents usable horsepower. So, if your boat is equipped with an engine rated to deliver a certain power at some definite speed, or r.p.m., and this speed is by no means approached, do not always blame the engine for failure to deliver its full quota of power. The chances are a propeller was selected for the best possible performance, regardless of how the engine may have been rated by the builder, but you may be sure you are not getting the full usable horsepower, which, after all, doesn't matter, as it is boat performance you want, and not engine revolutions.

"Horsepower" is a term representing a means of measuring energy, and is the amount of work that can be done in a given time. To be specific, it is the amount of work required to lift a load of 33,000 pounds one foot in one minute. From this definition, it will be noted that the element of time is a factor. If we were to take two engines, both rated alike as to horsepower, but one of them a light, high speed engine, and the other, a heavy duty engine, and put them both to the same task of lifting equal loads, it will be found that whereas the big engine does the job with ease, the little one cannot even budge its load. So we divide up the work, and instead of having our small engine attempt to do its job in one effort, we have it do the work piecemeal, taking smaller loads, which it handles quicker. After we are all through, and we add up the time required to do the work, we will find that in either case the total time consumed for completing the task was exactly the same. So, since both engines did the same amount of work, in the same space of time, they exerted the same effort, and therefore may be considered as developing the same power.

Engine manufacturers will usually supply, on request, a chart, or curve, showing the power developed by their engines at various speeds. These are not always readily understood, and many owners are led to believe that the engine speed as shown by the tachometer is truly indicative of the power developed at that speed. But that is not always true. Manipulation of the throttle will vary the speed, but will not give a true indication of the useful horsepower for each speed change. When an engine is installed in a boat, there is but one speed at which the power shown by the curve will actually be developed, and that is only when the throttle is wide open.

In testing engines for power, the builders vary the speed by varying the load, and not by making constant throttle adjustments, so that through the full range of speed, the engine is always pulling its maximum. A suitable brake, or dynamometer, by means of which the power is measured, is coupled to the engine, and is adjusted until, with wide open throttle, the power developed will just turn it over. A reading is taken, and interpreted in terms of horsepower. The load is then lightened, which permits the engine to speed up, and another reading is made. This process is repeated throughout the entire speed range, until maximum power is shown. After the peak load speed has been reached, there will be no increase of power, but instead there will be a dropping off. Throughout this test, the throttle is never touched. The results of the test are plotted, and a curve is drawn. This is known as a full load curve. To obtain a propeller load curve, the process is reversed. The dynamometer load is adjusted so that with the engine developing its maximum power, the throttle will be wide open so as to enable it to run at the speed at which peak horsepower is attained. Then, instead of reducing the speed by increasing the load, the speed is reduced by gradually closing the throttle. The results of this curve are far different from the full load curve, as will be noted by comparing the two curves in the illustration. It is therefore the propeller load curve that indicates how much power your engine develops in your boat with each change of speed, as governed by the position of the throttle, and this will only be accurate when the propeller that is fitted will allow the engine to turn up at exactly the speed at which the peak horsepower is developed, when operated at full throttle.

The reason the propeller load curve differs from the full load curve is because neither the useful nor the usable horsepower is utilized, as there is always a reserve that can be secured by increasing the throttle opening. Of course, in a boat, the load cannot be varied at will. The only additional load that can be imposed on the motor being caused by increasing the number of passengers in the case of a pleasure boat, or the cargo in the case of a work boat. The effort required by the propeller to drive the craft through the water is what determines the load on the engine.

Getting back now to the selection of an engine, it is reasonable to assume that for every design of boat, there is just one size and shape of propeller that will give best results, that this propeller must revolve at some definite speed, and that a definite horsepower is needed to drive it at that speed. It is then necessary to find a power plant that will produce the necessary effort, and turn the propeller at the required number of revolutions per minute. Since there are innumerable kinds of boats, and propeller types running into the hundreds, it is not always possible to find the exact engine that will, with the hull and wheel, make a one hundred per cent combination, so compromises must be effected and an engine must be selected that will give as near perfect results as can be expected under the circumstances. If a boat needs a heavy duty engine, of, say one hundred horsepower, at a speed of approximately 1,500 r.p.m., don't install one that has to operate at twice that speed in order to develop the power. The chances are, if the proper wheel is used for that particular boat, the higher speed motor will not even be enabled to produce half its power rating, and it is doubtful if it can turn the wheel at even half the required speed, and if a smaller propeller is used, which will give the motor a chance to turn up properly, it will not have the blade area so necessary in heavy displacement craft, but will only churn the water without doing much in the way of propelling the boat. Of course if you use a reduction gear engine, that is another matter, so long as you get the right amount of power, at the right speed, *at the propeller*. It is equally ridiculous to put a heavy slow speed engine into a runabout, express cruiser or similar type of boat where light weight is obviously necessary, and where only a fast turning propeller will give sufficient wheel travel to bring about the desired boat speed.

Closely related to horsepower is torque. Torque is best defined as turning effort, or pressure against resistance. This is usually expressed in terms of "foot pounds." Thus, if an engine is said to have a torque of 150 foot pounds it means that if a lever one foot long is attached to the engine shaft, at right angles thereto, it will exert a pressure against resistance, of 150 pounds. If the lever is two feet long, the pressure

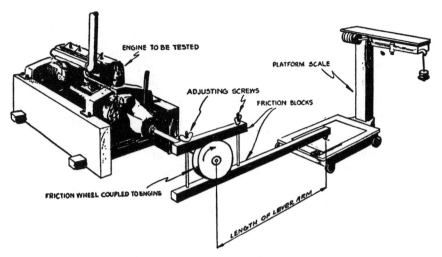

A simple rig to measure horsepower.

will be 75 pounds, the torque always being the product of the lever arm in feet, and the pressure in pounds. Engine testing brakes are constructed on the principle of such levers, which, however, are not securely fastened to the shaft, otherwise the motor could not run at all, but provision is made to allow slippage. The energy of the engine tends to rotate the lever, the end of which presses against a scalebeam, which in turn forms the resistance. The pressure against the scale is balanced by means of the counterpoises, and is read off directly in terms of pounds. The load variation is obtained by means of the adjustment of the slipping medium. In the simple prony brake, shown in the accompanying illustration, the band is tightened or loosened as desired, by means of a suitably provided adjusting screw.

Slow speed, heavy duty engines develop high torque at the lower speeds, while very much lower torque is developed in the high speed engine, regardless of its horsepower rating as compared with its heavy duty prototype. Where much effort is required to push a boat through the water, which in turn requires a large diameter propeller, we select an engine that has a high torque. It may therefore be readily noted that in some cases, horsepower is not of as much importance as torque. Although many boat builders do not understand the importance of torque, and do not generally select engines on the basis of torque values, they arrive at practically the same result by inquiring of the manufacturer about the sizes of propeller wheels that his engine will swing, and at what speed. This is the rule of thumb method of determining the suitability of an engine for a specific purpose.

In selecting an engine, it is first necessary to determine what is required of it. If pushing power is needed, and weight is no object, the heavy duty engine should, by all means, be the choice. It will be more economical of operation because of its high torque characteristics, enabling it to swing large diameter wheels without superfluous slip. If driving power is needed, in order to get a high rate of "wheel travel" then the high speed motor should be the right one to use. Its torque deficiency need not be a drawback, because a small propeller will be used, which does not require high torque.

After all, the many types of excellent engines now on the market are all built for specific purposes, and while compromises can frequently be effected, and are often necessary, it is always wise, before purchasing a motor, to determine exactly what the requirements are, and bearing in mind the illustration given by our equine example at the opening of these paragraphs, the rugged, powerful, but slow-moving draught horse for work, and the spirited, and swift thoroughbred for the saddle.

ON THE BAROMETER

by CAPT. E. ARMITAGE MC CANN

AUGUST, 1931

THE aneroid barometer is an instrument which measures the pressure of the air. It consists of a corrugated metallic chamber, partially exhausted of air and hermetically sealed. By an arrangement of levers and springs a hand is worked which indicates the pressure on a dial. The greater the pressure of the air, the more the chamber is contracted and the higher goes the hand; when the pressure is lessened the box expands and the hand shows less inches. These inches correspond to the height at which the column of mercury would stand in a mercurial barometer under similar conditions.

The aneroid, not being so reliable as a mercurial barometer, should be compared with one, as occasion offers, or with the standard readings as given in some of the daily papers, for the same time. That is, read yours at 8 A.M., note it down and then in next day's paper see what the standard then was, and note the error or adjust by the screw at the back of your instrument. A good aneroid is compensated for changes of temperature, and is so marked. The barometer will fall 1/10th inch for every 100 feet that it is above sea level.

When about to read it, give it a *gentle* tap in the center of the face, not on one side or the other and have it fixed so that it will not bang about with the motion of the vessel.

To foretell the weather you must study the thermometer in conjunction with your barometer, and in truth, the former will often give you longer notice than the latter. The clouds also are good weather prophets.

Meteorology is not an exact science and although the following hints are of fairly general application, they must not be absolutely relied upon, as local conditions and other causes may upset them. Even the Weather Bureau with all its scores of observers, synoptic weather maps and the like, can only tell you what will most likely occur in the way of weather.

The usual wording on a barometer has but little meaning; it is the rise and fall that matters.

Barometer Falling

In general—the barometer falls because the air is warm, moist and consequently light. This indicates moisture-bearing Southerly winds, with most likely rain, especially if the clouds are from the same direction.

A slow steady fall indicates a general and extensive storm.

When the glass begins to fall after dry weather expect unsettled or stormy weather especially in winter. In summer, warmer sultry weather, with showers.

For a fall with the weather warmer and damper, expect wind and rain, with S.E. to S.S.W. winds.

A fall with Northerly wind indicates rain or snow.

A fall with a dry atmosphere in winter indicates snow.

A fall after calm and heat in summer indicates squalls, thunder and rain.

If the barometer falls steadily with light E. or N.E. winds, expect rain with change to the S.E. with possibly a gale; especially if there is a short rise, this will veer to the S.W., the barometer continuing to fall. When the wind passes the S.W. point, the barometer will begin to rise, with heavy showers and strong W.N.W. or N.W. to follow, after which the sky will clear and the weather become colder.

A fall with increased temperature shows that the storm center is coming near, and will pass to the Northward.

With a low barometer and Southerly winds, if the weather gets cooler, expect a squall and sudden shift to N.W. or W. with rain or snow.

Southerly winds give longer warning than Northerly, especially Southwesterly—the first indication usually being mare's tails in the sky, followed by driving scud.

The force of the wind is proportionate to the rapidity and extent of the fall.

A barometer will fall more on a cloudy day than on a clear day.

Barometer Rising

In general—a barometer rises because the air is cold, dry and constantly heavy. This indicates drying Northerly winds and, usually, fine weather.

A slow steady rise, in general, indicates settled weather.

But a slight slow rise after a heavy storm predicts continued cloudiness and unsettled weather.

A slight but steady rise from low, before a storm, indicates a few days fine, with possibly fog on Spring mornings.

A steady rise above the average is a prognostic of a shift of wind to the N.W. or W. with cooler or drier weather.

With an average barometer, steady or rising, with the weather colder and air drier, expect N.W. to N.N.E. winds, or less wind and less rain or snow, if any.

A rapid but steady rise indicates strong Westerly or Northerly winds.

The strongest wind comes with a rapidly rising barometer.

The quicker the rise the more wind.

With a high barometer and rising thermometer, expect the wind to shift to the Southward.

With a high barometer and fresh E. to N.E. winds, expect rain or snow.

If the barometer rises with a Southerly wind, expect fine weather.

A rise when it is cold and moist indicates a Northerly wind with snow or rain.

A short rise with a lull in the wind, followed by a rapid rise, and shift of wind shows that the storm center is passing you.

Barometer Steady

With a high steady barometer, the weather will be dry and wind light for some days.

With a low steady barometer (say, 29.55) expect wet weather, with Southerly winds. The longer it remains low the greater the danger of storms following.

Barometer Fluctuating

A fluctuating barometer indicates quick changes of weather.

A quick rise is just likely to bring a gale as a sudden fall.

> *First rise after low,*
> *Indicates a stronger blow.*
> *Short notice soon past*
> *Long notice long last.*

Fluctuations are generally greater in the northern than the southern parts of the U. S. and in the eastern than the western.

Fluctuations are much greater in the winter than in the summer.

Thunderstorms

Small craft should always make for shelter on the first indication of an approaching thunderstorm, as, with its accompanying squall of wind, it is likely to be very much increased over water, whether sea, lake or river.

The usual indications are warm weather, usually dry but close, the wind from the East or South for several hours previous, then a gradual fall of the barometer, the piling up of cumuli-nimbus clouds, an abrupt fall of the barometer, then when the storm reaches you, a rapid rise with the wind shifting to W. to N.W. and a heavy drop in the temperature from 10 to 40 degrees.

If you get the wind before the rain, expect a short blow but if the rain before the wind expect a longer heavier gale.

HOW TO READ THE TIDE TABLE

by A. G. PELIKAN

JANUARY, 1943

To THOSE who are unaccustomed to reading tables of various kinds the interpretation and use of the Tide Table may at first seem complicated and confusing.

It is even difficult for some advanced students to determine the height of a tide at a certain time in the case where the duration of the tide between high and low goes from the P.M. of one day into the A.M. of another, and particularly where one minute after midnight causes a change in date.

In order to simplify the work as much as possible for the beginner, the accompanying tidal data form has been prepared by the author. The procedure for the use of this form is as follows:

PROBLEM: Required to find the height of the tide on a certain day at a given time, as for instance to find the height of the tide at Philadelphia on April 6 at 10:45 A.M.

Since Philadelphia is a reference station, no allowance for time correction needs to be made. The first step is to determine from the Tide Table the time between which high and low tide on the date given the desired time falls.

Since the time is 10:45 A.M. and the nearest high tide on this date is at 7:28 A.M. and the nearest low tide is at 2:33 P.M., then 10:45 A.M. is between the time of these two tides.

Next obtain the range of the tide by taking the difference between the height of the tide at high water and the height of the tide at low water.

Two other factors must be determined next before Table Number 3 in the Tide Tables can be used.

1. The duration of the rise or fall of the tide.
2. The time nearest to high or low water.

TABLE 3.—HEIGHT OF TIDE AT ANY TIME   291

Duration of rise or fall, see footnote	Time from the nearest high water or low water														
h. m.	h. m.	h. m.	h. m.	h. m.	h. m.	h. m.	h. m.	h. m.	h. m.	h. m.	h. m.	h. m.	h. m.	h. m.	h. m.
4 00	0 04	0 16	0 24	0 32	0 40	0 48	0 56	1 04	1 12	1 20	1 28	1 36	1 44	1 52	2 00
4 20	0 09	0 17	0 26	0 35	0 43	0 52	1 01	1 09	1 18	1 27	1 35	1 44	1 53	2 01	2 10
4 40	0 09	0 19	0 28	0 37	0 47	0 56	1 05	1 15	1 24	1 33	1 43	1 52	2 01	2 11	2 20
5 00	0 10	0 20	0 30	0 40	0 50	1 00	1 10	1 20	1 30	1 40	1 50	2 00	2 10	2 20	2 30
5 20	0 11	0 21	0 32	0 43	0 53	1 04	1 15	1 25	1 36	1 47	1 57	2 06	2 19	2 29	2 40
5 40	0 11	0 23	0 34	0 45	0 57	1 08	1 19	1 31	1 42	1 53	2 05	2 16	2 27	2 39	2 50
6 00	0 12	0 24	0 36	0 48	1 00	1 12	1 24	1 36	1 48	2 00	2 12	2 24	2 36	2 48	3 00
6 20	0 13	0 25	0 38	0 51	1 03	1 16	1 29	1 41	1 54	2 07	2 19	2 32	2 45	2 57	3 10
6 40	0 13	0 27	0 40	0 53	1 07	1 20	1 33	1 47	2 00	2 13	2 27	2 40	2 53	3 07	3 20
7 00	0 14	0 28	0 42	0 56	1 10	1 24	1 38	1 52	2 06	2 20	2 34	2 48	3 02	3 16	3 30
7 20	0 15	0 29	0 44	0 59	1 13	1 28	1 43	1 57	2 12	2 27	2 41	2 56	3 11	3 25	3 40
7 40	0 15	0 31	0 46	1 01	1 17	1 32	1 47	2 03	2 18	2 33	2 49	3 04	3 19	3 35	3 50
8 00	0 16	0 32	0 48	1 04	1 20	1 36	1 52	2 08	2 24	2 40	2 56	3 12	3 28	3 44	4 00
8 20	0 17	0 33	0 50	1 07	1 23	1 40	1 57	2 13	2 30	2 47	3 03	3 20	3 37	3 53	4 10
8 40	0 17	0 35	0 52	1 09	1 27	1 44	2 01	2 19	2 36	2 53	3 11	3 28	3 45	4 03	4 20
9 00	0 18	0 36	0 54	1 12	1 30	1 48	2 06	2 24	2 42	3 00	3 18	3 36	3 54	4 12	4 30
9 20	0 19	0 37	0 56	1 15	1 33	1 52	2 11	2 29	2 48	3 07	3 25	3 44	4 03	4 21	4 40
9 40	0 19	0 39	0 58	1 17	1 37	1 56	2 15	2 35	2 54	3 13	3 33	3 52	4 11	4 31	4 50
10 00	0 20	0 40	1 00	1 20	1 40	2 00	2 20	2 40	3 00	3 20	3 40	4 00	4 20	4 40	5 00
10 20	0 21	0 41	1 02	1 23	1 43	2 04	2 25	2 45	3 06	3 27	3 47	4 08	4 29	4 49	5 10
10 40	0 21	0 43	1 04	1 25	1 47	2 08	2 29	2 51	3 12	3 33	3 55	4 16	4 37	4 59	5 20

Range of tide, see footnote	Correction to height														
Ft.	Ft.	Ft.	Ft.	Ft.	Ft.	Ft.	Ft.	Ft.	Ft.	Ft.	Ft.	Ft.	Ft.	Ft.	Ft.
0.5	0.0	0.0	0.0	0.0	0.0	0.0	0.1	0.1	0.1	0.1	0.1	0.2	0.2	0.2	0.2
1.0	0.0	0.0	0.0	0.0	0.1	0.1	0.1	0.2	0.2	0.2	0.3	0.3	0.4	0.4	0.5
1.5	0.0	0.0	0.0	0.1	0.1	0.1	0.2	0.3	0.3	0.4	0.5	0.6	0.7	0.7	0.8
2.0	0.0	0.0	0.0	0.1	0.1	0.2	0.3	0.3	0.4	0.5	0.6	0.7	0.8	0.9	1.0
2.5	0.0	0.0	0.1	0.1	0.2	0.2	0.3	0.4	0.5	0.6	0.7	0.9	1.0	1.1	1.2
3.0	0.0	0.0	0.1	0.1	0.2	0.3	0.4	0.5	0.6	0.8	0.9	1.0	1.2	1.3	1.5
3.5	0.0	0.0	0.1	0.2	0.2	0.3	0.4	0.6	0.7	0.9	1.0	1.2	1.4	1.6	1.8
4.0	0.0	0.0	0.1	0.2	0.3	0.4	0.5	0.7	0.8	1.0	1.2	1.4	1.6	1.8	2.0
4.5	0.0	0.0	0.1	0.2	0.3	0.4	0.6	0.7	0.9	1.1	1.3	1.6	1.8	2.0	2.2
5.0	0.0	0.0	0.1	0.2	0.3	0.5	0.6	0.8	1.0	1.2	1.5	1.7	2.0	2.2	2.5
5.5	0.0	0.1	0.1	0.3	0.4	0.5	0.7	0.9	1.1	1.4	1.6	1.9	2.2	2.5	2.8
6.0	0.0	0.1	0.1	0.3	0.4	0.6	0.8	1.0	1.2	1.5	1.8	2.1	2.4	2.7	3.0
6.5	0.0	0.1	0.2	0.3	0.4	0.6	0.8	1.1	1.3	1.6	1.9	2.2	2.6	2.9	3.2
7.0	0.0	0.1	0.2	0.3	0.5	0.7	0.9	1.2	1.4	1.8	2.1	2.4	2.8	3.1	3.5
7.5	0.0	0.1	0.2	0.3	0.5	0.7	1.0	1.2	1.5	1.9	2.2	2.6	3.0	3.4	3.8
8.0	0.0	0.1	0.2	0.3	0.5	0.8	1.0	1.3	1.6	2.0	2.4	2.8	3.2	3.6	4.0
8.5	0.0	0.1	0.2	0.4	0.6	0.8	1.1	1.4	1.8	2.1	2.5	2.9	3.4	3.8	4.2
9.0	0.0	0.1	0.2	0.4	0.6	0.9	1.2	1.5	1.9	2.2	2.7	3.1	3.6	4.0	4.5
9.5	0.0	0.1	0.2	0.4	0.6	0.9	1.2	1.6	2.0	2.4	2.8	3.3	3.8	4.3	4.8
10.0	0.0	0.1	0.2	0.4	0.7	1.0	1.3	1.7	2.1	2.5	3.0	3.5	4.0	4.5	5.0
10.5	0.0	0.1	0.3	0.5	0.7	1.0	1.3	1.7	2.2	2.6	3.1	3.6	4.2	4.7	5.2
11.0	0.0	0.1	0.3	0.5	0.7	1.1	1.4	1.8	2.3	2.8	3.3	3.8	4.4	4.9	5.5
11.5	0.0	0.1	0.3	0.5	0.8	1.1	1.5	1.9	2.4	2.9	3.4	4.0	4.6	5.1	5.8
12.0	0.0	0.1	0.3	0.5	0.8	1.1	1.5	2.0	2.5	3.0	3.6	4.1	4.8	5.4	6.0
12.5	0.0	0.1	0.3	0.5	0.8	1.2	1.6	2.1	2.6	3.1	3.7	4.3	5.0	5.6	6.2
13.0	0.0	0.1	0.3	0.6	0.9	1.2	1.7	2.2	2.7	3.2	3.9	4.5	5.1	5.8	6.5
13.5	0.0	0.1	0.3	0.6	0.9	1.3	1.7	2.3	2.8	3.4	4.0	4.7	5.3	6.0	6.8
14.0	0.0	0.1	0.3	0.6	0.9	1.3	1.8	2.3	2.9	3.5	4.2	4.8	5.5	6.3	7.0
14.5	0.0	0.2	0.4	0.6	1.0	1.4	1.9	2.4	3.0	3.6	4.3	5.0	5.7	6.5	7.2
15.0	0.0	0.2	0.4	0.6	1.0	1.4	1.9	2.5	3.1	3.8	4.4	5.2	5.9	6.7	7.5
15.5	0.0	0.2	0.4	0.7	1.0	1.5	2.0	2.6	3.2	3.9	4.6	5.4	6.1	6.9	7.8
16.0	0.0	0.2	0.4	0.7	1.1	1.5	2.1	2.6	3.3	4.0	4.7	5.5	6.3	7.2	8.0
16.5	0.0	0.2	0.4	0.7	1.1	1.6	2.1	2.7	3.4	4.1	4.9	5.7	6.5	7.4	8.2
17.0	0.0	0.2	0.4	0.7	1.1	1.6	2.2	2.8	3.5	4.2	5.0	5.9	6.7	7.6	8.5
17.5	0.0	0.2	0.4	0.8	1.2	1.7	2.2	2.9	3.6	4.4	5.2	6.0	6.9	7.8	8.8
18.0	0.0	0.2	0.4	0.8	1.2	1.7	2.3	3.0	3.7	4.5	5.3	6.2	7.1	8.1	9.0
18.5	0.1	0.2	0.5	0.8	1.2	1.8	2.4	3.1	3.8	4.6	5.5	6.4	7.3	8.3	9.2
19.0	0.1	0.2	0.5	0.8	1.3	1.8	2.4	3.1	3.9	4.8	5.6	6.6	7.5	8.5	9.5
19.5	0.1	0.2	0.5	0.9	1.3	1.9	2.5	3.2	4.0	4.9	5.8	6.7	7.7	8.7	9.8
20.0	0.1	0.2	0.5	0.9	1.3	1.9	2.6	3.3	4.1	5.0	5.9	6.9	7.9	9.0	10.0

Obtain from the predictions the high water and low water, one of which is before and the other after the time for which the height is required. The difference between the times of occurrence of these tides is the duration of rise or fall, and the difference between their heights is the range of tide for the above table. Find the difference between the nearest high or low water and the time for which the height is required.

Enter the table with the duration of rise or fall, printed in heavy-faced type, which most nearly agrees with the actual value, and on that horizontal line find the time from the nearest high or low water which agrees most nearly with the corresponding actual difference. The correction sought is in the column directly below, on the line with the range of tide.

When the nearest tide is high water, subtract the correction.
When the nearest tide is low water, add the correction.

Tide table, showing range and duration.

321

The duration of rise or fall may be obtained by determining the time difference between the high water and low water for the given date.

Next take the time of the nearest tide and the time desired and the difference will give you the time nearest to the high water or low water.

We now have the three factors necessary to obtain the height of the tide at the time desired.

1. Duration of rise or fall 7.05
2. Time from the nearest high water or low water 3.17
3. Range of tide 5.1

Referring to Table Number 3 we find that:

1. The nearest number to 7.05 is 7.00
2. The nearest number to 3.17 is 3.16
3. The nearest number to 5.1 is 5.00
4. The correction is found in the column directly below the "time from the nearest high or low water" on line with the figure indicated in the "Range of Tide" column. Where the two columns intersect the correction is found, which in this case is 2.2.

Since the nearest tide to the time desired is at 7:28 A.M. which is high tide, the correction is subtracted from the height of the tide given for high tide which is 4.7. The answer for the height required is therefore 2.5 feet, which in turn must be added to the charted depth of the locality for which you have determined the height of the tide.

In the case of a substation the problem is the same, with the exception that the time difference and height difference is added or subtracted according to the corrections found for the particular substation in Table Number 2.

EXAMPLE: Find the height of the tide at Shelton on September 29 at 12:43 P.M. The reference station is Willets Point. After the time and height corrections have been made, the problem is the same as the first problem. See tidal data form.

Tidal Data Form

(Left form)

SUBSTATION Feb 3 TIME 10:45 a.m.
REFERENCE STATION Philadelphia

NEAREST HIGH TIDE AT REFERENCE STATION
HEIGHT 4.7

FROM TABLE NO. 2	7:30 a.m.	8:33 p.m.	-0.4	4.7
CORRECTION	NO CORRECTION			-0.4
				5.1

Time { Lower Tide → 2:33 p.m., 10:45 a.m., 7:38 a.m.
Different { High → 7:26 a.m., 7:26 a.m.
7.05 7.05 3.7 9th high tide
3.79
2 → 0. TIME OF FALL

FROM TABLE NO. 3 — HEIGHT OF TIDE AT ANY TIME

HEIGHT OF TIDE AT ANY TIME	7.05	7.00
HIGH TIDE, NEAREST TIDE—ADD OR SUB	3.7	3.46	2.2
HEIGHT OF TIDE	5.1	5.0

HEIGHT OF NEAREST TIDE—LOW TIDE—ADD 4.7
HEIGHT OF NEAREST TIDE—HIGH TIDE—SUBTRACT 2.2
CORRECTION 2.5
HEIGHT REQUIRED

(Right form)

SUBSTATION Shelton TIME Sept 29, 12:45 p.m.
REFERENCE STATION Millers Point

NEAREST LOW TIDE AT REFERENCE STATION
HEIGHT 0.8 4.5

FROM TABLE NO. 2	2:30 a.m.	8:57 p.m.	6.7	0.8	4.5
CORRECTION	-1.85	-2.30	-2.2	0.2
	3:48 a.m.	11:39 p.m.	4.6	0.8	4.3

Time { Lower Tide → 11:39 p.m., 12:43 p.m., 11:39 p.m.
Different { High → 3:48 a.m., 11:39 p.m.
4.19 1:14 gives last tide
2 → 0. TIME OF FALL

FROM TABLE NO. 3 —

HEIGHT OF TIDE AT ANY TIME	4.19	4.20
HIGH TIDE, NEAREST TIDE—ADD OR SUB	1.14	1.16	0.9
HEIGHT OF TIDE	4.3	4.5

HEIGHT OF NEAREST TIDE—LOW TIDE—402 0.2
HEIGHT OF NEAREST TIDE—HIGH TIDE—SUBTRACT 0.9
CORRECTION 0.9
HEIGHT REQUIRED 1.1

Tide data forms used in working out these problems.

ON MOTOR BOAT COMPASSES

by NEGUS

MAY, 1903

THE compass may not be often needed but, when it is required, it is like the Texan's gun. Few launch owners realize the importance of having a good compass on board, and few are acquainted with the errors that it may have, due to the attraction of the iron and steel in engines, anchors, steering gears, tanks, etc., or know how to use it to the best advantage.

The compass should be placed on a line parallel with the keel of the boat. It should be placed as far away as possible from the engine, tanks, or steering gears, and yet be in a place where it can be readily seen from the wheel. After a compass is once placed and its errors, if any, determined, the movable iron, such as anchors, chains, etc., should always be stowed in the same place and in the same manner.

To get a compass on board parallel to the keel, a good way is to stretch a fish line from the center point of the bow to the center of the stern, place the lubber lines of the compass under this line, or, if at the side, exactly parallel. Then make a mark, or put some catch to it so it can always be put in the same place. The lubber line is a black line in the bowl of the compass—usually there are four—and when steering the boat one of these lubber lines should be directly forward on line with the keel. This explanation is made, thinking that possibly some novices might not know what a lubber line is.

If the reader is well acquainted with compasses, and understands the use of taking azimuths, he need not read this article. The idea in a small launch is not to *correct* the compass, but simply to find its errors and apply them when a certain course is to be steered.

To *correct* the compass errors requires the service of a professional compass adjuster, and this is rather expensive for a small launch, and not necessary.

The best simple way is to take an object on the shore (far distant), it may be a lighthouse, a beacon, a chimney, a steeple, or any prominent object.

324

.... COMPASS on Board the
.... Captain ....
Date .... by ....

For Correct Magnetic.	STEER BY COMPASS.	For Correct Magnetic.	STEER BY COMPASS.
North.		North.	
N. by W.		N. by E.	
N.N.W.		N.N.E.	
N.W. by N.		N.E. by N.	
N.W.		N.E.	
N.W. by W.		N.E. by E.	
W.N.W.		E.N.E.	
W. by N.		E. by N.	
West.		East.	
W. by S.		E. by S.	
W.S.W.		E.S.E.	
S.W. by W.		S.E. by E.	
S.W.		S.E.	
S.W. by S.		S.E. by S.	
S.S.W.		S.S.E.	
S. by W.		S. by E.	
South.		South.	

A steering card.

Take your compass in your hands so as to lift it well above the deck, stand in some part of the launch as far away from the engine and tanks as possible. In this position there is very slight chance that your compass will have any error. As you hold the compass in front of your face, sight across it at the distant object on the shore, note the bearing of the compass, then place the compass back in the place where you intend using it for steering; after this is done, steer your launch straight for the same land object; if the compass reads the same as it did when you held it in your hand, it is correct and has no error on this course. If it shows an error, then make a note of this on your steering card. For instance, if your land object bore north, and your compass read in position north half east, you would always steer north half east when you wished to steer north. You may then select another object and keep repeating this performance until you have all the courses, but usually if you tested the compass in this way on north, south, east and west, you would probably have no other errors, and you would be satisfied that your compass was right on all courses.

To facilitate getting the first bearing, you can set up two pins on the box of your compass directly over the lubber line forward, and over the lubber line in the aft end of the box. Place these pins about ⅛ of an inch apart—you look at the object through the two sets of pins. When you can see the lighthouse directly in the center of these pins, the lubber line below gives you the reading of the compass. You can, of course, procure a more elaborate sight vane from any of the nautical instrument makers, but the above will answer very well.

This method would be still easier if you happen to have two compasses, as you do not have to keep shifting them in each reading.

ON CANVAS SAILS

by ERNEST RATSEY

APRIL, 1931

CANVAS is the topic to be discussed. There are two kinds, basically, a Southern grown American cotton which is white and an Egyptian grown cotton which is called brown Egyptian because of its reddish tint. The difference is really very marked. This brown Egyptian is getting lighter in color every year and the only feasible explanation I have heard for this change is that in the olden days the River Nile overflowed its banks when it had too much water in it and irrigated the fields, sending with the water a lot of the silt, which in itself is a reddish brown color. Now, since the Assouan dam has been built, nature no longer floods the fields but it is done by man instead and scarcely any silt goes with the water as most of it has settled to the bottom.

Don't confuse brown Egyptian with tanned canvas. This is a dye which I believe comes from India. This tanned canvas is used quite a good deal by the fishing boats and trawlers working off the Brittany coast and in the North Sea. This dye is supposed to preserve the canvas and, of course, it doesn't show the dirt or the mildew.

Now as to the weights of canvas. It is highly confusing to the layman to get it into his head why 8 oz. should be heavier than 7 oz. and yet No. 8 should be lighter than No. 7.

CLASSIFICATION OF CANVAS

No. 00		12 OZ.
" 0		10 OZ.
" 1		9 OZ.
" 2		8 OZ.
" 3		7 OZ.
" 4		6 OZ.
" 5		5 OZ.
" 6		4 OZ.
" 7		3 OZ.
" 8	Balloon Cloth	2 OZ.
" 9		1 OZ.

When considering the weight of sail canvas, the first thing to remember is that the standard width of cloth is $28\frac{1}{2}$ inches, so a piece of 8 oz. duck means that 1 yard $28\frac{1}{2}$ inches wide weighs 8 oz. You could also have 8 oz. duck 18 inches wide (or any other width for that matter) but that duck does not weigh 8 oz. per yard in that width, but it would weigh 8 oz. if it was $28\frac{1}{2}$ inches wide. Now you will notice on the chart that 1 oz. is the lightest and the numbers increase in weight as they go up until they get to 12 oz. After that canvas is denoted by numbers and it runs from No. 9 up to No. 00. That is where the confusion starts in most persons' minds, owing to the fact that the numbers here are diminishing yet the weights are increasing. Exactly why duck above 12 oz. is referred to by numbers instead of by ounces I don't really know.

In the old days flax was used a great deal for canvas. It is of a very soft nature and even when wet it remains that way but, of course, sails made from flax do not hold their shape owing to its softness, that is why it has been superseded by cotton. Egyptian cotton has a longer staple than Southern grown American cotton and it makes a stronger sail which seems to hold its shape better.

In a piece of canvas the threads running lengthwise in it are referred to as the "warp" and the threads running across it are referred to as the "weft." In the days when the cloths ran vertically in sails the canvas was made with the warp stronger than the weft, to take the vertical strain, but now in cross-cut sails this procedure is reversed and the weft threads are stronger than the warp.

The actual making of sails can be divided for simplicity's sake into four parts. First, the actual size of the sail is chalked out on the floor and the strips of canvas cut to cover the required area. The cloths are then taken to a long table (one edge of which is a straight edge) and here lines are drawn on each cloth to show the mechanics exactly how much the next cloth is to be lapped over when it is sewn on. The cloths are then spread out again alongside each other, all pulled out tight with an even tension and cross marks put on the selvages so that they will be sewn together as an even surface.

The second step is sewing the cloths together. If you refer to the chart you can visualize my next remark a little better. Up to 12 oz. in weight the seams are sewn usually by machine, but for canvas above that weight it should really be done by hand. A machine needle is round and in going through the canvas it merely punches a hole through, drawing after it a thread smaller in diameter than the needle itself; but the needle the sailmaker uses when sewing by hand is triangular to start with, tapering off round as it gets up towards the eye. When this is pushed through canvas instead of punching a hole through and splitting the threads, it eases its own way through and draws after it a very much heavier waxed thread. This thread sinks down into the canvas a trifle in being pulled through, whereas the thread following a machine needle lies on top of the canvas and is much more susceptible to the chafe from topping lifts, backstays, or any other wires that are apt to come up against it.

The third step is what is technically known as "rubbing down." This means that the sail having been sewn together is spread out and the necessary curves are marked on the sides to help give it the proper flow or draft. Incidentally this flow or draft is put into the sail little by little in all the stages of making as well as this rubbing down. Having marked all the curves, the excess canvas is cut off and the various tablings or hems and strengthening pieces are cut out and sewn on. Here again some are done by machine and some by hand, depending upon weight of canvas and the size of the sail.

The fourth and last step is finishing and it does not matter what kind or size of sail one is dealing with it all has to be done by hand. There is no machine for sewing on ropes.

You hear a lot about ordering sails in the winter time and you probably think that this is a lot of sales talk. In a way I suppose it is, but the real reason is that during the winter months where the steam heat is on and the loft is kept at an even temperature, the canvas as it goes through the various stages of manufacturing into a sail does not vary very much and in the end should turn out to be a smoother sail; whereas, in the summer, you may start a sail on a nice sunny day, have it blowing northeast with rain on the second day and get a dry nor'wester the third. This is really most disconcerting to the sail-maker because the canvas reacts very differently on each of these days, so you can see that it is a much simpler and should be a safer proposition making sails during the winter time.

I don't think the average racing skipper pays much attention to his gear and fittings. The principal reason that the sails set so well on the season's champions is that they were all treated carefully and that they had the correct gear on those boats to set the sails. It is quite possible that the boats in the various classes that they beat would have had just as good sails and probably better if only they had given them the care and attention that was shown on these winning boats.

ON CHARTERING A BOAT

by HENRY T. MENEELY

JULY, 1939

This may be elementary knowledge to many, but headaches that constantly arise out of improper charterings indicate that many of these factors are overlooked.

CHARTERING a boat is very much the same as renting a house, providing that the house is completely furnished and attended by a staff of servants paid by the owner. But—a house does not move from place to place (normally) and here is the big difference and where the ramifications and pitfalls enter the picture.

For those who are about to flip the page, let me get one important idea across. It is, simply, do not enter into a charter agreement with a minor. Such a contract would not be recognized in court and in case some difference of opinion should arise as an outcome from such an agreement, someone would have to bear all the grief. But, let us not delve into the unpleasant possibilities.

I will try to bring out the mechanics of the business of chartering a boat, by no means in complete detail, but enough to help a person who wants an introduction to the procedure.

The first and perhaps most important consideration is price. It is generally understood that a boat is worth, for charter, ten per cent of its value per month. This is too rough a way to figure a charter price, literally, but if we take a typical boat about three years old—one that is neither extravagant nor cheap and with normal equipment—appraise it at about seventy per cent of its new value, ten per cent of that value would be about right, more or less, depending on the condition of the boat, the demand for its size, and how well it can serve the purpose for which it is intended. Thus, an auxiliary yawl, say, to sleep four persons, no crew, that cost about $7,000 to build, is worth about $500 per month to charter. If the boat has a stateroom so that two couples can sleep in two separate cabins, then it is probably more desirable than a boat equipped with upper and lower berths all in the same cabin, and hence worth a little more. Also, a sailboat without power would not bring as much as one with an auxiliary, unless chartered for class racing, and so on and so on. Cost then, is largely a matter of informed opinion and comparison of relative values. Your broker is your best bet here.

The other main points to consider might best be enumerated. Assume then, you know just what you want and only care for details pertaining to its charter.

1. Price or value—discussed above.

2. Terms under which monies shall be paid: For charters of two weeks or less, the entire amount is usually payable in advance. For longer periods, a substantial amount should be paid in advance and the rest prorated and likewise paid in advance.

3. Delivery and redelivery: It should always be stated where and when the charter party takes possession and returns it.

4. Crew: A paid crew is generally supplied by the owner but works for the charter party except in case of emergency when the captain would take full charge as prescribed by law, in the interest of safety. However, the crew must be subordinate to the charter party and it is generally agreed that they may be discharged if deemed advisable by the charter party though it is generally stipulated that the captain and engineer can be discharged only with consent of the owner.

5. Insurance: This is up to the owner as a rule and he must have permission of the company carrying the risk before he can charter his boat under the protection of that company.

6. Running expenses: The charter party regularly assumes all expenses other than insurance and crew's wages during the charter term. He is also liable for any damage or repairs and replacements not due to ordinary wear and tear, except as might be covered by the insurance.

7. Navigation limits: It is a good thing to have it understood in a charter agreement just where the vessel may be taken. Limits are probably stated in the insurance policy and those limits are, usually, Eastport, Maine, to Norfolk, Virginia, in the summer, unless special dispensation is made in advance.

The above would seem to cover the main points. Other clauses in a complete agreement take up such matters as sub-chartering, defaults on any agreed points, etc. Incidentally, it is usually agreed that any differences arising from a yacht charter be referred to arbitration, which often relieves possibility of tedious and inconvenient court proceedings.

All of the above is merely to show some of the main points that ought to be considered in chartering a boat. Do not by any means feel you can draw up a complete form on the basis of only those points I have brought out. I merely state that all those things should be considered in every charter agreement. Often, too, justifiable exceptions can be and are made. For instance, there are occasions when a man charters a bare boat and puts his own crew aboard. This is called a "bare boat charter." Many yachts are too small to carry any crew.

It is not usually economical, unless a boat can be gotten for a very low figure, to charter for a term exceeding two months. For a greater length of time it might be cheaper to buy and resell. Many people, on the other hand, charter regularly for all summer because, regardless of the cost, they simply do not want to own a boat. Plenty of difference of opinion on this point, but most of the old-timers would prefer to own.

Any way you look at it, a vacation can hardly be more perfect than aboard a yacht. Figure the cost per person as compared with most anything else people normally do and you will be amazed how economical it can be. No hotels—no railroads—no extra expenses for theatres, etc. (providing you have the good sense to stay aboard) and the ladies find it difficult to go shopping unless you have the bad taste to stay too long at Newport.

So it goes, but you might as well look into the subject before planning your vacation. See your broker. I am sure he can help you.

THE WHYS OF MARINE INSURANCE

by H. W. LOWEREE

JANUARY, 1936

"FINE residence burned to the ground; fully covered by insurance." This is a common headline in the daily press as practically every home is insured against fire but when a yacht casualty is reported insurance is rarely, if ever, mentioned. While nearly all of the larger yachts are covered by marine insurance there are many owners of smaller craft who have overlooked this protection although a marine yacht policy covers practically every casualty including loss by fire.

Marine insurance is the oldest form of underwriting known and from it have sprung all other kinds of insurance protection. It was not, however, until recent years that the marine insurance companies would accept the risk of insuring yachts except those in the larger classes. Now it is possible to obtain this coverage on practically all types from the lowly dinghy to the largest yacht.

Among the "perils" covered by a marine yacht policy are: burning, sinking, stranding, collision, explosion, hauling or launching, theft of the vessel and salvage charges. In the event of collision the assured collects for the damage he sustains regardless as to who may have been at fault and if he is held legally liable for the damage to the other vessel the insurance company must also pay any claim up to the value of the vessel at fault. The policy covers the hull, fittings, fixtures and navigating equipment against practically every casualty wherever it may be, afloat or ashore, within the limits set forth with but few exceptions as will be later explained.

A few recent casualties, that are typical, will serve to illustrate the operation of marine insurance when a loss occurs:—A fire was discovered on a thirty-eight foot auxiliary that got beyond control of the crew. A commercial vessel came alongside and extinguished the fire which had damaged the interior, below decks, to a considerable extent. The damaged yacht was then towed to a shipyard where an estimate was obtained for repairing the hull and the figures checked by a representative from the insurance company. The amount agreed upon was $3,500. In addition to this there was equipment damaged or destroyed to the extent of $400, making a total of $3,900, which was paid but the underwriters were not yet through with this loss as the owners of the commercial vessel, that extinguished the fire, put in a claim for salvage which also had to be settled and paid by the insurance company. After receiving payment of the $3,900, the owner decided he would not have the yacht repaired and sold her as she stood for $750, thus realizing $4,650, on a $5,000 policy.

Another case was a forty foot cruiser insured for $10,000 which hit an obstruction one night and stove in a plank. The owner beached the yacht and notified his insurance company who immediately sent a wrecking derrick to raise the wreck and tow her to a shipyard. The yacht had to be reconditioned inside and out and several new planks installed at a cost of $3,000 which was paid in full. In addition the underwriter had to pay $200 for equipment and salvage charges bringing the loss up to approximately $4,000. In three weeks the yacht was again in commission in as good or in fact better condition than before the accident and the only loss to the owner was for personal effects not covered under the yacht policy.

Last summer an old yawl, valued at not over $400, dragged through a fleet of anchored yachts during a moderate squall because of being improperly anchored. This yawl was not insured and the only damage to her was loss of the bobstay, however, she fouled four yachts causing total damages of more than $1,000. Two of the damaged yachts were insured and collected in full. Two were not insured and the owner of one who suffered damages to the extent of $500 tried to libel the yawl but was unsuccessful and had to stand his own loss. If the yawl had been insured the underwriters would have been liable for the damages but only up to the amount of insurance carried. In other words, if a yacht insured for $500 causes damages of $5,000 to a vessel that is not insured the owner of the latter can collect only $500 from the underwriters.

Quite recently a fine power cruiser picked up a dinghy that had broken adrift from a yawl in quite heavy weather. In maneuvering to return the dinghy the yawl was struck with a heavy puff of wind causing her to crash into the cruiser with a resulting damage of $500. The owner of the yawl said he was sorry but the underwriter carrying the insurance on the cruiser had to pay the damages and then take the chance of trying to collect from the owner of the yawl or his insurance company—if the yawl was insured.

In the late fall of 1932 there was the highest tide ever recorded down on the east end of Long Island. A Marblehead cruiser had been hauled out and blocked up for the winter but the high water floated the yacht and when the tide receded she came down on a post that stove a hole in the bottom which cost the insurance company $500 and saved the owner the difficult problem of trying to get the ship-yard to make good.

It will be seen by these actual cases that the owner of an insured yacht is relieved of the difficulties of trying to collect from irresponsible parties, filing suits or liens and payment of exorbitant salvage charges as he collects from the insurance company regardless of who is at fault.

The marine yacht policy may appear to be a complicated document but it affords broad coverage and is free from technicalities. It is known as a "valued" policy, that is, a contract in which the value is established at inception and not after a loss.

The premium charge for yacht insurance may seem high but like all kinds of indemnity the cost is proportional to the loss and expense ratio. Rates are based on the type, value, age, speed, period in commission and waters navigated. For example, sailing vessels, without engines, are about 25% less than auxiliaries or gasoline powered yachts as there is less fire hazard but this may be offset by installation of an approved fire extinguishing system built into the engine compartment. Steam and Diesel yachts, not over ten years old, are written with a reduction of ¼% from the rates of gasoline yachts provided the "in commission period" does not exceed six months but otherwise take the same rates.

It would be difficult, in this article, to give a synopsis of rates as so many factors enter into the system of arriving at a figure that is fair to both parties in the contract.

In these latitudes the usual limits of navigation are confined to Atlantic coastwise and inland waters between Eastport, Maine, and Norfolk, Virginia, both inclusive. Vessels navigating beyond Eastport are charged with an additional premium and also for "ditch crawling" in the canals beyond Albany. If you make a canal cruise, better check your insurance.

There is a considerable increase in the rates for navigating south of Norfolk and all policies for this district contain the Florida Grounding Clause which reads as follows: "Not liable for any damage to propellers or machinery due to stranding, grounding or contact with any fixed or movable object between Jacksonville and Miami on the inland route. This, however, does not exclude claims under the collision clause."

Policies covering yachts navigating northern waters contain a warranty that the yacht is laid up and out of commission from November 1, to April 15 or May 1, according to class, but the "in commission period" may be extended by payment of an additional charge for each fifteen days in excess of this period. Yachts using southern waters may be written with a privilege for six months' navigation or a full year and the rate is adjusted accordingly.

All yachts, valued under $5,000, contain a clause to the effect that no losses are paid of less than $25 but this is not a deductible clause. If the loss exceeds $25 it is paid in full without deduction. All losses are payable, irrespective of percentage on policies of $5,000 and over.

Yachts valued at $10,000 or more receive suitable credit, at expiration of the policy, if less than six months in commission.

Marine insurance differs, in some respects, from other forms of indemnity because coastal and navigable waters, tributary thereto, come under Federal and International laws. For example: theft, by force, on the high seas, is an act of piracy which is a much more serious offense than when committed on land.

Theft of a yacht is covered and the underwriters are liable for any damage if the vessel is recovered. On the other hand if a pair of marine glasses or other equipment is "lifted" they would not be covered unless the yacht is broken into by force which is classed as assailing thieves and is an act of piracy.

The loss of dinghies has been the cause of some controversy. If the dinghy is stored on a float, detached from the yacht, and is stolen, it has been held that this is not an insurance loss. If it is moored to the yacht and the painter shows evidence of having been cut by thieves then it is an insurance loss. If it is being towed astern or carried on board and is lost through stress of weather it is covered under the policy.

"Average," is the trade term used for any partial loss and it may be "General" or "Particular." General average is any expense incurred, in an emergency, for the preservation of the vessel such as jettison of cargo or towing a disabled ship into port. Particular average is a loss applying to a particular interest as damage to a hull or fittings of a yacht which is payable to the owner.

If an insured yacht is damaged the usual procedure is to get an estimate from a reputable shipyard. This is presented to a "surveyor" employed by the insurance company who goes over the figures with the yard and passes on the claim. In the event of claims, repairs are paid for in full without deduction of new for old. In addition to paying for replacement of damages to hull and equipment the cost of towing and salvage charges, if any, are also paid in full.

A constructive total loss is one in which the expense of recovering and repairing the vessel shall exceed the insured value. There can be no abandonment of a damaged vessel to the insurance company unless the loss be total or constructively total and in which case the face value of the policy is paid in full. All legitimate claims are adjusted and paid promptly. In the event of a partial loss, repair work may be started immediately after the surveyor and yard agree upon a figure. After an accident any emergency work that will tend to reduce the cost of repairs may be immediately started but the insurance company should be notified of this fact.

All movable fittings up to 10% of the amount of the policy are covered against fire, when the yacht is out of commission, while stored elsewhere.

The yacht may be used for racing, but no loss will be paid on spars or sails that are lost or damaged during a race.

It is expressly stipulated that the yacht is used only for pleasure purposes and not engaged in any trade or illicit venture prohibited by law. It may be chartered or hired but only with the agreed consent of the underwriter. Carrying passengers or freight for hire puts the vessel in a commercial class.

To insure a yacht it is usual to require an application giving details of construction, value, name of builder, name of yacht, power plant, speed, age, waters intended to navigate, name and occupation of owner. From this information the underwriter, if he considers the risk desirable, will quote a rate and then have the yacht surveyed for the purpose of determining the value, condition, installation of power plant, cooking outfit, etc. If the surveyor passes on the risk the policy is issued.

As above stated the yacht policy covers practically any damage to the hull, fittings, fixtures and navigational equipment of the insured vessel but does not cover any personal effects of the owner or his guests. It does not cover personal injury or loss of life of employees or the public but this protection may be included by attaching a rider known as the "Protection and Indemnity clause." The additional charge for this protection ranges from 30 cents to 90 cents per $100 of liability with a minimum charge of $25. The limits of this liability are usually fixed at the value of the yacht but higher limits may be had if desired.

There are a few possible casualties that are not covered under the running down clause in the "hull" policy, such as damage to docks, buoys, telegraph cable or other fixed or movable things, goods or property but these are all included in the protection and indemnity clause.

Under Federal law, in the event of collision with another vessel, the owner of the vessel at fault can be held for damages but not to exceed the value of his vessel, after the accident. In other words, if an outboard runs down and sinks a palatial yacht that is not insured, the owner would have no recourse in the courts, for damages sustained, because the value of the vessel at fault would be practically nil.

There is some agitation, at the present time, to try to have this law changed owing to recent collisions at sea involving steamships.

There is also the Federal Longshoremen's and Harbor Worker's Compensation Act to be considered which provides compensation, in case of injury, for certain classes of workmen on vessels. This additional coverage may be added to the "hull" policy at small cost by endorsement. There does not seem to be much liability on the part of yacht owners under this law as it appears that negligence, on the part of the owner, must be proven to substantiate any claim.

Speed boats with a maximum speed of more than twenty-five m.p.h. are written under a special form at considerably higher rates than cruisers. These policies contain the following clause: "Not liable for any loss or damage to the rudder, propeller, shaft or machinery unless caused by stranding, sinking, burning or collision with another vessel." It is evident that this clause excludes only damage caused by striking, with the propeller or rudder, some floating or fixed obstruction and is to prevent the many small claims which might arise from bent propellers and broken rudders. All claims for loss or damage caused by or resulting from any accident during any official race or speed test are also excluded.

Outboards are also written as a separate class under a special policy. The hull or motor may be written separately or combined. The motor is covered against loss by fire, theft, damage by collision, total loss from marine perils, including loss overboard. The motor is also covered while in transit as well as when stored anywhere ashore.

A breach of warranty in a marine policy, such as cruising beyond the geographical limits stated therein, going into commission before the date specified or remaining in commission after the date or chartering the yacht without permission of the underwriter, are grounds for denying liability, provided a loss occurs during such period of violation only.

ON BREWING COFFEE

I CHEERFULLY endorse the statement that perfect coffee can be made in a tea kettle, when you let it boil the right way. Which is, watch it as it comes up, and the moment it reaches a full boil, snatch it off the hot spot and let it simmer a minute before you add the cold water. Reason: continued boiling would carry away in steam the very volatile oil on which the pleasant aroma of coffee depends; yet the solution *must* come up to full boiling temperature, at least briefly, to extract the full flavor of the bean. A kettle is a damned awkward piece of equipment to use on a small stove, and to stow on a small boat. Why get two? Men who buy all their equipment on Madison Avenue and its offshoots may not know it, but it is still possible to buy the standard American coffee pot anywhere else in the country. I mean the pot that is just that: a pot, equivalent to a kettle, completely free of all percolators, drippers, or other fancy gadgets. The same thing that is official equipment in many millions of American homes, regardless of the increase in the plethora of complicated coffee concoctors. Being of a shape evolved by experience of generations—a truncated cone, broad on the base— it does not upset easily; takes up the minimum of space; and is easier to handle and pour from than a kettle. It should be of enamel ware, and the old-fashioned blue-edge white enamel is the best. Sure, I know enamel ware is likely to get chipped on a boat in time, but that doesn't affect the inside, and no metal utensil is ideal for either tea or coffee. Most important detail: be sure it is cleaned of every trace of old coffee and grounds before starting a fresh brew. Back in the tall timber it is the quaint custom to add one spoonful of fresh coffee to the old grounds, and more water, and boil hard, repeating this process again and again. People who have run up against such rotgut in roadside lunch rooms are very stupid in blaming it on the kind of utensil used, rather than the method. I'll fight the world on the proposition that the standard coffee pot, properly used, can produce as good coffee as the most complicated percolators yet invented.

JOHN G. HANNA.

ON SEASICK REMEDIES

OF REMEDIES for seasickness there is no end. All of you probably know a man who has a friend whose Uncle Henry's first wife was cured by so-and-so—but unfortunately it never seems to work for you. Well, you will have to admit that anything which has been tried by the doctors of a famous passenger line in over 1,000 cases, with invariable success, *must* be good. And if it is pleasant to take, cheap and everywhere available, you probably want to hear of it.

It is nothing more than ordinary Karo corn syrup, a popular table delicacy obtainable at any grocery. You take two tablespoonfuls of this at the first sign of uneasiness and repeat as often as necessary. Take it in lemonade, milk, coffee, water or straight. The medical reason for it is simple. All distress is primarily due to a condition of extreme acidosis, which in plain terms is a lack of the necessary amount of sugar in blood and muscles. And Karo is largely dextrose, the kind of sugar that is absorbed directly, without need of digestive changes, and is not likely to ferment in the stomach, as large quantities of ordinary sugar will. The old plan of taking soda bicarb failed because it only neutralized what acid might be in the stomach, but could not correct the real cause of distress—lack of adequate sugar in the blood. Incidentally, though doctors do not all agree as to the best medicine, they do agree that the common notion that it is best not to eat before or during an attack is the worst possible thing you can do, since deprivation of all food quickly increases acidosis—still further lowers the blood sugar content. It is best to eat all you can of all you like, particularly fruits and vegetables, avoiding only—as instinct usually tells a sick person—all fats and greasy foods. That instinct checks perfectly with the medical reasoning, for it is well known fats develop acid substances in the course of digestion.

J.G.H.

ON WEIGHING ANCHORS

It might be a good idea to weigh all your anchors. Sure, I know all anchors are weighed more or less regularly all the time. But I mean to place the anchor on the platform of the ingenious machine of Mr. Fairbanks which indicates the number of pounds avoirdupois of metal contained in said ground hook. And this operation should preferably be performed before you weigh out some ounces of gold, or whatever you are using for money today, in payment for the anchor. Recently I purchased an alleged 60-pound anchor, and thought I had cheated the express agency, as the transportation charge was for only 50 pounds. But when we weighed it, in spite of a nice large black 60 painted on the fluke, it registered just 50 pounds and a few ounces. It bore the trade mark of a supposedly very honest manufacturer, too. Anchors are rough forged or cast work, and nobody expects them to be of exact weight. A tolerance of plus or minus 5 per cent is always allowable. But 20 per cent is a very bad shortage, and may be enough to lose your boat if it ever comes to a bad pull when every last ounce is needed.

J.G.H.

ON SEA-GOING PIPE TOBACCO

THOMAS R. MARSHALL, one of the best Vice-Presidents this country ever had, is well remembered for his declaration that what this country most needed was a good five cent cigar. That need has been filled, I am told by experts in that line, and I rise to declare that the greatest need at present is a good *sea-going* pipe tobacco. All tobacco in this country is made for use on the arid plains of Kansas or the torrid steam-heated cliff-dwellings of New York. To keep it from getting too dry, manufacturers mix molasses and other things with it to attract and hold as much moisture as possible. Very good in such places. But take that tobacco aboard a boat, and in a day or two it absorbs so much moisture from sea air that it becomes unburnable. Or if it can be kept burning over a hot fire of matches, the excess moisture turns into steam that is no good for anybody's tongue. What is needed is some straight tobacco, without an hygroscopic substance added, that will remain reasonably combustible at sea. There's a fortune waiting for the first manufacturer who will read and heed this plea. J.G.H.

ON YACHTING CAPS

ANYONE who ventures around yacht clubs, public yacht docks, and such places, is bound to see many painful sights. Being a patient old man, I just grin and bear most of them. But one always makes me move to the lee rail. I refer to the hundreds of men you see wearing either work clothes or any old kind of lounging clothes, and also a full dress formal yachting cap. Faugh! It's as disgusting a spectacle as to see a laborer in greasy overalls wearing a silk opera hat. I doubt if a single one of the men misusing the yacht cap would make such an ass of himself as to appear publicly in the overalls and silk hat get-up, yet he blandly goes around day after day in a get-up equally offensive to good taste. I never could figure why. Canvas work hats are the proper thing to wear when swabbing or painting the old barge. For those hours when you are just loafing around in slacks and any old kind of shirt, sea duty caps, with small, soft crowns, can be had, if you feel you must look very hotsy totsy salty. Hard as it may be to resist the temptation to show the girls you have the price of a formal yacht cap, if not a yacht, still it is better to put it away until you don the type of coat, trousers, collar and tie accepted as formal yachting dress. Mind you, I'm just an old clam digger, and I don't urge anyone to go formal, ever, if he doesn't want to. Point I am making is, there is but one choice for a man of any self-respect: either go *all* the way, or none. Mismatched rag bag combinations are definitely out. J.G.H.

ON DRINKING SALT WATER

THE professor of physiology in one of the country's greatest medical colleges has favored me with some interesting facts relating to the drinking of more or less salty water. I quoted a suggestion from an English paper that some salt water be mixed with fresh to increase the total quantity of drinkable fluid available in a lifeboat that has not enough to sustain life in its crew for the long time required to reach land. The doctor states that sea water is normally about three per cent salt, whereas the salt concentration in human blood is only 0.9 of one per cent, and in sweat, 0.2 of one per cent. This latter is the strongest concentration in water advised as beneficial for use under conditions of heat and hard work. In a normal person the drinking of solutions as strong as 0.5 of one per cent will, he says, cause marked diuresis—that is, the water will be lost from kidneys as fast as ingested. That, however, may not be the case in the severely dried-out body of a man near death from thirst. He estimates that, ordinarily, one part sea water to fifteen parts fresh is the most that can be added to produce a perfectly satisfactory and harmless drinking water. No doubt true, but the object is not to produce an ideal drink. It is to find a mixture which, while far from ideal, unpleasant in taste, and inclined to gripe, nevertheless will keep life in tortured bodies for the final day or two necessary to reach land or rescue. Quite possibly, in some known cases, the increase of a ten-gallon supply to eleven by adding one gallon sea water would have meant the precious extra day of life for all hands.

J.G.H.

Warren Sheppard

INDEX

INDEX

Jean-Pierre de Caussade on reaching holiness by abandoning one's soul to God:

"In reality, holiness consists of one thing only: complete loyalty to God's will."

"Perfection is neither more nor less than the soul's faithful cooperation with God."

"Our only satisfaction must be to live in the present moment as if there were nothing to expect beyond it."

"You are seeking for secret ways of belonging to God, but there is only one: making use of whatever he offers you."

"If we only have sense enough to leave everything to the guidance of God's hand we should reach the highest peak of holiness."

"The great and firm foundation of the spiritual life is the offering of ourselves to God and being subject to his will in all things."

"The truly faithful soul accepts all things as a manifestation of God's grace, ignores itself and thinks only of what God is doing."

"Let us love, for love will give us everything."

"If we are truly docile, we will ask no questions about the road along which God is taking us."

"God truly helps us however much we may feel we have lost his support."

"The more God takes from the abandoned soul, the more is he really giving it . . . the more he strips us of natural things, the more he showers us with supernatural gifts."

"To all his faithful souls, God promises a glorious victory over the powers of the world and of hell."